Rescuing the Dinner Hour

Easy Meals for Busy People

Peggy K. Glass

FONT & CENTER PRESS • P.O. Box 95 • Weston, MA 02193

Published by
Font & Center Press
P.O. Box 95
Weston, Massachusetts 02193

Cover design by Denise Bergman
Author's photograph by Gene Ritvo © 1994

Library of Congress Cataloging-in-Publication Data
Glass, Peggy K.
Rescuing the dinner hour : easy meals for busy people / Peggy K. Glass.
p.   cm.
Includes index.
ISBN 1-883280-04-4 : $15.95
1. Cookery.   I. Title.
641.5--dc20   94-31718
                                                      CIP

First Printing 1994
Printed in the United States of America on recycled paper

1   2   3   4   5   6   7   8   9   10

Acknowledgements

Rescuing the Dinner Hour began with happy childhood memories that inspired a personal way of living, a food career, a more public newspaper column, and now, a second cookbook.

The bookmaking process is consuming, exhilarating, and terrifying . . . a private process that becomes more real as you talk to the computer, try to be yourself, put things on paper you do without thinking, consider possibilities and alternatives . . . watch the ideas take shape, become focused, refocused . . . and slowly a book emerges. What is an essential part of your life becomes accessible, exposed, and open to scrutiny.

Along the way, there are so many people who give encouragement just when it's needed most, who offer help, or are simply friends . . . and who need to be thanked.

First, my family near and far, for without them there would be no memories or a desire to create more. Thank you to Jane and Burton Kohn who made Indianapolis dinner hours special . . . and to my sisters and brother, Laurie, Nancy, and Sandy, who shared happy times, good food, and fine music at our dinner table. At home in Newton, cooking and family life have been inseparable. We all share the surprises and adventure of making new foods, and take comfort in old family favorites. My family has been a collective guinea pig in the testing process, and they always come back for more. Rebe admires the presentation and always offers thoughtful critiques and creative ideas. Adam has a discriminating palate and an intuitive sense of what's good. And Noah never hurts my feelings even when he'd prefer beef tenderloin and mashed potatoes to my latest creation. I am forever grateful to Len for his thoughtful, kind, and patient words and his loving support of our family and me.

There are friends who have cheered me on for years: Lorie and Richard; Donna and Alec; Cindy and Bill; Deborah and Jon; Laurie and Bob; Susan and John; Ed, Trude, and Elio; Lucienne; Peggy and Fred . . . friends who love to eat, to cook, and to watch me cook!

Thanks to the Newton Graphic (Harte-Hanks Community Newspapers) for allowing me to try out ideas on their pages, and for letting me be their hometown cook these past years. Ilene Horowitz at Font & Center Press has made book publishing a collaborative process from beginning to end . . . thank you.

And I'm grateful to be in your kitchens, and hope I can make your dinner hours easier and more fun. Please let me hear from you.

P.K.G.

Table of Contents

Beef, Lamb & Pork
85–98

Seafood
99–116

Pasta
117–138

Grains, Potatoes & Beans
139–156

Sauces, Dressings, Marinades, Relishes, Dips & Spreads
157–172

Sandwiches
173–190

Breads, Coffeecakes & Rolls
191–204

Cakes, Pies, Cobblers, Crisps, Cookies & Bars
205–236

Tips & Basic Recipes
237–272

Basic Recipes
240–272

Eggs
240–241

Vegetables
241–242

Salads
243–244

Chicken
245–246

Introduction

*T*hese days, as the dinner hour gets later and more chaotic and there is less time and energy for home cooking, I think back with longing to the dinners of my childhood. My family gathered to share good home-cooked food—usually delicious and sometimes, even adventurous. Dinnertimes were occasions to celebrate good news and achievements. They were comforting to us as we discussed our daily activities, world events, and personal disappointments. Dinnertimes were an essential part of family life.

The memory of those special meals was the impetus for my weekly column in the *Newton Graphic* (Harte-Hanks Community Newspapers, Newton, Massachusetts) and, ultimately, for this book. Today, dinnertime is more important than ever as a refuge from the pace of contemporary life. It is a way of connecting and sharing with family and friends. But it is an uphill battle to make it happen.

Rescuing the Dinner Hour is a user-friendly book of more than 200 recipes. It is a book for cooks on the run; harried moms and dads whose impatient children want to know "what's for dinner?"; families who value time together but seem to have too little of it; beginning cooks who need some basic recipes and an understanding of cooking techniques; and even experienced cooks looking for new ideas.

These recipes are healthy, fun, and easy to make. They use contemporary ingredients such as arugula and radicchio in salads, dried cranberries with meats, roasted vegetables in lasagnas, and oven-dried tomatoes in sandwiches. They broaden our palate with international spices and ethnic twists. Enjoy dry-rub spice marinades, Indian Carrot Slaw, Peking Ravioli, Mexican Dinner Waffles, and chicken recipes from Tangier, Bombay, Havana, Normandy, South Africa, and South America. There are lots of pasta dishes, hot and cold; creative dinner sandwiches from Desert Pizzas to Falafels; and a variety of cold salads for the long hot summer. When you'd rather bake than cook, there are easy desserts to end a simple meal.

Since my goal is to make the cook's job more manageable, the recipes emphasize stir-frying, grilling, and quick-cooking foods rather than long-simmering stews and roasts. Quick breads and canned beans make more sense for easy dinners than yeast breads and dried beans. These recipes are neither meat and potatoes nor gourmet, but everyday food for family and friends, and even for entertaining.

Each recipe is accompanied by an illustrated set of measuring spoons. After you've tried a recipe, use these measuring spoons as a rating system. For example, color in all four spoons if you thought the recipe was terrific. This will help you when you're looking for something to make for dinner.

I've written **Rescuing the Dinner Hour** not just as a busy mother, wife, and friend, but as a cooking teacher who has spent years helping other cooks. The reference chapters (Staples, and Tips & Basic Recipes) and chapter introductions explain different cooking methods and special techniques, such as defooting scallops, roasting peppers, and preparing artichokes. They discuss varieties of vegetables, grains, and potatoes, and offer tips on making faster lasagna, preventing cookies from burning on the bottom, and how to know when shrimp, meat, and cakes are done.

Each recipe, whether a soup, pasta, chicken, bread, or dessert, is the focus of the menu at the bottom of the page. My menus are suggestions for a colorful plate, an ethnic alliance, a healthy balance, or a seasonal match—with a minimum of fuss. If the menu suggests a roast chicken, cook it the way you usually do or use the recipe located on the page number given in parentheses or buy a prepared rotisserie chicken. If the menu suggests an apple pie, you might even try your own favorite or bake a ready-made pie crust with canned fruit filling or go to the bakery or decide you'd just as soon eat an apple. Be flexible in creating a dinner everyone will like. Remember, the first taste is with the eyes, so present the food in an appealing way—with colorful garnishes on attractive serving platters.

The Tips & Basic Recipes chapter offers information about cooking equipment, utensils, storage, and terminology. But more than anything else, it is a collection of recipes every cook should have. You may already know how to poach chicken for salads, boil rice or make a rice pilaf, whip up an omelet, devein and cook shrimp, whisk together a vinaigrette dressing, or make a pie crust—or you may not. The Basic Recipes are a handy reference guide either to learn from or to refresh your memory. Once they're part of your repertoire, you can be as creative as you wish.

In **Rescuing the Dinner Hour** I've tried to make dinnertime more enjoyable for everyone, especially the cook, so that even when life is hectic, we can savor good food together. I hope the book provides you with some inspiration as well as recipes and menus that will help you in the kitchen. The dinner hour is worth your time and effort, because it is a nightly gift of love that makes family and friends feel special. It reaps great rewards and creates lifelong memories. Armed with this book, the rescue of your dinner hour should be easy—and delicious too!

Staples in My Kitchen

When I think of staples, I think of the basic, singular, quality foods on my pantry shelves and in the refrigerator and freezer that I use frequently in making most of our meals. These may be somewhat different in your kitchen since they reflect what you like to cook and your family likes to eat. I have included some helpful tips about the quality and storage of certain staples rather than list them all.

Artichoke Hearts	Artichoke hearts and other vegetables that are processed, taste much better from a glass jar than a can. To eliminate the can taste, soak the vegetables in water and drain.
Baking Powder and Baking Soda	Keep these fresh and replace a few times a year. You can test the efficacy of baking powder by adding 1 teaspoon to $1/4$ cup of hot water. It should fizz and bubble. To test baking soda, add 1 teaspoon of vinegar to $1/4$ cup of hot water. When you add 1 teaspoon of baking soda it should fizz and bubble. These tests show the reaction of baking powder in water and baking soda with acid to produce carbon dioxide bubbles that make baked goods rise.
Beans	Cooked and canned beans make the cook's work much faster. They come in 16-ounce and 19-ounce sizes. Use either size in recipes that call for 2 cups of cooked beans.
Black Pepper	In my kitchen I always use freshly ground black pepper from a pepper mill. Rather than measure the pepper precisely, I grind the peppercorns and season the food according to taste. When recipes in the book call for pepper, it is always freshly ground black peppercorns.
Brown Sugar	This should stay soft in its plastic bag or box if you close them tightly. If the sugar gets hard, store a folded, damp paper towel in the bag or box to soften.

Butter	I prefer salted butter for cooking and bread and unsalted butter for baking. I use butter in moderation rather than margarine. The hydrogenation process that turns liquid fats into solid form also changes the structure of margarine into trans-fats that are unhealthy. In cooking, mono-unsaturated oils—olive and canola—are the healthiest choices. In baking, oil cakes and crusts are healthier than butter, although not as tasty.
Buttermilk	Buttermilk is a wonderful, soothing drink with hot spicy foods, but mostly it's one of my favorite ingredients in baking. Milk is cultured with an acid-producing bacteria to produce a thickened buttermilk with a unique piquant taste. Don't substitute milk for buttermilk in recipes—it won't produce the same results. It's better to use thinned yogurt in its place, or to acidify and curdle milk (add a few teaspoons of lemon juice or vinegar for every cup of milk). Store cartons of buttermilk in the refrigerator in small plastic sandwich bags that cover the bottom half since these containers tend to leak, or transfer the buttermilk to a glass jar.
Cheese Ravioli	These are a staple in the freezer that make a quick dinner with almost any sauce or topping.
Chicken Breasts	Skin and bone chicken breasts, package them in twos in small, heavy plastic bags, and freeze, or buy them on sale already skinned and boned.
Chocolate	Chocolate picks up the flavors of its neighbors, so it should be kept in a clean plastic container and stored in a dark place, at room temperature, away from strong smelling foods. Semisweet chocolate is the easiest to find and comes in chips. Bittersweet chocolate is often referred to as dark chocolate and **is** sweetened, but retains a strong, rich, chocolaty flavor. Find a candy supplier and buy a ten-pound block to share with a friend. Break it up with a hammer and store it in chunks. Unsweetened chocolate is used for baking.
Cocoa	Dutch or European-style unsweetened cocoa has a richer flavor than American (Hershey's or Nestlés) unsweetened cocoa. It has also been alkalized, a process that neutralizes the acid and eliminates the need for baking soda in baking.

Flour	There really are differences in flour because of the wheat it comes from and the way it's processed. The protein or gluten in flour makes some flours better for cakes and others better for bread. All the recipes in the book use all-purpose, unbleached white flour unless something else is specified.
Ginger Root	Buy it fresh but in small quantities as needed since as it doesn't keep for more than a week or two before drying out.
Heavy Cream or Whipping Cream	I buy ultra-pasteurized cream since it keeps well and I don't use it often. Moderation is the key here. Aside from sweetening and whipping these creams for desserts, cream adds a wonderful, rich finish to soups and sauces. There is sufficient butterfat in heavy cream to prevent it from curdling when you boil it down to make a sauce. Don't try the same with half-and-half or light cream or they will curdle.
Natural Peanut Butter	This contains no sugar or added oil—just peanuts. If the oil separates and rises to the top, stir the peanut butter and oil together and refrigerate it.
Nuts	Freezing prevents nuts from becoming rancid. Wrap well in a heavy plastic bag or store in an airtight container.
Onions, Garlic, Shallots	Replace these when the onions and shallots begin to grow green sprouts and the garlic gets soft.
Parmesan Cheese	Buy aged shredded or grated Parmesan cheese of the best quality available in the cheese case. It is a dry, salty cheese that should keep for weeks. Buy it in a whole piece if you have a cheese grater or machine strong enough to grate it as you need it. Romano cheese is a bit less costly but also sharper in flavor.
Peas (tiny ones) and Corn Kernels	Frozen peas and corn are easy to measure if you buy them in plastic bags.
Pimientos/Roasted Peppers	Pimientos are a variety of red pepper that come already roasted and cut or chopped in convenient jars. They're a handy staple for adding color and flavor (pages 165 and 170).

Rice	There are many varieties of rice. The most useful is long-grain white rice. This is what is used in the recipes in this book unless otherwise specified.
Spices	Find a good spice shop where spices are fresh and you can buy any amount you like. Label jars or containers and keep the spices out of the sun. Replace them occasionally since they tend to lose their flavor.
Tomato Paste	Tubes of paste can be kept in the refrigerator, or open both ends of a can and push the paste into a small plastic bag. Store in the freezer and cut off chunks as needed.
Whole Wheat Flour	Freezing prevents it from becoming rancid.

Soups & Chowders

W hen time is of the essence, soups and chowders can be wholesome one-dish dinners, not just a prelude to them. They're easy to make ahead, they freeze well, and, if you make a lot, you'll have enough for another dinner. Usually they just need a good loaf of bread and maybe a salad to accompany them.

Chunky meat or vegetable soups served with homemade croutons in large wide soup bowls are rustic and hearty fare. Vegetable soups can be puréed and/or creamed. When filled pasta or gnocchi are added, they become a whole meal.

Soups needn't be just cold weather fare. In the summer heat, chilled gazpacho soup may be all you need for a quick meal. Chilled fruit soups served in goblets can take the place of fruit or a dessert in a menu, or can be a satisfying drink with chicken salad or sandwiches.

Most hearty soups begin by sautéing chopped vegetables (onions, garlic, carrots, celery, etc.) in oil or butter, adding chicken or beef broth, tomatoes, and a starch (potatoes, pasta, grains), then flavoring with herbs or spices. Meat bones enrich the broth and add flavor as well as protein.

Canned Broth vs Homemade Stocks?

Canned broth is fast and easy. It comes in 14½-ounce cans, so I usually add enough water to make 16 ounces when recipes call for 2 cups. This also cuts down slightly on its saltiness.

The advantage of homemade stocks is that the long, slow cooking extracts the protein from the meat bones and cartilage, and produces a gelatin (protein) rich and flavorful stock. But few of us have the time for this luxury. An alternative is to make chicken soup (page 9) then strain it and cook it down to concentrate the flavor. Add salt only after the soup is cooked. It's easier to defat the stock when it's chilled. If you've boned a number of chicken breasts, or have lots of chicken bones or a chicken carcass from a roasted chicken, add them to a pot of water with aromatics (onion, carrot, celery, parsley), simmer partially covered for a few hours, and strain. Cool and store in 2-cup portions in the freezer in labeled plastic containers. This takes very little effort and adds much more flavor to foods than water.

Grandma's Chicken Noodle Soup

The aroma of chicken soup cooking in the kitchen is enough to make one feel that all is right with the world . . . even in the dark and sub-zero temperatures of winter. This comfort food and elixir is loved in every culture, and changes with the herbs, spices, or seasonings added to it. Here's a basic chicken soup recipe to please everyone, and sure to chase away winter cold(s). You may want to remove the cooked chicken breast for another use: Chicken Salad (page 52), Fried Rice (page 144), Pilaf (page 252), Biryani (page 60), or for chicken sandwiches. Use the remaining chicken in the soup.

1 3–4-pound chicken
1 14-ounce can chicken broth (for extra flavor)
Water to cover the chicken
1 large onion, peeled and quartered
2 celery stalks
2 carrots, peeled and cut into chunks
1/4 bunch of fresh parsley
Salt to taste
8 ounces broad egg noodles

♦ Trim the chicken of all excess fat and skin. Place the chicken, breast side down, in a large pot. Add the canned chicken broth and water to cover. Bring to a boil slowly, and skim the surface of foam as it appears.

♦ Add the onion, celery, carrots, and parsley, and simmer, covered for 1 hour.

♦ Let the soup cool slightly before removing the chicken and vegetables.

♦ Pour the broth through a fine mesh strainer and skim the fat from the surface. Taste and season with salt.

♦ Dice the carrots, remove the chicken from the bones, and return both to the soup.

♦ Cook the noodles in boiling salted water, drain, and add to the soup.

♦ Taste and adjust the seasoning.

Serves 6 to 8

NOTE: To stretch the soup, you may add an additional can of chicken broth and a can of water.

MENU

Grandma's Chicken Noodle Soup
Raw vegetables with a dip (pages 168–171)
Sliced challah
Fresh pineapple and banana skewers

Red Tomato & Pepper Soup with Tortellini

Here's a soup as colorful as it is delicious. Serve it without the tortellini as a fine first course. Small cheese ravioli can be substituted for the tortellini.

3 tablespoons butter
1 small onion, chopped
1 red pepper, seeded and chopped
1/8 teaspoon cayenne pepper or to taste
1 1/2 teaspoons paprika
1 teaspoon cumin
1/2 teaspoon coriander
1 28-ounce can Italian whole tomatoes in purée
4 cups chicken broth
3 tablespoons chopped cilantro or flat leaf parsley
1/2 pound cheese tortellini, cooked according to directions and drained
1/2 cup sour cream

♦ In a large saucepan, melt the butter over low heat. Sauté the onion for about 5 minutes, stirring often, until softened but not colored. Add the red pepper and continue to sauté for 3 minutes, stirring often. Stir in the spices and sauté for 1 minute longer.

♦ Add the tomatoes with purée and the stock and slowly bring to a boil. Cover and simmer for 30 minutes, stirring occasionally.

♦ Ladle batches of the soup into a blender and purée, starting on low speed and increasing to high.

♦ Return the soup to the saucepan. Stir in the cilantro and season to taste with cayenne pepper.

♦ Add the cooked tortellini to the soup and simmer for a few minutes to warm.

♦ Ladle the soup into shallow bowls and garnish with sour cream and a sprig of cilantro.

Serves 4

MENU

Red Tomato & Pepper Soup with Tortellini
Green salad vinaigrette with radiccio, watercress, and croutons (page 261)
Poundcake with custard (page 264) and strawberries

Spinach & White Bean Soup

If there's a vegetarian in your house, or you're trying to eat healthier, this is the perfect soup to make for cold weather dinners. Vegetables and complex carbohydrates (potatoes, beans, and oats) give it color, texture, and flavor galore.

2 tablespoons olive oil
1 large onion, chopped
1 clove garlic, minced
1 large carrot, peeled and finely chopped
1 celery stalk, finely chopped
4 cups chicken or vegetable broth
3 cups water
1 medium potato, peeled and diced—keep in water to cover until cooking time
3 cups chopped fresh spinach leaves (or 1 10-ounce package frozen chopped spinach)
¼ cup quick rolled oats
2 cups cooked small white beans, drained (1 16- or 19-ounce can)
Salt and pepper to taste
Freshly grated Parmesan cheese

♦ In a large soup pot over low heat, sauté the onion, garlic, carrot, and celery in the oil for about 10 minutes, stirring often to prevent the vegetables from coloring.
♦ When the vegetables are soft, add the broth and water and bring to a boil. Simmer, covered, for 20 minutes.
♦ Stir in the potato and spinach and simmer for 10 more minutes.
♦ Stir in the oats and beans and heat to boiling. Taste and adjust the seasoning with salt and pepper.
♦ Serve with a generous topping of freshly grated Parmesan cheese.

Serves 6

MENU

Spinach & White Bean Soup
Breadsticks and butter
Gingerbread cake (page 209) and applesauce (page 268)

Tomato-Basil Gazpacho Soup

Gazpacho soup takes advantage of the summer garden's harvest—tomatoes, cucumbers, peppers, herbs—all blended together into a delicious cold soup that works as a refreshing lunch, a dinner soup awaiting the grilled entree, or even as a brunch drink—spiked with vodka. I like to flavor this cold soup with basil, but you could give it a Mexican twist with cilantro, a hot pepper, some cumin, and chili powder.

3 large summer tomatoes,
   peeled, seeded, and
   chopped
1 cup seeded and
   chopped cucumber
1/2 green pepper, chopped
1/4 cup chopped red
   onion
1 small clove garlic
1/4 cup chopped parsley
3 tablespoons chopped
   fresh basil
1 8-ounce can tomato
   sauce
1/4 cup red wine vinegar
2 tablespoons olive oil
1 teaspoon salt
1/8 teaspoon cayenne
   pepper or to taste
Black pepper to taste
Croutons (page 261)

♦ Combine all the gazpacho ingredients in a blender or processor bowl. Blend until nearly smooth, or process with on/off turns until blended but still chunky. Purée the soup if you plan on drinking it.

♦ Adjust the seasoning and chill thoroughly before serving.

♦ Serve in pretty, shallow soup bowls or goblets with an ice cube. Top with a handful of croutons at the last minute.

Serves 4 to 6

MENU

Tomato-Basil Gazpacho Soup
Grilled chicken breasts (page 246)
New potatoes, partially cooked, oiled and grilled
Grilled summer squash on skewers
Fruit cobbler (228)

Chunky Chili Soup

This recipe combines two favorites in a hearty, spiced soup that's just right for chilly evenings.

2 tablespoons vegetable
   oil
1 large onion, chopped
2 cloves garlic, minced
1 jalepeño pepper, seeded
   and minced
1 tablespoon chili pow-
   der, or more to taste
1 teaspoon cumin
1/2 teaspoon oregano
1 bay leaf
1 28-ounce can whole
   Italian tomatoes
2 tablespoons tomato
   paste
4 cups chicken broth
1 cup water
3/4 cup elbow macaroni
2 cups cooked dark red
   kidney beans, drained
   (1 16- or 19-ounce can)
3 tablespoons chopped
   fresh coriander
Salt and pepper to taste
1 cup grated Colby or
   Longhorn cheddar
   cheese

♦ In a large pot, heat the oil over low heat and add the onion, garlic, and jalepeño pepper. Simmer for about 10 minutes until the onion is very soft, stirring often to prevent the vegetables from coloring.
♦ Stir in the chili powder, cumin, oregano, and bay leaf, and cook for another minute.
♦ Add the tomatoes with the juice, tomato paste, and chicken broth, and bring to a boil. Simmer partially covered for 15 minutes, stirring and breaking up the tomatoes.
♦ Cook the macaroni in a large pot of boiling salted water until tender, according to the package directions, drain, and add to the soup.
♦ Add the beans and simmer for a few minutes to heat thoroughly.
♦ Stir in the coriander. Taste and adjust the seasoning with salt and pepper. Remove the bay leaf.
♦ Ladle into bowls and sprinkle with grated cheese.

Serves 6 to 8

MENU

Chunky Chili Soup
Cornbread (page 260)
Celery sticks (with peanut butter filling)
Fresh grapes or other seasonal fruit

Seafood Chowder

*U*se whatever seafood you like in this chowder, as long as it's fresh. Bottled clam broth is a useful staple in the pantry for soups and chowders such as this one as well as for quick sauces. Serve this with a hearty bread such as Focaccia—the round, flattened, chewy Italian bread that's brushed with olive oil and sometimes flavored with rosemary before baking. It's delicious plain or dipped in olive oil.

3 tablespoons butter
2 onions, chopped
2 celery stalks, chopped
1/2 teaspoon fennel seeds
1 teaspoon anchovy paste
3 medium all-purpose
   potatoes, peeled
   and diced
2 tablespoons flour
2 8-ounce bottles clam
   broth
2 cups milk
2 pounds boneless fish
   chunks
1/2 pound scallops
1/2 cup heavy cream
3 ripe tomatoes peeled,
   seeded, and choppped
   (or 1 1-pound can
   whole peeled tomatoes,
   drained and chopped)
1/4 cup minced fresh
   parsley
Salt and pepper to taste

♦ In a large heavy saucepan, melt the butter over low heat and add the onions and celery. Sauté for 5 minutes, stirring often, until softened. Add the fennel seeds, anchovy paste, and potatoes and continue to sauté a few minutes longer, stirring to mix well.

♦ Whisk in the flour and cook for 1 minute. Whisk in the broth and milk and bring to a simmer. Add the fish and scallops and simmer for about 3 minutes until cooked through.

♦ Add the cream and tomatoes and heat thoroughly, but don't let it come to a boil. Stir in the parsley and season to taste with salt and pepper. Ladle into soup bowls and serve hot.

Serves 6 to 8

MENU

Seafood Chowder
Focaccia bread
Mixed green salad vinaigrette
Spumoni

Tiger's Carrot Soup

Here's a soup that is filled with familiar, seasonal tastes, and an elusive ingredient to intrigue your curious tasters. Serve it as a simple start to a holiday feast, topped with cinnamon croutons (easily made with cinnamon swirl bread, buttered, trimmed, and cut into cubes, then baked in a 300°F oven until browned and crisp). Or this can be a complete dinner with the addition of a few cooked cheese ravioli. The color is wonderful!

4 tablespoons butter
1 onion, chopped
1 pound carrots or winter squash, peeled and cut into chunks
1 medium potato, peeled and cut into 1-inch cubes
2 tablespoons peanut butter
¼ teaspoon curry powder
¼ teaspoon cayenne pepper
½ teaspoon sugar
5 cups chicken broth
2 tablespoons chopped cilantro
½ cup heavy cream, optional

♦ In a large pot, melt the butter and add the onion. Sauté for 5 minutes over low heat, stirring often, until softened.

♦ Add the carrots, and the potato, and continue to sauté for 3 minutes.

♦ Stir in the peanut butter, curry powder, cayenne, and sugar. Add the broth and bring to a boil.

♦ Cover and simmer until the carrots and potato are soft, about 20 minutes.

♦ Purée in batches in a blender, starting on low speed and increasing the speed to high.

♦ Return the soup to the pan and adjust the seasoning. The soup can be prepared ahead of time up to this point.

♦ At serving time, heat the soup to boiling. Stir in the cilantro and the cream and heat for a minute. Ladle into soup bowls and serve hot.

Serves 6 to 8

MENU

Tiger's Carrot Soup
Grilled chicken wings (page 81)
Broccoli (page 242)
French rolls
Warm apple cider in a mug
Sugar cookies (page 266)

Fidel's Black Bean Soup

Bean soups take a long time to make if you begin with dried beans that may require hours of cooking. When speed is an essential dinnertime ingredient, try this unusual black bean soup made with canned beans. The seasoning has a hint of the Caribbean. Serve with a spoonful of sour cream or yogurt and a sprinkle of cilantro.

2 tablespoons olive oil
1 medium onion, finely chopped
1 large clove garlic, minced
2 stalks celery, finely chopped
1 green pepper, seeded and chopped
1 jalepeño pepper, seeded and chopped
2 teaspoons cumin
$^1/_8$ teaspoon cinnamon
1 1-pound can whole peeled tomatoes, drained
4 cups chicken broth
4 cups cooked black beans, drained (2 16- or 19-ounce cans)
Juice of 1 lime
Salt and pepper to taste

Toppings: sour cream or yogurt, chopped fresh cilantro, homemade croutons (page 261)

- In a large heavy pot, heat the oil over low heat. Sauté the onion, garlic, celery, and peppers, stirring frequently for about 15 minutes until very soft. Don't let the vegetables color.
- Add the cumin, cinnamon, tomatoes, chicken broth, and beans. Bring to a boil, cover, and simmer for 30 minutes.
- Transfer the soup to a blender in small batches and process on low to medium speed until nearly smooth.
- Return to the pot, add the lime juice, and adjust the seasoning with salt and pepper. The soup should be fairly thick.
- Serve hot or cold with a spoonful of sour cream or yogurt and a sprinkling of cilantro, accompanied by a bowl of homemade croutons.

Serves 8

MENU

Fidel's Black Bean Soup
Grilled chicken (page 82)
Green beans
Garlic bread
Baked custard (page 264) or tapioca pudding

Vegetable-Lentil Soup

This is a dinner you can easily prepare ahead of time since you can walk away to do other things while it simmers. Lentils need no pre-soaking in this hearty, healthy soup. Red lentils cook in just 30 minutes.

3 tablespoons vegetable oil
1 medium onion, finely chopped
1 clove garlic, minced
1 small jalepeño pepper, seeded and finely chopped
1 large celery stalk, finely chopped
1 small carrot, peeled and finely chopped
1 small green pepper, seeded and finely chopped
2 tablespoons flour
1 cup red lentils, rinsed well and picked over
4 cups beef broth
4 cups water
2 tablespoons tomato paste
2 tablespoons fresh lemon juice
Salt, black pepper, and cayenne pepper to taste
Plain yogurt for the topping

• In a large pot, add the oil and sauté the onion, garlic, jalepeño pepper, celery, carrot, and green pepper over low heat, stirring to prevent them from coloring, for about 10 minutes.
• Stir in the flour and sauté for 1 minute. Add the lentils, broth, and water, and bring to a boil.
• Skim the surface of the soup. Stir, scraping the bottom, and simmer covered for 30 minutes until the lentils are soft.
• Stir in the tomato paste and simmer for 5 more minutes.
• Purée half the soup and stir it into the remaining soup to thicken it. Add the lemon juice, salt, black pepper, and cayenne pepper to taste.
• Ladle into soup bowls and serve with a spoonful of yogurt.

Serves 6 to 8

MENU

Vegetable-Lentil Soup
Pita Crisps (page 262)
Cucumber sticks
Citrus fruit salad (page 268)

Italian Pasta & Bean Soup

Similar to Italian minestrone, this soup is filled with vegetables, pasta, and beans (fagiole). Fennel is the magic ingredient that gives the soup a unique and rich flavor.

6 tablespoons olive oil
1 large onion, chopped
2 cloves garlic, minced
1 cup chopped celery
1 cup chopped fennel
  (about half a small
  bulb)
1 jalepeño pepper, seeded
  and minced
1 carrot, peeled and
  chopped
2 14-ounce cans chicken
  broth
2 cups water
1 1-pound can whole
  peeled tomatoes
1/2 teaspoon oregano
2 cups cooked white
  beans, drained (1
  16- or 19-ounce can)
Salt and pepper to taste
1 cup elbow macaroni or
  fuscelli
2 cups julienned spinach
  or escarole leaves
1/2 cup freshly grated
  Parmesan cheese

- In a large heavy pot, heat 3 tablespoons of the olive oil and sauté the onion and garlic over low heat for about 3 minutes, stirring often, until soft but not colored.
- Add the celery, fennel, pepper, and carrot and continue to sauté for about 5 minutes, stirring, until the vegetables are softened.
- Add the chicken broth, water, tomatoes with their juice, and the oregano. Bring to a boil, cover, and simmer for 20 minutes, breaking up the tomatoes.
- Add the beans, cover, and continue to simmer for 10 minutes.
- Mash the soup a bit with a potato masher or the back of a large spoon to thicken the soup. Taste and adjust the seasoning.
- Cook the pasta in a large pot of boiling salted water until tender according to the package directions. Drain and add to the soup. Stir in the remaining 3 tablespoons of olive oil.
- At serving time, heat the soup to a simmer and add the spinach leaves, stirring until wilted. Serve in bowls with a generous sprinkling of Parmesan cheese.

Serves 4 to 6

MENU

Italian Pasta & Bean Soup
Crusty Italian bread
Grapefruit brulée (half, topped with brown sugar, and briefly broiled)

Chilled Berry & Fruit Soup

Fruit soup can be a summer refresher made with seasonal fruit at its peak, or a winter treat made mostly with dried fruit. The color, flavor, and consistency will vary according to your choice of fruits and cooking liquids.

In the summer:

2 pounds fresh fruit (peaches, plums, nectarines, pears, cherries, strawberries) pitted, cored, and cut into 1-inch pieces

3 cups of liquid (a combination of water and orange juice, or some cider or grape juice)

In the winter:

3/4 pound dried fruit (apricots, peaches, pears) cut into 1-inch pieces

6 cups of liquid (a combination of water, orange juice, or some cider or grape juice)

2 strips of lemon zest
1 cinnamon stick
1/2 cup sugar, or to taste
2 cups buttermilk
1/2 pint raspberries or small blueberries

- ◆ Combine the fruit, liquid, lemon zest, and cinnamon stick in a medium saucepan and bring to a boil. Cover and simmer until the fruit is soft, 15 to 30 minutes.
- ◆ Remove the cinnamon stick.
- ◆ While hot, purée the soup in a blender in small batches, beginning on low speed and increasing the speed until the soup is smooth.
- ◆ Add the sugar to taste, and stir to dissolve.
- ◆ Cool before stirring in the buttermilk. Depending on the consistency, you may want to thin the soup with more fruit juice or a fruit liqueur.
- ◆ Cover and chill.
- ◆ At serving time, stir the soup and ladle it into pretty glass bowls. Top with fresh berries, and a sprig of mint or strip of orange zest.

Serves 8

MENU

Chilled Berry & Fruit Soup
Grilled lamb chops (page 247)
Sautéed spinach
Risotto (page 252)
Biscotti (page 231) and cappuccino

Summer Corn Chowder

This chowder's so good I make it in every season—with native corn in the summer, with southern corn that's available nearly all year, or even with frozen corn kernels. The cilantro gives the chowder a great finish and color.

3 tablespoons butter
1 small onion, finely chopped
1 red or orange pepper, seeded and finely chopped
1 celery stalk, finely chopped
2 tablespoons flour
2 cups light cream
4 cups boiling chicken broth
Corn kernels from 3 ears of fresh corn, cut and scraped (about 2 cups)
Cayenne pepper to taste
1/4 teaspoon cumin
Salt and black pepper to taste
1 teaspoon sugar
2 tablespoons chopped cilantro or flat Italian parsley

♦ Melt the butter in a large saucepan. Add the onion, pepper, and celery and sauté for about 10 minutes over low heat, stirring often to prevent the onion from coloring.
♦ Stir in the flour and cook a few minutes.
♦ Add the cream and bring to a boil, stirring to prevent any lumps.
♦ Add the hot broth and corn, and simmer for 10 minutes.
♦ Season with cayenne, cumin, salt, pepper, and sugar. Stir in the fresh cilantro and serve hot.

Serves 4 to 6

MENU

Summer Corn Chowder
Boiled lobsters (page 249) or shrimp (page 248)
Cherry tomatoes
French bread
Frozen yogurt sundaes

Vegetables

*P*roduce departments today are a visual delight, filled with an array of colors and choices year-round. They've become international culinary adventures that transport our minds and taste buds to other cultures and climates in minutes. With nutrition guidelines suggesting five servings of fruits and vegetables a day, this is a wonderful opportunity to expand your vegetable horizons and try something new. A trip through the produce department brings back memories of the past (turnips, rutabagas, parsnips, cabbage), tastes of the future (mesclun greens, frisee, sun-dried tomatoes, arugula, turnips, kumquats, peppers of every color from sweet to fiery) and of adopted cultures (bok choy, pomegranates, long beans, kim chee, cilantro, broccoli rabe). If you don't know what to do with these new vegetables, ask the people buying them or talk to the produce manager who wants to sell them and they will happily explain their use and cooking needs. Be adventurous!

So much of vegetable cookery is understanding cooking methods to maximize the freshness and simple goodness of the vegetables you choose to make and that your family likes to eat or learns to like.

Cooked Vegetable Techniques

Blanching. This means cooking for just a minute or two, or until *al dente* (crisp-tender), in boiling water, and then plunging into ice water to chill rapidly and stop the cooking. Blanched vegetables make a wonderful salad with a vinaigrette dressing drizzled over them at serving time. The brief cooking takes the bite out of julienned carrots, and brings out the beautiful green color of snow peas, sugar snap peas, green beans, and asparagus, and the yellow of corn. Be sure to chill the green vegetables immediately to stop the cooking so they'll stay green. Unfortunately, cooked green vegetables turn a terrible khaki color when an acid (lemon or vinegar) dressing is poured over them, so wait until serving time to dress them. Parsley also discolors in an acid dressing, but much less when it's coarsely cut than when it's finely chopped.

Boiling vs. Steaming. In boiling, the vegetables are cooked **in** boiling, salted water, and in steaming, the vegetables are cooked **over** simmering/boiling water that produces steam. Fewer vitamins are lost in the steaming process. You'll need a basket or steaming device to hold the vegetables over the water.

Sautéing vs. Stir-Frying. Sautéed vegetables are cooked in a little fat (oil or butter) over moderate or low temperatures. Sautéed vegetables usually don't require long cooking. Fresh spinach is sautéed in just minutes. Sautéed onion and garlic begin soups, sauces, and meat dishes. Stir-fried vegetables are quickly cooked in a little oil over high temperatures. Chinese woks are often used as the vessel, although a deep, heavy sauté pan will do as well. For longer-cooking vegetables (broccoli or carrots), stir-frying is sometimes combined with steaming. After a quick stir-fry, a little liquid (water or broth) is added, the pan covered, and the vegetables steamed to the desired doneness.

Grilling vs. Roasting. Both grilling and roasting require high temperatures, either on a hot grill or in the oven. Since vegetables have no natural fat to protect them from the heat, it's important to brush the vegetables with oil or a vinaigrette dressing before cooking. For roasted peppers, see page 242.

Buying and Storing

For taste and nutrition, fresh vegetables are the best. That's why I first consider native, seasonal produce that supports our local farms as well. But frozen vegetables have become part of our contemporary life, and some do nearly as well as fresh, and much better than canned: corn kernels, petite peas, and spinach.

Preparing Vegetables

In cutting vegetables, the descriptive terms range from coarsely chopped to minced, and may be more specific: cubed, diced, or julienned.

Raw vegetables are the easiest to prepare for quick dinners. Cut up a colorful assortment to serve on a platter with a dip, flavored olive oil, or plain and simple. Storing raw vegetables in ice water in the refrigerator keeps them crunchy, but also drains them of nutrition. It's best to store them in small plastic bags and eat them up quickly. Any of these can be added to green salads.

- Cut **cucumbers** in sticks, or score the skin lengthwise with a fork and cut into rounds. The long English (sometimes called European) or pickling cucumbers aren't waxed and have fewer seeds.
- **Carrots** keep well and are as good raw as cooked. Large carrots are as tasty and sweet as small ones.
- **Peppers** just need to be cored. The seeds mostly come out with the core if you cut around the top and pull.
- **Celery** is best and least stringy if you peel the stalks with a paring knife or a vegetable peeler.
- **Radishes** add bite, whole or sliced, and just need to be rinsed and the top greens removed.
- **Cherry** or **plum tomatoes** are often the best tomato choice out of season.
- **Jicama** is a large brown rounded root that tastes like a fresh water chestnut, or a cross between a cucumber and a coconut. Peel the skin to get to the white vegetable. Cut it into thin slices and eat it plain or with salt.
- **Purple-topped turnips** have a sharp flavor that grows on you.
- **Snow peas**, also know as Chinese pea pods or sugar snap peas, are delicious raw as well as blanched or sautéed. The pods are eaten as well as the peas. Remove the strings by pinching the ends and pulling off the string.

For a bit more sophistication on a crudité platter, include:

- **Cauliflower** cut into bite-size flowers.
- **Broccoli.** The tops should be cut off and cut into bite-size flowers and the

stalks should be peeled with a paring knife or vegetable peeler and cut into sticks or diagonally sliced rounds. Blanching brings out the green color.

- **Fennel** stalks have an anise or licorice taste and a celery-like texture.
- **Belgian endive** leaves are pale yellow-white with a slightly bitter taste.
- **Asparagus**, raw or blanched, is a great addition when it is in season.

Serve the vegetables with a modified Italian *bagna caulda*—olive oil warmed with mashed garlic, and salted to taste. An authentic *bagna caulda* would include mashed anchovies as well.

Year-Round Basics

Fresh **garlic** and **ginger** are best bought in small quantities as needed and kept loose in a dry dark spot—not in plastic. Plastic holds moisture in and doesn't allow any air circulation. Fresh ginger can be peeled and stored in a jar of sherry and kept in the refrigerator, but it changes the flavor and texture and limits its use.

Onions, shallots, garlic, and **leeks** are all vegetables from the lily family. Most noted for their flavoring of other dishes and in soups and stews, they can also be baked or roasted alone as a vegetable side dish.

Celery, parsley, fresh herbs, watercress, and **leafy greens** (spinach, kale) are best stored without ties, wrapped loosely in paper towels, and then put in an open plastic bag. The paper absorbs any moisture, and the open plastic bag still allows the vegetables to breathe. If the paper towels get very wet, re-wrap the greens in dry ones. Parsley has either curly or flat leaves. I prefer the slightly stronger flavor of the flat Italian parsley although the curly seems easiest to chop in large quantities.

It's best to keep **mushrooms** in the refrigerator in a paper bag, not plastic, so they can breathe and are less likely to mold. Buy them as you need them since they don't do well after a few days. Before using them, wipe any dirt from the mushroom with a clean damp sponge. If you have an excess of mushrooms, you can slice them, sauté them in butter or oil until the juices are evaporated, cool, and freeze in portions in a plastic container or plastic bag for future soups, stews, or sauces.

Hot chili peppers can be intimidating in their intensity and the warnings to wear rubber gloves in handling them. For the timid, chili peppers come processed in a can, but you'd be missing so much flavor and variety. When choosing fresh hot peppers ask about the taste and intensity of each. Jalepeños are the most readily available year-round and add just enough fire to dishes.

Summer Favorites

Tomatoes. There's no doubt about a real garden tomato: it smells like a real tomato, looks uniformly red, and tastes sweet and tart at the same time without being mealy or hard. It's no wonder that tomatoes are one of the most frequently used and loved vegetables, and a staple in every kitchen, either fresh or canned at their peak.

Fresh tomatoes should be kept out of the refrigerator where they lose their flavor. To ripen them, put them in a paper bag, not in the sun, where the natural ethylene gases can work their magic.

Whatever the variety, red or yellow, cherry or Italian plum, tomatoes are the essence of summer and a delight to the taste buds raw or cooked in so many ways.

In the summer the skin of ripe garden tomatoes will peel right off without the ice water/boiling water plunges. In the winter when tomatoes are of such poor quality, it's best to use canned tomatoes for cooking purposes and use plum or cherry tomatoes for salads.

Whole Italian plum tomatoes have more taste and better texture than regular whole, peeled tomatoes. Crushed tomatoes with added tomato purée come in a chunky variety that is a staple for sauces and cooking in the winter. Tomato paste is a quick thickener of sauces, with an intense tomato flavor. Most recipes call for just a tablespoon or two.

If a recipe calls for tomatoes *concassée*, it means peeled, seeded, and chopped tomatoes. You can seed tomatoes by cutting them in half horizontally—like a grapefruit. This exposes the seed pockets. Turn the tomato upside down and squeeze gently to force the seeds out.

Green beans from my garden have spoiled me for green beans elsewhere. Before the sun gets too hot in July and August, I'm in the garden picking bags of straight, thin 3-inch beans that taste as good raw as they taste steamed or boiled for just a few minutes. Cooked green beans are wonderful hot with butter and a sprinkle of celery seeds, or chilled in ice water (to retain the green color) and served as part of a summer Niçoise salad, or chilled and topped with chopped garden tomatoes and a drizzle of mustardy vinaigrette, or pickled for winter dinners. We never seem to tire of them.

Peas seem such a waste since you eat the peas and throw away the pods. Allow about 1 pound of peas in the pod for 1 cup of shelled peas. Snow peas and sugar snap peas are early and late summer garden vegetables since they do well in cooler weather. They're perfect for stir-fry dishes and quick sautés.

Peppers of every color and hotness have become the rage. They're the beginning vegetable (with onions, garlic, carrots, and celery) for soups and stews, a crudité platter essential because of the variety of color, and everyone's current favorite when roasted and served with goat cheese on sandwiches, or in composed salads vinaigrette. The colorful (red, yellow, orange, purple) Holland peppers are much meatier than other sweet peppers. You can recognize them by their price and the thick whole stems that match the dense heavy peppers.

Corn is no longer a brief summertime treat. New varieties have starch blockers that keep the corn tasting sweet and freshly picked, even when it's been shipped from Florida in the winter. The golden kernels are like bursts of sunshine that add sweetness and color to any dish they grace.

Winter Favorites—Root Vegetables

Celery root is a knobby, brown, lumpy vegetable that's delicious when peeled, julienned, blanched, and tossed with vinaigrette dressing.

Carrots are good raw, but cooking brings out their natural sweetness.

Parsnips look like white carrots. They're great cooked with carrots and mashed, or braised (sautéed, then simmered with liquid until soft).

Fennel (*finocchio*) is also known as anise and has a delicate licorice flavor. Fennel adds flavor and interest to a dish when sautéed with onions, celery, and carrots in soups and stews.

Purple-topped turnips are a gentle version of the regular turnip. They' re great cooked in stews, as a flavor enhancer in soups, or cooked and mashed alone, or with potatoes and other root vegetables.

Squash. Winter squashes keep very well and can be so colorful, that they're fun to have around whether you eat them or not. They're dense and take longer to cook than the summer varieties, so different cooking methods are better for these: boiling, baking, and microwaving. The most popular winter squashes are **acorn, butternut**, and the wonderful **spaghetti squash** that pulls out in strands that look like spaghetti. Some winter squashes are so big and the skin so thick, that produce departments will cut and even peel them for your convenience.

The most common and useful summer squashes are **yellow** and **zucchini**. They cook in minutes, so do best sautéed briefly, or combined with other quick-cooking vegetables (snow peas, peppers, onions) and stir-fried.

Year-Round Favorites

Cruciferous Vegetables. These include broccoli, cauliflower, Brussels sprouts, and cabbage. They have become new favorites especially because of their cancer fighting reputations. They're as versatile as they are delicious.

Leafy Greens. Spinach, escarole, arugula, watercress, and dandelion greens may be eaten raw in salads or used as a base for grilled or roasted foods. Chard, kale, broccoli rabe, turnip greens, dandelion greens, beet greens, and spinach can be steamed, stir-fried, or sautéed. Before washing the greens, store them loosely wrapped in paper towels in an open plastic bag, and refrigerate. The towels will absorb the moisture and the greens will keep longer.

Corn-Off-the-Cob

Corn-on-the-cob is delicious in its simplicity. Corn-Off-the-Cob is an irresistible treat, especially for the diners if not the cook. The pepper and parsley make this a beautiful dish as well.

6 ears of fresh corn,
  husked
1 tablespoon butter
1 red pepper, seeded and
  diced
1½ teaspoons sugar
Salt and pepper to taste
2 tablespoons chopped
  Italian parsley

♦ Cut the kernels off the cob with the sharp edge of a knife, and scrape any remaining pulp with the flat side of the knife. You should have about 4 cups of kernels. Standing the corn up and cutting into a large deep bowl avoids a mess!
♦ Heat the butter in a medium-size sauté pan and sauté the pepper for 1 minute. Add the corn and sugar and cook for about 3 minutes, stirring, until creamy and hot. Stir in the parsley. Taste and season with salt and pepper.

Serves 4 to 6

MENU

Grilled salmon steaks (page 248)
Corn-Off-the-Cob
Caesar Salad (page 35)
Chilled coffee in a wine goblet with a scoop of ice cream

Curried Eggplant

Curried Eggplant is a fast answer to week-day dinners, and a healthy choice if you're staying away from meat. Any leftovers are great as a topping for pasta.

1 medium eggplant, cut into ³/₄-inch cubes to make about 6 cups
1 teaspoon salt
6 tablespoons vegetable oil
1 onion, coarsely chopped
2 cloves garlic, minced
2 teaspoons grated fresh peeled ginger root
2 teaspoons curry powder
1 teaspoon cumin
¹/₂ teaspoon tumeric
4 cardamom pods, pinched to expose the seeds, or ¹/₄ teaspoon ground cardamom
1 tablespoon sugar
²/₃ cup water
3 tablespoons soy sauce
Salt, black pepper, and cayenne pepper to taste

- Toss the eggplant cubes with the salt and place in a colander or strainer. Put a small plate on top of the eggplant and weight with a heavy can. Drain the eggplant for 30 minutes and rub with paper towels to dry.
- Heat 4 tablespoons of the oil in a large heavy sauté pan. Over medium-high heat, sauté the eggplant for 5 to 10 minutes until nearly soft. Stir often with a flat-bottom spatula to prevent sticking. Remove from the pan and reserve.
- Add the remaining oil to the pan and set over low heat. Sauté the onion, garlic, and ginger for 5 minutes, stirring often, until softened but not colored. Add the spices and continue to sauté for a few minutes. Add the sugar, water, and soy sauce, and simmer for 1 minute.
- Return the eggplant to the pan, cover, and simmer for about 15 minutes until the eggplant is very soft and the sauce is thickened. Add more water and cook longer if needed, until the eggplant is very soft.
- Remove the cardamom pods and adjust the seasoning with salt, pepper, or cayenne.
- Serve hot over rice.

Serves 4

MENU

Curried Eggplant
Rice Pilaf (page 252)
Chopped cucumbers in plain yogurt
Tapioca pudding

Autumn Vegetable Stew

Autumn's harvest brings a cornucopia of nutritious and colorful vegetables that cook together in a seasonal stew. Vary the vegetables according to their availability and your taste.

3 tablespoons butter
1 onion, coarsely
  chopped
1 teaspoon curry powder
2 large carrots, peeled
  and cut into matchstick
  julienne
1/2 head cauliflower,
  broken into bite-size
  pieces
1 baking potato (russet or
  Idaho), peeled and cut
  into 1/2-inch cubes
1 pound butternut or
  buttercup squash,
  peeled and cut into
  1-inch cubes
1 1/2 cups chicken broth
Salt, black pepper, a
  grating of nutmeg, and
  cayenne pepper to taste
1/2 cup frozen petite peas

♦ Heat the butter in a large sauté pan and add the onion. Sauté over low heat for about 5 minutes, stirring often, until very soft, but not colored. Stir in the curry powder, then add the julienned carrots, cauliflower, potato, and squash, and sauté for a few minutes. Add the chicken broth and bring to a simmer. Partially cover and cook for about 15 minutes until the vegetables are tender. Be sure the carrots and cauliflower are tender even if the potato is falling apart.

♦ Season to taste with salt, black pepper, nutmeg, and cayenne pepper. Stir in the peas and heat thoroughly.

Serves 6

MENU

Autumn Vegetable Stew
Roast pork (Roasting Chart, page 247)
Pear tasting
Gingerbread cake (page 209)

Roasted Summer Vegetables

Insalata and Panino *seem to be on the menu of every Italian res-*
taurant. Insalata is a salad, not just of greens, but usually composed
of roasted or grilled vegetables for a light lunch or appetizer. Panino is
an Italian sandwich made on flat chewy focaccia bread, filled with grilled
vegetables or chicken, tomato, and sometimes topped with melted cheese. Both are
easy dishes to make at home and can begin with these flavorful summer vegetables. My
original plan was to grill the vegetables, but a rainy day necessitated the oven-roasting,
and the results were so good, I've been roasting them ever since. Sweet seasonal Vidalia
onions are perfect for this dish, and eggplant slices are delicious too. The peppers add
sweetness and color, and the plum tomatoes are even better than the commercial sun-
dried tomatoes. With fresh mild goat cheese and crusty bread, this is perfect picnic fare
as well as a refreshing dinner.

¹/₄ cup olive oil
2 Vidalia or other sweet
  onions, peeled and cut
  into 1-inch slices
8 ripe plum tomatoes, cut
  in half
2 red peppers, cut in half
  and seeded
Salt and pepper to taste
3 tablespoons Balsamic
  vinegar
Fresh chopped basil or
  parsley

+ Preheat the oven to 425°F. Lighly oil a large shallow roasting pan or jellyroll pan with some of
  the oil.
+ Arrange the vegetables close together, cut side up,
  in the pan. Drizzle with oil, rubbing it over the
  surface of the vegetables to cover completely.
  Sprinkle liberally with salt and pepper.
+ Roast the vegetables in the middle of the hot oven
  for about 1¹/₄ hours.
+ Reduce the heat to 400°F for the last 30 minutes
  if the vegetables darken too much. The onions
  will caramelize, the peppers will sweeten and
  soften, and the tomatoes will reduce in size and
  intensify in flavor.
+ Cool slightly, remove to a serving platter, and
  sprinkle with vinegar and fresh basil or parsley.
  Serve at room temperature or with bread and
  fresh cheese.

Serves 4 to 6

MENU

Roasted Summer Vegetables
Focaccia bread
Fresh goat cheese
Chocolate cake (page 265)
Iced cappuccino

Garden Vegetable Melange

Served at room temperature, and full of Mediterranean panache, this mixture of vegetables is perfect for picnics or for dinnertime with a simple grilled chicken. It cooks itself while you're outdoors doing better things. The handful of rice absorbs the juices and thickens the ratatouille-like dish. Substitute a 28-ounce can of plum tomatoes, drained and coarsely chopped, if fresh ones aren't at their peak.

1 large onion, thinly sliced

1 clove garlic, peeled and skewered with a toothpick

1 small eggplant cut into ³/4-inch cubes

1 large green pepper, seeded and cut into 1-inch pieces

1 medium zucchini or yellow squash, cut into ¹/4-inch rounds

4 garden tomatoes, peeled, seeded, and chopped

¹/4 cup olive oil

2 tablespoons rice

Salt and pepper to taste

1 bay leaf

1 cup cooked chick peas, drained

1 tablespoon tiny, brined capers, drained, optional

Small, black, oil-cured olives, optional

+ Preheat the oven to 350°F.

+ In a large roasting pan, add the vegetables and toss to mix. Pour the oil over the vegetables, toss, and sprinkle with the rice. Season with salt and pepper, and add the bay leaf. Cover tightly with foil and bake about 1 hour, stirring a few times, until the vegetables are tender and the liquid has mostly been absorbed by the rice. It will thicken more as it cools.

+ Remove the garlic and the bay leaf. Stir in the chick peas, capers, and olives, and adjust the seasoning. Serve warm or at room temperature.

Serves 6

MENU

Grilled chicken (page 83)
Garden Vegetable Melange
French bread
Chocolate chip cookies (page 232)

Tomato Tart Italienne

This tomato tart, similar to a quiche, takes advantage of a bumber crop of garden tomatoes. The custard is flavored with basil, oregano, scallions, and Parmesan cheese. Homemade pie crusts are always best, and fast to make, especially if you prepare the dough in the processor ahead of time, refrigerate, and roll it out at dinnertime. Prebaking the pie crust—baking it "blind"—is an added step but worth the effort.

Dough for a 9-inch pie crust
  (page 262):
1¼ cups flour
¼ teaspoon salt
6 tablespoons shortening
3–4 tablespoons ice water

2 eggs
1 tablespoon flour
1 cup light cream
2 tablespoons chopped
  fresh basil
½ teaspoon salt
½ teaspoon dried
  oregano
2 scallions, thinly sliced
  with some green, to
  make ¼ cup
2 medium-size ripe
  garden tomatoes,
  peeled and thinly sliced
¼ cup freshly grated
  Parmesan cheese

+ Combine the flour and salt in a large bowl. Cut in the shortening with a pastry blender or 2 knives until it resembles coarse meal. With a fork, stir in the water until it forms a dough. Turn onto a lightly floured surface and gently knead until a ball forms. Enclose it in plastic wrap, and chill.
+ On a lightly floured surface, roll out the dough to form a 13-inch circle. Fit it into a lightly greased 9-inch pie plate, pressing it into the bottom and sides. Trim the edges and crimp.
+ Preheat the oven to 400°F.
+ Line the bottom and sides of the dough with foil and weight with dried beans. Bake in the middle of the oven for 10 minutes. Remove the beans and foil and prick the bottom with a fork. Continue to bake for 5 minutes until lightly colored. Reduce the oven temperature to 375°F.
+ In a small bowl, whisk together the eggs and flour, and then add the cream and spices. Sprinkle the scallions over the bottom of the baked pie shell.
+ Remove the seeds and excess juice from the tomato slices. Drain on paper towels. Arrange in overlapping circles around the bottom of the crust.
+ Pour the custard over the tomatoes and sprinkle with the cheese. Bake on the bottom shelf of the oven for about 40 minutes or until set in the middle.
+ Cool for 10 minutes before cutting and serving.

Yields 1 9-inch tart

MENU

Beef steaks, broiled or grilled (page 247)
Tomato Tart Italienne
Romaine and endive salad
Cupcakes

Salads

G reen salads are year-round favorites and can be found at our dinner table nearly every night. We never tire of them because there are so many choices of greens to combine, so many interesting ingredients to add, and innumerable ways to *dress* the salad. Consider a variety of greens for color, texture, and flavor:

Iceberg is almost passé, but still fun if you like the crunchy texture. I usually cut it into wedges and serve it with Russian (page 259) or Blue Cheese Dressing (page 259), or shred it for Cowboy's Nachos (page 181) or tacos.

Bibb, or **Boston Bibb** is a soft and buttery head lettuce that is wonderful cut in half, drizzled with vinaigrette, and sprinkled with crumbled blue cheese.

Green leaf, red leaf, and **romaine** lettuces are the basis of any mixed green salad. The red seems to be a bit more perishable. Be sure to store these properly for added shelf life as you would any leafy greens. Remove the ties, wrap loosely in paper towels, and put in an open plastic bag. Wash and dry the lettuce in a salad spinner as you need it for a salad. If you've washed and dried more than you need, or you want to clean the lettuce ahead of time, layer the dried leaves between paper towels in a plastic bag, and refrigerate. The paper towels will absorb moisture that causes the lettuce to deteriorate. It's important to dry lettuce before serving because salad dressing will have a hard time coating wet leaves and excess water will dilute the salad dressing.

Additions to mixed green salads can be:

> **frisee**—pale green, curly leaves that are slightly bitter
> **arugula**—small, dark green leaves with an elusive, peppery taste
> **mesclun**—a very delicate mix of tiny greens and herbs
> **fresh spinach**—remove the tough stems
> **watercress**—remove the thick stems
> **radicchio**—a tight head of beautiful red leaves
> **Belgian endive**—small stalks of delicate, slightly bitter white/yellow leaves
> **shredded cabbage**
> **sliced mushrooms**
> **cucumbers**
> **tomatoes**—cherry tomatoes work best in mixed green salads since the juice is enclosed in the tomato
> **other vegetables**—carrots, peppers, sliced scallions, sprouts, and celery
> **croutons**—homemade are the best and they use up day-old French or Italian bread (page 261)
> **cheese**—crumbled blue cheese or grated Parmesan
> **sunflower seeds**

In the summer, fresh fruit is a refreshing surprise in a lettuce salad, and in the spring, I pick violets from my unsprayed yard for a colorful and tasty addition to the greens. Even young dandelion greens add a sharp and bitter touch to salads, but only if there are no pesticides in your yard. If used in moderation, the bitter greens—escarole and chicory—are a nice contrast to the sweeter greens in a mixed salad, and work well with a sharp, mustardy vinaigrette dressing.

A good salad dressing can be as simple as 1 part acid (red wine vinegar, Balsamic vinegar, or lemon juice): 3 parts oil (olive oil or a combination with vegetable oil), salt, and pepper. For more information on dressings see Tips and Basic Recipes, page 258.

Vegetable and **main dish salads** are synonymous with warm weather since they feature cold vegetables, pasta, grains, potatoes, seafood, or chicken, and combine them with a vinaigrette or mayonnaise-based dressing. The raw or cooked ingredients can be jazzed up with ethnic flavors or zippy additions to make them versatile and easily assembled for fast dinners. Pasta salads seem to taste best the day they are made, so prepare the ingredients in advance, toss them together just a few hours before serving, and chill them. Cold seems to dull the flavors of salads that tasted perfectly seasoned when you made them. Taste before serving and be prepared to add more salt and pepper or even a bit more dressing.

Caesar Salad

Classic Caesar salad dressings are made with raw egg yolks (to thicken) and anchovies (for flavor). By substituting mustard and mayonnaise for thickening, and Worcestershire sauce for the anchovies, you can achieve the same consistency and taste without the health risk of raw eggs, or the objection by some to anchovies. Caesar salads are always made with romaine lettuce (crunchy and sweet), homemade croutons, and freshly grated, or, even better, shaved Parmesan cheese.

1 large head romaine lettuce, washed, dried and torn into bite-size pieces
1 clove garlic, finely minced to a paste
2 tablespoons fresh lemon juice (about 1/2 lemon)
3 tablespoons mayonnaise
2 teaspoons Worcestershire sauce
1 rounded teaspoon Dijon mustard
1/2 teaspoon salt
Pepper to taste
1/2 cup olive oil
1/3 cup freshly grated Parmesan cheese
2 cups homemade croutons (page 261), or more if you like

+ Put the prepared lettuce in a large salad bowl.
+ Prepare the dressing in a small bowl by combining the garlic, lemon juice, mayonnaise, Worcestershire sauce, mustard, salt, and pepper. Whisk to mix well. Slowly add the olive oil while whisking to make a thickened dressing.
+ At serving time, add enough dressing to the lettuce to coat it lightly. Top with the Parmesan and croutons, toss, and serve immediately.

Serves 6

MENU

Grilled salmon steaks (page 248)
Grilled vegetable skewers (summer squash, cherry tomatoes, and peppers)
Couscous (page 250)
Caesar Salad
Chocolate Fondue with fresh fruit (page 235)

Indian Carrot Slaw

If you tire of cabbage slaws, try one with carrots and some intriguing Indian ingredients that add texture as well as great flavor combinations. You may never go back to coleslaw.

4 large carrots, about
  1 pound
¹/₄ cup dried coconut
  flakes*
¹/₄ cup pistachio nuts,
  chopped
¹/₄ cup currants
2 tablespoons sugar
2 teaspoons minced
  crystallized ginger
¹/₂ teaspoon ground
  cardamom
¹/₄ teaspoon cinnamon
¹/₂ cup mayonnaise
1 tablespoon sour cream
  or plain yogurt

♦ Peel and grate the carrots into a large bowl. Add the coconut, nuts, currants, sugar, ginger, cardamom, and cinnamon, and stir to mix thoroughly.
♦ In a small bowl, combine the mayonnaise and sour cream. Add enough of the mayonnaise mixture to bind the carrots. Taste and adjust the seasoning.
♦ Store covered in the refrigerator. Stir the slaw before serving.

Serves 4 to 6

* Available in natural food stores, dried coconut is sometimes labeled *dessicated* and is not nearly as sweet as the sweetened flaked coconut used for baking.

MENU

Grilled lamb chops (page 247)
Boiled red potatoes
Indian Carrot Slaw
Pita Crisps (page 262)
Apple pie (page 223)

Sweet & Tart Vegetable Salad

*V*inegar and sugar turn this vegetable salad into a refreshing, tart-sweet side dish that complements this rich menu of potato pancakes and pot roast. It's perfect for a picnic menu as well.

1 long English cucumber
1/2 small green cabbage
    (about 3/4 pound)
1 sweet onion, cut in half
    and thinly sliced
Salt

For the dressing:
1/2 cup cider vinegar
2 tablespoons vegetable
    oil
3–4 tablespoons sugar
1 teaspoon salt
1/4 teaspoon cayenne
    pepper

1 green pepper, seeded
    and julienned
1 red pepper, seeded and
    julienned

♦ Score the cucumber, running the tines of a fork down the length of the cucumber. Cut into very thin slices.
♦ Shred the cabbage with a knife to make about 3 cups.
♦ Layer the cucumber, cabbage, and onion in a large strainer and sprinkle well with salt. Put a small plate on top of the vegetables and weight them with a heavy can. Let them sit for at least an hour, tossing a few times. This will eliminate some of the water and wilt the vegetables. Wash well with water and drain, patting with paper towels to dry.
♦ In a small bowl, combine the vinegar, oil, sugar, salt, and cayenne.
♦ In a large bowl, combine the wilted vegetables and peppers with the dressing, tossing to coat thoroughly. Pack in a glass jar and chill in the refrigerator.

Serves 6 to 8

MENU

Pot roast (page 90)
Potato pancakes (page 152) with Applesauce (page 268)
Sweet & Tart Vegetable Salad
Challah

Tabouleh

Tabouleh is the ever-popular Middle Eastern bulgur (cracked wheat) salad that's loaded with flavor and nutrition. This salad is easy to transport, safe for picnics, and doesn't wilt in hot weather. For a fast, low-calorie meal, mix a little tuna fish into the tabouleh and serve it in a pita pocket with a wedge of lemon. Chop the parsley coarsely so that it will stay a beautiful green in the salad.

1 cup medium- or fine-cut bulgur wheat
1 cup cold water
¼ cup fresh lemon juice (about 1 large lemon)
¼ cup olive oil
3 scallions, finely chopped
1 cup coarsely chopped parsley
2–3 tablespoons chopped fresh mint
1 large garden tomato, peeled, seeded, and chopped
Salt and pepper to taste

♦ Combine the bulgur wheat and water in a large bowl. Set aside for 30 minutes until the water is absorbed and the grains are softened.
♦ Add the lemon juice and oil and stir to coat. Stir in the scallions, parsley, and mint. Drain the excess juice from the chopped tomatoes and add them to the salad. Stir to combine and season with salt and pepper to taste. Add a bit more lemon juice or oil if the salad seems dry.

Serves 4 to 6

MENU

Grilled marinated beef (page 93)
Tabouleh
Green salad vinaigrette
Frozen yogurt with Chocolate Sauce (page 264)

Armenian Salad

When tomato season is at its peak, try this wonderful Armenian Salad, similar to Tabouleh, as a condiment for sandwiches or even as a topping for pasta. A little goes a long way since it's intensely flavored and spiced. For a treat, spread just a little of the salad on an opened pita bread round. Top with a little crumbled Feta cheese, a drizzle of olive oil, and bake in a hot oven (450°F) until crisp. Voilà, an Armenian pizza!

3 garden tomatoes, peeled, seeded, and chopped
1/2 bunch parsley, stems removed and coarsely chopped
1 sweet onion, chopped
3 scallions, finely chopped
1 tablespoon tomato paste
1 tablespoon fresh lemon juice
2 tablespoons olive oil
2 tablespoons chopped fresh mint
1/2 teaspoon salt
1/4 teaspoon cayenne pepper
Black pepper to taste

+ Drain the tomatoes of excess juice and add them to a large bowl.
+ Add the remaining ingredients and stir to mix well. Taste and adjust the seasoning.
+ Store the salad in a glass jar or plastic container in the refrigerator.

Serves 4 to 6

MENU

Grilled lamb chops—rub with olive oil, garlic, salt, and pepper (page 247)
Armenian Salad
Grilled or baked potatoes (page 254)
Peppermint ice cream

Pennsylvania Dutch Coleslaw

Cabbage is one of the cruciferous vegetables that are important for healthy diets, so it's a good idea to eat lots of coleslaw year-round. This is just one of many coleslaw variations. The cooked dressing has no oil and is thickened with flour and an egg yolk. It's tart and sweet at the same time—and a real Pennsylvania Dutch specialty.

3½ tablespoons sugar
1 tablespoon flour
1 teaspoon salt
½ teaspoon dry mustard
Pinch of cayenne pepper
1 egg yolk
¼ cup cider vinegar
¼ cup water
2 tablespoons heavy
  cream
1½ pounds green
  cabbage, shredded to
  make about 6 cups
1 carrot, grated
1 celery stalk, thinly
  sliced
3 scallions, finely
  chopped

♦ In a small heavy saucepan, combine the sugar, flour, salt, mustard, and cayenne pepper. Whisk in the egg yolk, then slowly whisk in the vinegar and water. Cook over low heat, stirring often, for about 6 minutes, or until the dressing is smooth and thick and begins to bubble in the center.

♦ Remove from the heat, stir in the cream, and cool. You may want to strain it if there are any lumps.

♦ In a large bowl, combine the cabbage, carrot, celery, and scallions. Pour the dressing over the cabbage mixture and toss to combine thoroughly. Refrigerate and serve chilled. Toss again before serving.

Serves 6

MENU

Grilled hot dogs or sausages
Potato Salad (page 244)
Pennsylvania Dutch Coleslaw
Fresh blueberries or raspberries in a waffle cone or cup with vanilla yogurt topping

Spinach & Shrimp Salad

Here's a spectacular salad with enough goodies to make it a meal in itself. The sesame dressing is unusually good and full of flavor. Cooked shrimp, crabmeat, or even grilled chicken can be added to make this an elegant dinner. Dry the spinach well and add the dressing at serving time so the spinach doesn't get soggy.

³/₄ pound fresh spinach, washed, dried, and tough stems removed
2 celery stalks, sliced
1 red pepper, seeded and julienned
2 scallions, sliced
¹/₂ English cucumber, sliced
³/₄ pound cooked shrimp, peeled and deveined
1 cup firm tofu cubes
1¹/₂ cups bean sprouts
Red onion rings

For the dressing:
3 tablespoons rice wine vinegar
1 tablespoon Balsamic vinegar
¹/₄ cup mayonnaise
1 teaspoon dry mustard
¹/₂ teaspoon powdered ginger
¹/₂ teaspoon salt
Pepper to taste
¹/₂ cup vegetable oil
2 tablespoons roasted sesame oil
2 tablespoons sesame seeds, lightly toasted

♦ Combine the salad ingredients in a large bowl.
♦ For the dressing, whisk together the vinegars, mayonnaise, dry mustard, ginger, salt, and pepper in a small, deep bowl.
♦ Combine the oils and add them very slowly to the dressing ingredients, whisking constantly, until an emulsion forms. Stir in the sesame seeds.
♦ At serving time, add enough dressing to the salad to coat the spinach lightly.
♦ The dressing recipe makes enough dressing for 2 salads. Refrigerate the remainder in a glass jar to use another time.

Serves 4 to 6

MENU

Spinach & Shrimp Salad
Crusty French bread
Brownies with ice cream (page 233)
Iced tea

Vegetable-Pilaf Salad

Pasta salads, especially those based on vinaigrette dressings, are just right for summer picnics or dinner buffets. Add your choice of vegetables to this versatile rice pilaf salad.

2 tablespoons vegetable oil
1/4 cup vermicelli or thin spaghetti, broken into 1-inch pieces
2 cups rice
4 cups boiling water
2 teaspoons salt
1 10-ounce package frozen mixed vegetables
3 tablespoons red wine vinegar
1/2 cup olive oil
4 scallions, cut into thin diagonal slices
4 plum tomatoes, diced
1/2 cup chopped parsley
1 green or red pepper, seeded and chopped
Salt and pepper to taste

Optional additions:
Cooked chick peas
Pitted black olives
Jalepeño pepper, seeded and minced
Chopped fresh herbs

♦ In a sauté pan, heat the oil over low heat and add the vermicelli, stirring, until it changes color. Add the rice and cook, stirring, until the rice is very hot and the vermicelli is golden. Add the boiling water, cover, and simmer for 10 minutes.

♦ Top with the frozen vegetables, cover and continue to simmer for about 15 minutes until all the liquid is absorbed and the rice is tender.

♦ Uncover, cool for 15 minutes, and add the vinegar and oil. Use a fork to mix together.

♦ When completely cool, toss with the remaining ingredients and any additions you like. Season with salt and pepper. Serve at room temperature.

Serves 8

MENU

Grilled chicken (pages 82, 83)
Vegetable-Pilaf Salad
French bread
Chocolate Fondue with strawberries and bananas (page 235)

Garden Vegetable & Rice Salad

Here's a summer salad loaded with colorful vegetables from the garden—tomatoes, peppers, corn, and peas.

1 cup frozen petite peas
  or garden fresh ones
2 tablespoons fresh lime
  or lemon juice
2 tablespoons red wine
  vinegar
1/2 cup olive oil
1 clove garlic, minced
3 scallions, chopped with
  some green
2 large garden tomatoes,
  peeled, seeded, and
  diced
1 red pepper, seeded and
  chopped
1 orange or green pepper,
  seeded and chopped
8 marinated artichoke
  hearts, rinsed and cut
  in half
Chopped fresh herbs,
  optional
1 cup rice
2 cups salted water or
  chicken broth
1 cup corn kernels cut
  from 2 ears of fresh
  corn
1/4 cup chopped parsley
Salt and pepper to taste

- If you are using frozen peas, run them under boiling water to defrost them. If you are using fresh peas, cook them for 1 minute and chill them in ice water. Drain the peas and reserve them.
- In a large bowl, combine the lime juice, vinegar, oil, garlic, and scallions. Add the tomatoes, peppers, artichoke hearts, herbs, and reserved peas.
- Combine the rice and water or broth in a medium-size saucepan. Bring to a boil, stir, cover, and cook for about 15 minutes until the liquid is absorbed and the rice is tender.
- Uncover the pan, add the corn, and set aside. The corn will cook slightly from the heat of the rice.
- When the rice is cool, add it to the bowl of vegetables and stir to mix thoroughly. Stir in the parsley. Season with salt and pepper to taste. Serve at room temperature.

Serves 8

MENU

Marinated and grilled shrimp on skewers (page 180)
Garden Vegetable & Rice Salad
Foccacia bread
Blueberries and cream

Tartar Potato Salad

This potato salad is bursting with flavor from brined buds of the caper bush, cornichons (little French pickles), and salty pimiento-stuffed green olives—all available in most markets.

2 pounds (about 4 or 5) all-purpose red or white potatoes
3 tablespoons red wine vinegar
1 teaspoon sugar
Salt and pepper to taste
2 celery stalks, chopped

For the sauce:
3/4 cup mayonnaise
2 tablespoons tiny, brined capers, drained
2 tablespoons coarsely chopped cornichons or dill pickles
2 tablespoons chopped pimiento-stuffed green olives
2 tablespoons of the caper or cornichon brine
1 tablespoon Dijon mustard
1 shallot, minced
Pinch of sugar
Pinch of cayenne pepper

♦ Cook the potatoes in boiling salted water for about 20 minutes until tender but not mushy. While hot, peel the potatoes, cut them into chunks, and place in a large bowl. Sprinkle with vinegar, sugar, salt, and pepper. Toss gently to mix. Cover and let the potatoes cool. Add the celery to the potatoes.

♦ Combine the sauce ingredients in a small bowl. Fold enough of the sauce into the cooled potatoes and celery to coat them well. Season with salt and pepper to taste.

Serves 6 to 8

MENU

Grilled salmon or swordfish steaks (page 248)
Tartar Potato Salad
Garden green beans
Lemon sorbet with fresh berries and mint

German Caraway Potato Salad

*W*arm *potato salad with sausages may be the perfect dinner for chilly evenings. This dressing is sweet and tart, with caraway seeds for added flavor and bacon for saltiness. If you skip the bacon, use 2 tablespoons of vegetable oil for sautéing the onions.*

2½ pounds (about 6 or 7) all-purpose red or white potatoes
4 slices bacon, cut into 1-inch pieces
½ cup finely chopped onion
½ teaspoon caraway seeds
2 tablespoons flour
½ cup cider vinegar
½ cup water
⅓ cup sugar
1 teaspoon salt, or more to taste
Pepper to taste
Snipped chives for garnish

♦ In a large pot of boiling salted water, cook the potatoes for about 20 minutes until they are tender. Peel the potatoes and cut them into thick slices. Put the potatoes in a large bowl.

♦ Cook the bacon in a large sauté pan until crisp. Remove the bacon to a paper towel to drain. Leave 2 tablespoons of bacon fat in the pan.

♦ Over low heat, sauté the onion in the bacon fat (or use vegetable oil) until softened. Add the caraway seeds and sauté for 1 minute without browning the onion. Add the flour and sauté for another minute. Stir in the vinegar, water, sugar, and salt. Bring to a boil, whisking, and simmer for 1 minute until thickened.

♦ While the dressing is hot, pour it over the potatoes and toss gently. Season to taste with more salt and pepper. Garnish with the reserved bacon and chives and serve at room temperature.

Serves 8

MENU

Sausages and mustard
German Caraway Potato Salad
Dill pickles
Cherry pie

Oriental Noodle & Pepper Salad

This noodle salad sparkles with color and travels well for a picnic. Fresh noodles are available in most produce departments, in Chinese or Japanese varieties. You can buy them fresh and freeze them in the package for a later time. Colorful peppers are irresistible especially in the summer. You can roast them (page 242) and freeze them to enjoy even when they're out of season. But in their abundance, eat them raw or with dips, or add them to greens, pasta, vegetables, rice, or chicken salad.

³/₄ pound green cabbage, about half a small head

For the dressing:
¹/₃ cup vegetable oil
3 tablespoons rice wine vinegar
2 tablespoons sugar
1 teaspoon salt
Black pepper to taste
Pinch of cayenne pepper

1 12-ounce package fresh Chinese noodles
3 scallions, white and green part, thinly sliced
¹/₂ red pepper, seeded and julienned
¹/₂ orange pepper, seeded and julienned
¹/₂ green pepper, seeded and julienned
3 tablespoons sesame seeds

♦ Shred the cabbage with a knife to make about 3 cups and place in a large bowl.

♦ In a small saucepan, combine the dressing ingredients and bring to a simmer, stirring until the sugar is dissolved. Pour the dressing over the cabbage, stir, and set aside for 5 minutes to cool.

♦ Cook the noodles in a large pot of boiling water according to the package directions until tender. Drain, run under cold water to chill, and drain well.

♦ Add the noodles to the cabbage along with the scallions and peppers. Mix well to coat all the ingredients. Cover and refrigerate for a few hours. Toss again before serving. Season with salt and pepper.

♦ At serving time, toast the sesame seeds in a dry sauté pan, stirring often, until lightly colored—don't let them burn. Sprinkle over the salad and serve at room temperature.

Serves 8

MENU

Oriental Noodle & Pepper Salad
Baked chicken (page 245)
Fresh fruit on bamboo skewers
Brownies (page 233)

Pasta, Pepper & Bean Salad with Feta Cheese

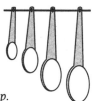

Some of the charm of pasta is in the names and shapes they conjure up. Bowtie pasta comes in small and large sizes and is also known as farfalle or butterfly pasta. In this salad, some of the beans are frozen and some are canned for convenience. The dressing is robust in flavor and the cheese adds a great finish.

1/2 pound large bowtie or farfalle pasta

1 9-ounce package frozen French-cut green beans

1 1-pound can chick peas

1 1-pound can dark red kidney beans

1 red pepper and 1 yellow pepper, seeded and chopped

3 celery stalks, finely chopped

1/4 cup finely chopped red onion

1/4 cup coarsely chopped Italian parsley

1 cup crumbled Feta cheese (about 4 ounces)

For the dressing:

1/4 cup red wine vinegar

2 tablespoons Dijon mustard

1 clove garlic, minced

1 teaspoon salt

1/2 teaspoon oregano

Pepper to taste

2/3 cup olive oil

- Cook the pasta in a large pot of boiling salted water according to the package directions until tender. Drain well, run under cold water to cool, and drain again. Transfer to a large bowl.
- Put the frozen beans in a strainer, run under hot water to defrost, and drain well. Add the beans to the bowl.
- Drain the canned beans, rinse, and drain well. Add to the bowl.
- Add the peppers to the bowl with the celery, onion, parsley, and cheese, and mix well.
- To make the dressing, combine the vinegar, mustard, garlic, salt, oregano, and pepper in a medium-size bowl. Add the oil slowly, whisking constantly, until a thick, emulsion forms.
- Add enough dressing to the salad to bind and coat well. Toss and taste. Season with additional salt and pepper to taste. Serve at room temperature. If you refrigerate the salad, take it out 15 minutes before serving so it can warm up slightly. Toss before serving.

Serves 8 to 12

MENU

Grilled tuna (page 248)
Pasta, Pepper & Bean Salad with Feta Cheese
Crusty Italian bread
Fruit Salad (page 268)
Chocolate chip cookies (page 232)

Twist 'n Shout Pasta Salad

Here's a fun pasta salad for summertime dinners. The twist *comes from twist pasta, also known as rotini or fuscelli. And the* shout *comes from hot peppers that give the salad a real zing. The intensity of the shout will depend on the number of jalepeños and the amount of cayenne pepper you use. The pasta, colorful peppers, corn kernels, and tomatoes are tossed with a creamy cumin-lime dressing. Pasta salads are best the day they're made, and chilled but not cold.*

3 ears of fresh corn
12 ounces twist, rotini, or
    fuscelli pasta
1 red or orange pepper,
    seeded and chopped
1 green pepper, seeded
    and chopped
2 jalepeño peppers,
    seeded and minced
4 plum tomatoes, diced
    and drained of excess
    juice
4 scallions, white and
    green, thinly sliced
1/4 cup coarsely chopped
    cilantro

For the dressing:
1/4 cup fresh lime juice
    (about 2 limes)
1 rounded tablespoon
    Dijon mustard
3 tablespoons mayonnaise
1 teaspoon ground
    cumin
1 teaspoon salt
1 teaspoon sugar
1/4 teaspoon cayenne
    pepper
1/2 cup olive oil

♦ Bring a large pot of water to boil. Husk the corn and add to the pot. Simmer for 2 minutes. Remove the corn, reserve the water, and run the corn under cold water to cool. Cut the kernels off the cob and add to a large bowl. This should make about 1 1/2 cups of kernels.

♦ Return the pot of water to a boil and cook the pasta according to the package directions until tender. Drain well, run under water to cool, and drain again. Add to the bowl with the peppers, tomatoes, scallions, and cilantro. Toss to mix well.

♦ To prepare the dressing, add the lime juice, mustard, mayonnaise, cumin, salt, sugar, and cayenne to a medium-size, deep bowl. Add the oil slowly, whisking constantly to make a thickened emulsified sauce. Pour over the salad ingredients and toss. Taste and adjust the seasoning with salt and cayenne pepper. Serve, or cover and refrigerate. Remove from the refrigerator 15 minutes before serving to warm slightly. Toss before serving.

Serves 8 to 12

MENU

Grilled steaks or chops (page 247)
Twist 'n Shout Pasta Salad
Garlic Bread (page 261)
Cheesecake with fresh fruit topping (page 267)

Tex-Mex Macaroni Salad

*A*dd *some spice and color to your summer cookouts. This maca-roni salad adds some new ingredients and spices to the more tradi-tional ones. When you cook corn-on-the-cob, add a few extras, cut the kernels off the cobs, and reserve for this spicy macaroni salad, corn chowder (page 20), Garden Vegetable Rice Salad (page 43), Summer Scallop & Corn Sauté (page 103), or corn/tomato relish.*

2 ears of fresh corn, husked

8 ounces elbow macaroni

2 large garden tomatoes, peeled, seeded, and chopped

1 1-pound can dark red kidney beans, drained

1/2 cup minced red onion

1/2 cup chopped parsley or cilantro

1 red or orange pepper, seeded and chopped

1 celery stalk, finely chopped

1 cup mayonnaise

1/3 cup hot prepared salsa

1 teaspoon ground cumin

1/8 teaspoon cayenne pepper, or to taste

Salt and black pepper to taste

♦ Cook the corn in a large pot of boiling water for about 2 minutes. Remove the corn and reserve the cooking water. Cool the corn and cut the kernels from the cobs to make about 1 cup. Add to a large bowl.

♦ Return the water to a boil and cook the macaroni according to the package directions until tender. Cool in cold water, and drain well. Add to the bowl with the corn.

♦ Drain the tomatoes of excess juice. Add them to the bowl with the beans, onion, parsley, pepper, and celery.

♦ In a small bowl, mix the mayonnaise, salsa, and spices together, and combine with the salad ingredients. Toss to mix well. Taste and adjust the seasoning with salt and pepper.

Serves 8

MENU

Hamburgers
Tex-Mex Macaroni Salad
Mixed green salad vinaigrette
Pecan pie (page 226)

Ginger-Lemon Chicken & Rice Salad

For a festive summer dinner or celebration you may need a simple chicken salad for a buffet table. This one combines chicken breasts and rice with lemon and ginger flavors. The poaching liquid from the chicken is used to cook the rice. Serve the salad at room temperature, not cold, for maximum flavor.

8 cups water

Aromatics: celery stalk, ½ onion, knob of fresh ginger root, salt, and pepper

5 chicken breast halves

2 cups rice

For the dressing:

⅓ cup fresh lemon juice

⅓ cup olive oil

¼ cup minced crystallized ginger

¼ cup thinly sliced scallions, white and green

½ cup coarsely chopped parsley

Zest of 2 lemons, julienned

1 teaspoon dry mustard

Salt and pepper to taste

Blanched snow peas for garnish

- In a large sauté pan, combine the water and aromatics and bring to a boil. Cover and simmer for 20 minutes.
- Trim the chicken of all excess fat and skin. Add to the sauté pan, skin side down, and return to a simmer. Cook over low heat for 5 minutes. Cover and remove from the heat. The chicken will continue to cook as it sits. In about 40 minutes, when the chicken has cooled, remove the bones and skin. Cut the chicken into 1-inch pieces and set aside.
- Strain the cooking liquid and add 4 cups to a saucepan. Stir in the rice, bring to a boil, cover, and simmer for 15 minutes, until the liquid is absorbed. Remove the cover, cool for 15 minutes, and fluff with a fork. Add the rice to a large bowl with the chicken pieces.
- In a small bowl, combine the dressing ingredients, stirring well to mix thoroughly. Add to the chicken and rice and mix with a fork. Adjust the seasoning, adding more lemon juice and oil if needed.
- Serve on a pretty serving platter garnished with snow peas.

Serves 8

MENU

Ginger-Lemon Chicken & Rice Salad
Mini croissants
Fruit Salad (page 268)
Cookies and finger pastries

Caribbean Chicken Salad with Mango & Orange

Here's a colorful summer chicken salad with fruit. It has a cumin and lime-flavored vinaigrette dressing that's tossed with poached chicken, oranges, and mangoes, and served on a bed of lettuce, watercress, or arugula. The oven-poached chicken has great flavor and texture, and is a technique worth using for any chicken salad.

1 tablespoon butter
4 chicken breast halves
1/4 cup minced shallots
Salt and pepper to taste
1/2 cup dry white wine
2 navel oranges, skin and
  white pith removed
  and cut into bite-size
  pieces
1 large ripe mango,
  peeled and cut into
  cubes
3 tablespoons minced red
  onion
1/4 cup coarsely chopped
  cilantro

For the dressing:
1/4 cup fresh lime juice
  (about 2 limes)
2 teaspoons Dijon
  mustard
1 teaspoon ground cumin
1/2 teaspoon salt
Pepper to taste
1/3 cup olive oil
Brunch of watercress or
  arugula, tough stems
  removed

♦ Preheat the oven to 450°F. With half the butter, lightly grease a shallow glass baking dish large enough to hold the chicken breasts in a single layer.

♦ Trim the chicken of all excess fat and skin. Arrange the chicken in the baking dish, skin side up. Sprinkle with the shallots, season with salt and pepper, and pour the wine in the dish. With the remaining butter, grease the parchment paper and place it, buttered side down over the chicken.

♦ Bake for about 20 minutes until the chicken is firm and opaque throughout. Set aside to cool completely before you remove the bones and skin from the chicken. Cut the chicken into 1-inch pieces and add to a large bowl with the oranges, mango cubes, onion, and cilantro.

♦ In a small bowl, whisk together the lime juice, mustard, cumin, salt, and pepper. Slowly add the oil, whisking until thickened.

♦ Pour the dressing over the chicken and fruit and toss. Refrigerate until serving time.

♦ Divide the greens between 4 dinner plates. Mix the chicken salad and arrange over the greens.

Serves 4

MENU

Caribbean Chicken Salad with Mango & Orange
Crusty rolls
Sangria (page 270)
Oatmeal cookies (page 230)

Chicken Salad with Peanut Dressing

Everyone loves this spicy peanut sauce that works so well with chicken, tofu, peppers, and snow peas. The chicken can come from a whole simmered chicken, or you may prefer to poach (page 245) or oven-poach (page 246) chicken breast halves. Prepare the ingredients ahead of time and refrigerate, but wait until serving time to assemble and toss.

4 cups cooked chicken
1/2 pound extra firm tofu, cut into 1/2-inch cubes
2 peppers, red and yellow, seeded and julienned
1 jalepeño pepper, seeded and minced
1/4 pound snow peas, strung, blanched, and julienned
1/4 cup chopped fresh cilantro or flat parsley
Mixture of mesclun, arugula, and watercress

For the dressing:
1/3 cup rice wine vinegar
1/4 cup peanut butter
4 teaspoons sugar
2 teaspoons salt
1 tablespoon dry mustard
1 teaspoon powdered ginger
1/8 teaspoon cayenne pepper
2/3 cup vegetable oil

1/2 cup cocktail peanuts, coarsely chopped

♦ Cut the chicken into 1-inch pieces and add to a large bowl. Gently press the cubes of tofu to eliminate the excess water and add to the bowl. Add the peppers, snow peas, and cilantro. Reserve the peanuts to garnish the top just before serving.
♦ To make the dressing, add the vinegar, peanut butter, sugar, salt, mustard, ginger, and cayenne to a processor or other deep bowl. With the motor running, slowly add the oil through the feed tube, or whisk in the oil until thickened and smooth.
♦ Refrigerate until ready to assemble the salad.
♦ At serving time, arrange the greens on a decorative serving platter. Add enough dressing to coat the salad ingredients, tossing to mix well. Arrange the salad on top of the greens. Sprinkle with the chopped nuts and serve.

Serves 8

MENU

Chicken Salad with Peanut Dressing
Rice cakes
Melon platter
Mint iced tea

Shrimp & Orzo Salad

*I*t's *easy to add vegetables and seafood to pasta salads to make them one-dish meals. Use cooked shrimp or crabmeat for this summer standby. Orzo is a rice-shaped pasta that is often overlooked, and seems to surprise everyone with its goodness. As with most pasta salads, this one is best assembled and tossed a few hours before serving.*

³/₄ pound orzo

For the dressing:
1 cup mayonnaise
¹/₄ cup chicken broth
2 tablespoons fresh
   lemon juice

1¹/₂ pounds shrimp,
   cooked, shelled, and
   deveined
Grated zest of 1 lemon
2 celery stalks, thinly
   sliced
1 orange or yellow
   pepper, seeded and
   julienned
2 scallions, white and
   green parts, thinly
   sliced
¹/₄ cup fresh snipped dill
1 tablespoon tiny, brined
   capers, drained
Salt and pepper to taste
Cherry tomatoes and
   fresh dill for garnish

+ Cook the orzo in boiling salted water according to the package directions until tender. Drain, rinse in cold water to chill, and drain again. Transfer to a large bowl.
+ Combine the dressing ingredients in a small bowl and whisk until smooth. Refrigerate until ready to assemble the salad.
+ Add the shrimp, lemon zest, celery, pepper, scallions, dill, and capers to the orzo in the bowl. Toss to mix the ingredients. Add enough dressing to the salad to coat well, mixing thoroughly. Taste and adjust the seasoning with salt and pepper. Reserve any extra dressing to serve on the side.
+ Transfer the salad to a decorative serving dish or platter and garnish with tomatoes and a sprig of fresh dill.
+ Serve at room temperature or chilled, but not cold.

Serves 8

MENU

Shrimp & Orzo Salad
Croissants and assorted cheeses
Strawberries and confectioners' sugar
Lemon-limeade

Seafood Pasta Salad with Curry Dressing

More hot weather salads to keep you cool and please your diners—this one with crabmeat, twist pasta, grapes, and almonds tossed with a curried dressing. You'll like the flavors and variety of textures and colors.

8 ounces fuscelli or twist pasta
1 pound crabmeat
1 8-ounce can sliced water chestnuts, drained
3 celery stalks, finely chopped
1¹/₂ cups green or red seedless grapes, halved
¹/₄ cup chopped parsley
2 scallions, white and green, thinly sliced
1 jalepeño pepper, seeded and minced
¹/₂ cup currants
3 tablespoons minced crystallized ginger

For the dressing:
1 cup mayonnaise
¹/₄ cup orange juice
2 teaspoons sugar
1 teaspoon curry powder
¹/₂ teaspoon paprika
¹/₂ teaspoon cumin
¹/₂ teaspoon ginger
¹/₄ teaspoon tumeric
Salt and pepper to taste

¹/₂ cup slivered almonds

- Cook the pasta in boiling salted water according to the package directions until tender. Drain, rinse in cold water to chill, and drain again. Add to a large bowl with the crabmeat, water chestnuts, celery, grapes, parsley, scallions, pepper, currants, and ginger. Toss to mix well.
- To make the dressing, combine the mayonnaise, juice, sugar, and spices in a small bowl. Whisk until smooth. Refrigerate if you are making it ahead of time.
- Add enough dressing to the salad to bind the ingredients. Transfer to a serving platter.
- Lightly toast the almonds and sprinkle over the salad at serving time.

Serves 6 to 8

MENU

Seafood Pasta Salad with Curry Dressing
Pita Crisps (page 262)
Iced tea and Sugar Cookies (page 266)

Shrimp & Tortellini Salad

Tortellini adds interest and substance to another summer salad. The shrimp gives the salad its elegance, but you could use chicken instead, or add more vegetables and serve it as a side dish for a grilled dinner.

1 15-ounce package frozen cheese tortellini, or 9 ounces fresh tortellini
1 pound cooked medium or large shrimp, peeled and deveined
1 red pepper, seeded and chopped
3 celery stalks, chopped
3 scallions, green and white part, thinly sliced,
3/4 cup coarsely chopped Italian parsley

For the dressing:
1/2 cup mayonnaise
3 tablespoons cider vinegar
1/4 cup olive oil
1 tablespoon Dijon mustard
Salt and pepper to taste

Cherry tomatoes and parsley for garnish

♦ Cook the tortellini according to the directions until tender. Drain, run under cold water to cool, and drain well.
♦ In a large bowl, combine the tortellini, shrimp, pepper, celery, scallions, and parsley.
♦ In a small bowl, whisk the mayonnaise, vinegar, oil, and mustard together until smooth. Add enough dressing to the salad ingredients to coat well. Toss the salad. Taste and add salt and pepper to taste.
♦ Transfer to a pretty serving platter and garnish with cherry tomatoes and a few sprigs of parsley.

Serves 6 to 8

MENU

Shrimp & Tortellini Salad
Crusty Italian bread
Green salad vinaigrette
Fruit pie

Chicken

*C*hicken is a staple in most kitchens today. Since it is so versatile, it is one of the perfect foods for quick and healthy dinners. Chicken's bland flavor means that it needs and loves other ingredients, marinades, and ethnic spices. The only way to ruin the white meat of chicken is to overcook it. Dark meat (the leg and thigh) is less delicate and fattier, and the texture seems to improve with longer cooking.

It's good to know how to cut up a whole chicken for some recipes, although you can buy cut-up chicken parts. Regardless of how you buy chicken, it needs to be trimmed of excess fat and excess skin.

Handle chicken with care, since bacteria spreads rapidly in raw poultry. Cut on a plastic, not wooden, board that you can put in the dishwasher. Sanitize the board and knife with hot soapy water, then scrub with salt and rinse again. Defrost chicken in the refrigerator, and don't refreeze it.

The cooking methods for chicken include:

Roasting—Roasted chicken is usually a whole chicken, cooked in a high-temperature oven or on a rotisserie. The skin gets browned and crisp, and the inside stays juicy and moist.

Baking—Coated with crumbs or simply seasoned, chicken pieces are baked in a 350°F oven for an hour with very little attention paid to them.

Frying—Coated in flour or a protective batter and cooked in hot oil to cover, fried chicken is not the healthiest preparation for chicken. If I have a craving for fried chicken, I usually indulge at a take-out shop, or go to the frozen food section of the supermarket.

Grilling—This has traditionally been a favorite summer cooking technique, but since the invention of the stove-top grill, you can grill all year-round. Marinate the chicken parts for at least one hour so they have time to absorb the flavors. Chicken breasts can easily be overcooked in this high-heat method, so watch them carefully and take them off the grill before the legs and thighs are done. In the winter, my beloved stove-top grill cooks boned and skinned chicken breasts in ten minutes, leaving me time to make a festive rice, potato, or vegetable dish. These grilled chicken breasts are perfect for the ubiquitous Chicken Caesar Salad.

Stir-Frying—This is a high-heat cooking method for boned and skinned chicken pieces. Stir-fried dishes usually include vegetables.

Sautéing—Boned and skinned chicken breasts are cooked on each side in butter or oil in a sauté pan over medium-low heat.

Poaching—This is a gentle way to cook chicken breasts, usually for chicken salads. Chicken is added to a simmering, flavorful liquid and cooked briefly until it is opaque throughout. Two poaching methods are described in Basic Tips & Recipes on pages 245–246.

Hunter's Chicken

*I*ry *some of the more exotic and flavorful shitaki, brown, or porto-bella mushrooms to give this dish a hearty and robust country flavor.*

1 4-pound chicken, cut into 8 pieces
Salt and pepper to taste
3 tablespoons vegetable oil
2 tablespoons butter
1 small onion, chopped
1/2 green pepper, chopped
1 clove garlic, minced
1/4 teaspoon thyme
6 ounces mushrooms of your choice, sliced to make about 3 cups
2 tablespoons flour
1 1-pound can peeled tomatoes
1/2 cup chicken broth
3 tablespoons chopped parsley

- Trim the chicken of all excess fat and skin, and season with salt and pepper.
- Heat the oil in a large sauté pan.
- Over medium-high heat, brown the chicken on all sides and set aside.
- Pour off any oil in the pan and reduce the heat to low. Melt the butter and add the onion, pepper, and garlic. Sauté, stirring, for about 5 minutes, until the vegetables are soft but not browned.
- Add the thyme and mushrooms and continue cooking until the mushrooms exude their juices. Add the flour, stir well, and cook for 1 minute.
- Drain the tomatoes and chop them coarsely before adding them to the pan. Stir in the chicken broth and bring to a boil. Return the chicken pieces to the pan, cover, and simmer for about 35 minutes, until the chicken is cooked through. Season the sauce with salt and pepper.
- Serve the chicken over noodles with some of the sauce and a sprinkling of parsley.

Serves 6

MENU

Hunter's Chicken
Noodles
Avocado and citrus fruit salad with French dressing
Poundcake with ice cream

Chicken & Rice Biryani

I've learned to love Indian Biryani dishes with the flavorful rice, spices, nuts, and chicken. In this American version, the chicken may come from one simmered whole chicken (page 9) or from four poached chicken breast halves (page 245–46). The rice is cooked in a flavored broth, and the two are combined with peas and toasted cashews. Like Chinese fried rice, this Indian fried rice is a colorful, not-too-exotic, one-dish dinner everyone will like.

4 cups cooked chicken
3 cups chicken broth
1/2 teaspoon tumeric
1 cinnamon stick
3 cardamom pods, pinched to expose the seeds
2 whole cloves
1 1/2 cups rice
3 tablespoons butter
1 large onion, chopped
1/2 teaspoon cumin seeds
1 1/2 teaspoons curry powder
1/8 teaspoon cayenne pepper
1/2 cup frozen petite peas
1/4 cup currants
1/2 cup lightly toasted cashews, coarsely chopped
Fruit chutney (pages 166–167)
Bottled hot sauce

♦ Cut the chicken into chunks and reserve.
♦ Heat the chicken broth in a heavy saucepan with the tumeric, cinnamon stick, cardamom, and cloves. Cover and simmer for 5 minutes to bring out the flavors. Add the rice, bring to a boil, stir, cover, and simmer for 15 to 17 minutes, until the liquid is absorbed. Remove the cinnamon stick, cardamom, and cloves that float to the top. Cool uncovered, then fluff with a fork.
♦ In a large sauté pan over low heat, melt the butter and sauté the onion for about 4 minutes until soft, stirring constantly. Add the cumin seeds, curry powder, and cayenne, and sauté for 1 minute, stirring. Add the peas and currants and heat through. Add the reserved chicken and rice, stirring together gently. Add a bit more chicken broth as needed to moisten. Taste and adjust the seasoning with salt and pepper.
♦ At serving time, add the cashews. Serve with fruit chutney and hot sauce on the side.

Serves 6 to 8

MENU

Chicken & Rice Biryani
Cucumber sticks dipped in cumin-and-salt-seasoned yogurt
Fruit chutney (pages 166–167) and hot sauce
Ginger cookies and tea

Chicken Jambalaya with Shrimp & Ham

Jambalaya is a colorful, Cajun-inspried chicken and rice dish. The shrimp and ham add an elegance that makes jambalaya fancy enough for company. Prepare this dish just before you serve it so the rice doesn't get mushy when reheating.

1 4-pound chicken, cut into 8 pieces
2 tablespoons vegetable oil
4 tablespoons butter
1 cup finely chopped onion
2 cloves garlic, minced
1 cup finely chopped green pepper
1 celery stalk, finely chopped
¼ cup finely chopped parsley
1½ cups rice
3 cups boiling water
1 cup peeled, seeded, and chopped tomatoes, or 1 1-pound can peeled tomatoes, drained and chopped
¼ teaspoon cayenne pepper
½ teaspoon thyme
1 bay leaf
Black pepper to taste
¼ pound boiled ham, julienned
½ pound shrimp, peeled and deveined

♦ Trim the chicken of all excess fat and skin.
♦ Heat the oil in a large sauté pan and brown the chicken on all sides. Remove the chicken and set aside.
♦ In the same pan, melt the butter and add the onion. Sauté over low heat for 5 minutes, stirring often. Add the garlic, pepper, and celery and continue to sauté a few more minutes. Add all but 1 tablespoon of parsley and the rice. Sauté until the rice is hot.
♦ Pour the boiling water over the rice, add the tomatoes, and stir in the spices and seasoning. Return the chicken to the pan. Bring the liquid to a boil, cover, and simmer for 30 to 35 minutes, until the chicken is cooked, the rice is tender, and the liquid has been absorbed.
♦ Add the ham and shrimp to the rice, cover, and continue to cook for about 5 minutes, until the ham is hot and the shrimp is pink and cooked.
♦ Fluff the jambalaya with a fork to distribute the ingredients and serve from the pan sprinkled with the reserved tablespoon of parsley.

Serves 6 to 8

MENU

Chicken Jambalaya with Shrimp & Ham
Vegetable sticks with a Blue Cheese Dressing (page 259)
Carrot cake (page 212)

Chicken Tangier

*N*orth African dishes love to combine meats or poultry with fruits to make stews called tajines. Here the chicken is combined with chick peas and pitted prunes in a honey sweetened tomato sauce. Absolutely delicious!

1 4-pound chicken, cut into 8 pieces
2 tablespoons flour
3 tablespoons vegetable oil
2 tablespoons butter
1 onion, finely chopped
1 large clove garlic, minced
1½ cups chunky-style crushed tomatoes
1 cup chicken broth
1 cinnamon stick
1 teaspoon cumin
¼ teaspoon tumeric
½ cup pitted, bite-size prunes
1 cup cooked chick peas, drained
2 tablespoons honey
Salt, pepper, and nutmeg to taste
Chopped parsley for garnish

♦ Trim the chicken of all excess fat and skin and dust the chicken pieces with flour.
♦ In a large sauté pan, heat the oil over medium-high heat and sauté the chicken until it's lightly browned. Set aside. Wipe out the pan and reduce the heat to low.
♦ Melt the butter and sauté the onion and garlic for 5 minutes, stirring, until softened but not colored. Add the tomatoes, broth, cinnamon, cumin, and tumeric. Cover and simmer for 5 minutes.
♦ Return the chicken to the pan, cover, and simmer for 20 minutes. Add the prunes and chick peas, cover, and simmer for 10 more minutes.
♦ Stir the honey into the sauce and season with salt, pepper, and a grating of nutmeg.
♦ Serve the chicken garnished with a sprinkle of parsley

Serves 4

MENU

Chicken Tangier
Noodles
Broccoli (page 242)
Whole strawberries with vanilla yogurt and brown sugar for dipping

Chicken Mambazo

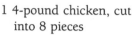

*O*ne dish meals can make dinner time so much simpler, especially when other activities intrude on the dinner hour. The flavors and spices of Africa make a classic chicken and rice dish so much more interesting. This is one of those recipes you can prepare ahead and reheat in the microwave at dinner time.

1 4-pound chicken, cut into 8 pieces
2 tablespoons vegetable oil
2 tablespoons butter
1 onion, chopped
1/4 cup minced shallots
2 tablespoons minced fresh peeled ginger root
1 carrot, finely chopped
1 red or yellow pepper, seeded and chopped
1 teaspoon tumeric
1 cup rice
2 cups boiling water
1 1/2 teaspoons salt
1 large ripe tomato, peeled, seeded, and chopped
Pepper to taste

+ Trim the chicken of all excess fat and skin.
+ Heat the oil in a large sauté pan over medium-high heat. Brown the chicken pieces on all sides and set aside.
+ Reduce the heat to low, wipe out the pan, and add the butter. Sauté the onion and shallots for 3 minutes, stirring to prevent browning. Add the ginger, carrot, and pepper, and continue to sauté for 3 more minutes.
+ Stir in the tumeric and then the rice. Sauté for 3 more minutes, stirring, until the rice is hot.
+ Add the boiling water and salt, and stir well. Add the tomatoes. Arrange the browned chicken pieces in the pan.
+ Bring to a boil, cover well, and simmer over low heat for about 25 minutes, until the chicken is cooked and the rice is tender. There will be some excess liquid for a sauce. Season with pepper to taste.
+ Cool for 5 minutes, fluff with a fork, and serve.

Serves 6

MENU

Chicken Mambazo
Cucumber spears
Biscuits (page 261)
Butterscotch pudding

Chicken & Shrimp Olé

Chicken & Shrimp Olé is similar to the popular Spanish paella but without the rice. It's loaded with flavor and enough ingredients to please everyone.

1 4-pound chicken, cut into 8 pieces
Salt and pepper to taste
1/3 cup olive oil
1 small onion, finely chopped
2 cloves garlic, minced
1 green pepper, seeded and chopped
1 red pepper, seeded and chopped
8 plum tomatoes, chopped
1/2 cup hot water
1/2 teaspoon saffron threads, crumbled
1/2 pound large shrimp, shelled and deveined
3/4 cup frozen petite peas

♦ Trim the chicken of all excess fat and skin and season with salt and pepper.
♦ In a large sauté pan, heat half the oil until hot. Over medium-high heat, brown the chicken pieces on all sides and set aside.
♦ Wipe out the pan, reduce the heat to low, and add the remaining oil. Sauté the onion and garlic for about 4 minutes, stirring often to prevent them from coloring. Add the peppers and sauté for a few more minutes. Add the tomatoes and sauté for another minute. Mix the water and saffron together and add to the pan.
♦ Bring to a boil and return the chicken to the pan, skin side up. Cover and simmer for about 25 minutes until the chicken is cooked through and tender. Add the shrimp and peas. Simmer for a few more minutes until the shrimp is pink and opaque throughout.
♦ Adjust the seasoning with salt and pepper and serve hot.

Serves 6

MENU

Chicken & Shrimp Olé
Rice (page 252)
Sautéed summer squash
Carrot sticks
Baked custard (page 264)

Southwest Baked Chicken

*B*aked, cornmeal-coated chicken is so easy, you can walk away for the hour it takes in the oven. Marinating it in lime juice and spices first gives the chicken added flavor.

1 4-pound chicken, cut into 8 pieces

For the marinade:
¼ cup fresh lime juice
1 clove garlic, minced
1 teaspoon chili powder
1 teaspoon salt
½ teaspoon cumin
Pepper to taste

3 tablespoons flour
¼ cup yellow cornmeal
½ teaspoon paprika
2 tablespoons butter

+ Trim the chicken pieces of all excess fat and skin.
+ In a glass or plastic dish, combine the lime juice, garlic, chili powder, salt, cumin, and pepper. Stir to mix well. Add the chicken, turning to coat the pieces on all sides. Cover and refrigerate for at least 1 hour.
+ Preheat the oven to 375°F. Lightly oil a shallow baking dish large enough to hold the chicken in a single layer.
+ On a piece of wax paper, combine the cornmeal, flour, and paprika.
+ Remove the chicken from the marinade and pat dry with paper towels. Roll in the cornmeal mixture, coating all sides. Place in the prepared baking dish, skin side up, and dot with bits of the butter.
+ Bake in the upper half of the oven for 1 hour, or until browned and crisp.

Serves 4

MENU

Southwest Baked Chicken
Sautéed zucchini and corn
Beans and rice (page 155)
Frozen fruit juice bars

Braised Chicken & Apples Normandy

Normandy is well-known for its apples and cream. Here they're combined in a French-style chicken dish. You can substitute chicken breasts for the more economical chicken pieces and cook it in half the time.

1 frying chicken, cut into 8 pieces
Salt and pepper to taste
2 tablespoons vegetable oil
2 tablespoons butter
1/4 cup minced shallots
1/2 cup chicken broth
1/2 cup apple cider
Pinch of dried thyme or a sprig of fresh
2 Golden Delicious apples, peeled, cored, and cut into eighths
1/3 cup heavy cream
1 tablespoon red currant jelly
Grating of nutmeg
Snipped chives or green scallion rings for garnish

♦ Trim the chicken pieces of all excess fat and skin, and season with salt and pepper.
♦ Heat the oil in a heavy sauté pan over-medium high heat. Brown the chicken on all sides and set aside.
♦ Pour off any excess oil in the pan. Reduce the heat to low, add the butter and sauté the shallots for about 5 minutes, stirring often, until soft but not colored. Stir in the broth and cider, and add the thyme. Scrape the bottom of the pan and bring the liquid to a simmer.
♦ Return the chicken to the pan, cover, and simmer for 20 to 30 minutes. Remove the chicken pieces as they are done and keep them warm.
♦ Add the apples to the sauce, increase the heat, and reduce the liquid by half. Add the cream, and continue to cook until the sauce is thickened and the apples are tender. Stir in the currant jelly.
♦ Return the chicken and any accumulated juices to the sauce and heat. Taste and adjust the seasoning with salt, pepper, and a grating of nutmeg.
♦ Serve over noodles garnished with a sprinkling of chives or scallions.

Serves 4 to 6

MENU

Braised Chicken & Apples Normandy
Noodles
Spinach salad
Vanilla Cake (page 265)

Chicken Havana

*E*ven chicken can become tedious without some new combination
of ingredients, a marinade, or some unusual spices to turn this
dinner staple into a wonderful new food. Cinnamon and cumin work
their magic in this spicy tomato sauce.

6 chicken breast halves
3 tablespoons olive oil
1 large onion, chopped
1 clove garlic, minced
1 jalepeño pepper,
    seeded and minced,
    or to taste
1 green pepper, seeded
    and chopped
1 teaspoon cumin
1/4 teaspoon cinnamon
1/2 bay leaf
Juice of 1 lime (about
    2 tablespoons)
1 1-pound can whole
    tomatoes, drained and
    coarsely chopped
Salt, black pepper, and
    cayenne pepper to
    taste
2 tablespoons chopped
    cilantro or parsley

+ Trim the chicken breasts of all excess fat and skin.
+ Heat the oil in a large sauté pan over medium heat,
and lightly brown the chicken on both sides. Set
aside.
+ On low heat, add the onion, garlic, and peppers
to the pan and sauté for about 5 minutes, stirring
often, until soft but not colored.
+ Stir in the cumin, cinnamon, bay leaf, lime juice,
and tomatoes. Simmer for 5 minutes.
+ Return the chicken to the pan, cover, and simmer
for about 15 minutes until the chicken is opaque
throughout but still juicy and tender.
+ Taste the sauce and adjust the seasoning with salt,
black pepper, and cayenne pepper. Garnish the
top with cilantro or parsley and serve hot.

Serves 4 to 6

MENU

Chicken Havana
Spaghetti squash
Crusty rolls
Strawberries in Custard Sauce (page 264)

South American Chicken Stew

Here's a cheerful dish, filled with a medley of flavorful ingredients and gorgeous colors. It's inspiration is a South American Indian stew known as locro, made with peppers, corn, and squash, and flavored with cumin and cilantro. Serve the stew in large, shallow soup bowls and let the rice soak up the plentiful juices.

4 chicken breast halves
2 tablespoons vegetable oil
1 small onion, chopped
1 clove garlic, minced
1 celery stalk, chopped
1 small red pepper, seeded and chopped
1 small jalepeño pepper, seeded and minced
1/2 teaspoon cumin seeds
1 teaspoon chili powder
1 teaspoon ground cumin
1 14 1/2-ounce can chicken broth
1 1-pound can whole tomatoes, drained and coarsely chopped
3 cups peeled butternut squash, cut into 1-inch cubes (about 3/4 pound)
1 cup corn kernels, frozen or fresh (cut from 2 ears)
3 tablespoons chopped cilantro, or parsley
Salt and black or cayenne pepper to taste

♦ Trim the chicken of all excess fat and skin.
♦ In a large, deep sauté pan, heat the oil over medium heat and lightly brown the chicken on both sides. Set aside.
♦ Wipe out the pan, lower the heat, and cool the pan. Sauté the onion, garlic, and celery for about 3 minutes, stirring to prevent them from coloring. Add the peppers and cumin seeds, and sauté for a few minutes. Add the chili powder and ground cumin, and stir in the chicken broth and tomatoes.
♦ Bring to a simmer and return the chicken to the pan. Add the squash to the broth, poking the cubes around the edges and between the chicken.
♦ Cover and simmer for about 15 minutes until the chicken is cooked through and the squash is tender. Add the corn and simmer for 1 more minute.
♦ Taste and adjust the seasoning with salt and black or cayenne pepper. Sprinkle with cilantro and serve with rice.

Serves 4

MENU

South American Chicken Stew
Rice (page 250)
Crusty rolls
Citrus and pineapple salad

Braised Satay Chicken with Carrots & Peppers

A colorful combination of chicken and vegetables in an Indonesia-inspired sauce.

4 chicken breast halves
2 tablespoons vegetable oil

For the sauce:
¼ cup orange juice concentrate
½ cup chicken broth
2 tablespoons soy sauce
2 tablespoons brown sugar
1 tablespoon peanut butter
2 teaspoons sesame oil
2 wedges peeled fresh ginger root
Pinch of dried red pepper flakes
1 clove garlic, minced

2 carrots, cut in thin ¼-inch diagonal slices
1 red pepper, cored and cut into 1-inch pieces
1 green pepper, cored and cut into 1-inch pieces
2 scallions, thinly sliced

+ Trim the chicken of all excess fat and skin.
+ Heat the oil in a large heavy sauté pan, and lightly brown the chicken over medium heat for 1 minute on each side.
+ In a bowl combine the orange juice concentrate, chicken broth, soy sauce, brown sugar, peanut butter, sesame oil, ginger, pepper flakes, and garlic.
+ Pour the sauce over the chicken and add the carrots. Bring the liquid to a boil, cover, and simmer over low heat for about 15 minutes until the chicken is cooked through. Remove the chicken and keep warm.
+ Raise the heat to medium, add the peppers to the carrots and sauce, and cook uncovered for 10 minutes until the vegetables are tender and the sauce has reduced and thickened. Add a few tablespoons of water if it reduces too much.
+ Return the chicken to the pan to warm and glaze with the sauce.
+ Remove the ginger and serve with scallions sprinkled over the top.

Serves 4

MENU

Braised Satay Chicken with Carrots & Peppers
Rice (page 250)
Sorbet and Sugar Cookies (page 266)

Citus Chicken Breasts

In midwinter when the produce section is looking grim, there is always citrus fruit to add zip and zest to the dinner menu. Don't substitute half-and-half or even light cream for the heavy cream— the acidic citrus juices will cause them to curdle. When cooking chicken breasts, it's important to remember that simmering is **not** boiling. It's the slow cooking technique that produces tender chicken.

6 chicken breast halves
2 tablespoons butter
¼ cup minced shallots
1 cup chicken broth
Juice of 1 lime
Juice of ½ lemon
Juice of ½ orange
1 tablespoon cornstarch
⅓ cup heavy cream
¼ cup chopped parsley
  for garnish
Lemon, lime, or orange
  rounds for garnish

* Trim the chicken breasts of all excess fat and skin.
* Melt the butter in a large sauté pan and lightly brown the chicken over medium heat, 1 minute on each side. Remove the chicken and reduce the heat to low.
* Sauté the shallots, stirring, until softened but not colored. Add the chicken broth and citrus juices and simmer. Add the chicken, return to a simmer, cover, and cook for 12 to 15 minutes until opaque throughout, depending on the size of the breasts. Remove the chicken to a serving platter.
* Remove 2 tablespoons of the liquid to a small bowl. Mix with the cornstarch until smooth and return to the pan. Whisk in and cook for a few minutes until the juices are thickened. Stir in the cream. Pour the sauce over the chicken and garnish with the parsley and citrus rounds.

Serves 4 to 6

MENU

Citrus Chicken Breasts
Noodles
Caesar Salad (page 35)
Everyone's favorite candy bar

Chicken Almondine with Indian Yogurt Sauce

*P*reparing ethnic dishes always gives me an excuse to visit unusual markets to replenish my supply of spices and special ingredients. Ethnic markets are a fast and inexpensive—if not totally satisfying—way to transport yourself to a new and exotic culture. Ask questions about unfamiliar foods and be open to new smells, tastes, and adventures.

4 chicken breast halves, boned and skinned
1 clove garlic, flattened with the side of a knife
1 large wedge of fresh ginger root, flattened with the side of a knife
3 tablespoons vegetable oil
1 teaspoon garum masala*
¹/₂ teaspoon tumeric
¹/₄ teaspoon cayenne pepper
³/₄ teaspoon salt
¹/₂ cup slivered almonds
2 tablespoons butter
1 cup plain yogurt
1 tablespoon flour
¹/₂ teaspoon cumin

- Trim the chicken breasts of all excess fat.
- Wipe the chicken dry and put it in a bowl with the garlic and ginger.
- In a small bowl, mix together the oil, garum masala, tumeric, pepper, and salt. Rub into the chicken. Cover and marinate for 1 hour.
- In a large sauté pan, toast the almonds, stirring constantly, until they are lightly colored. Remove with a slotted spoon and reserve.
- Remove the garlic and ginger from the chicken.
- In the same sauté pan, melt the butter and sauté the chicken over low heat until the surface is opaque, about 1 minute on each side. Shake the pan to prevent the chicken from sticking.
- Combine the yogurt, flour, and cumin. Add to the chicken and stir. Cover and simmer for 8 to 10 minutes until the chicken is cooked through and tender. The only trick is not to overcook the chicken. Season the sauce with salt and cayenne pepper.
- Top the chicken with the almonds and serve hot over rice.

Serves 4

* A blend of cardamom, cinnamon, cumin, and cloves, available in most spice stores and Indian markets.

MENU

Chicken Almondine with Indian Yogurt Sauce
Rice (page 250)
Carrots, julienned and cooked
Pita Crisps (page 262)
Fresh strawberries with confectioners' sugar

Avgolemono Chicken & Rice

This is a Greek-inspired chicken and rice dish flavored with lemon and garnished with capers, dill, and black olives. Leftovers make a good salad for lunch the next day. Cut the chicken into chunks, add julienned red pepper, and toss. Drizzle with olive oil, add more fresh snipped dill, salt, and pepper.

4 chicken breast halves, boned and skinned

2 tablespoons flour seasoned with salt and pepper

3 tablespoons olive oil

1 cup rice

2 cups chicken broth, heated

1 clove garlic, peeled and skewered on a toothpick

Juice of 1 large lemon (about ¼ cup)

Grated zest of 1 large lemon

2 tablespoons fresh snipped dill

1 tablespoon tiny, brined capers, drained

Imported black olives (oil-cured, marinated, or brined)

♦ Trim the chicken breasts of all excess fat.

♦ Lightly pound the chicken breasts to an even thickness between 2 sheets of wax paper. Dust with the seasoned flour.

♦ In a large sauté pan, heat the oil over medium heat and sauté the chicken for just a few minutes on each side until nearly cooked through. The chicken will continue to cook as it waits for the rice, so don't over cook it. Set the chicken aside and cover.

♦ Add the rice to the pan, and sauté for a few minutes. Add the chicken broth, garlic, lemon juice, and zest, and stir. Bring to a boil, cover, and simmer for 15 to 18 minutes until the rice is tender and most of the liquid is absorbed.

♦ Return the chicken and any accumulated juices to the pan, and top with the dill, capers, and olives. Cover and cook for just a minute to warm the chicken. Remove the garlic and serve hot from the pan.

Serves 4

MENU

Avgolemono Chicken & Rice
Sugar snap peas and red pepper strips, sautéed
French bread
Brownies (page 233)

Chicken Picante

"*Picante*" *indicates that a dish has tart tastes like lemon and vinegar-brined capers. Mushrooms and artichoke hearts are buried treasures in this favorite chicken dish.*

6 chicken breast halves, boned and skinned

2 tablespoons flour, seasoned with salt and pepper

3 tablespoons butter

1/2 cup dry white wine

1/2 pound mushrooms, thinly sliced

1 10-ounce package frozen artichoke hearts, cooked and drained

1 cup chicken broth

1/4 cup fresh lemon juice

Beurre manie—1 tablespoon flour kneaded into 1 tablespoon softened butter

3 tablespoons tiny, brined capers, drained

3 tablespoons minced parsley

♦ Trim the chicken breasts of all excess fat.

♦ Lightly pound the chicken breasts to an even thickness between 2 sheets of wax paper. Dust with the seasoned flour.

♦ In a large sauté pan over medium heat, melt the butter and sauté the chicken breasts in 2 batches, for a few minutes on each side, until nearly cooked through. Remove and keep warm.

♦ Add the wine to the pan, scrape the bottom, and cook over medium heat for a few minutes until the wine is reduced to a few tablespoons. Add the mushrooms and cook until soft. Add the artichoke hearts, chicken broth, and lemon juice. Heat to a simmer and add the *beurre manie*, stirring until the sauce is thickened.

♦ Return the chicken and any accumulated juices to the pan and warm. Add the capers and parsley and serve from the pan over noodles.

Serves 4

MENU ◦

Chicken Picante
Noodles
Cucumber and carrot sticks
Fruit pie

Chicken in Indian Masala Sauce

For those who like Indian spices, but not too much fire, this mellow red sauce is just right. This dish is similar to the well-loved Chicken Tikka Masala. Here, the chicken cooks in the sauce rather than in a tandoori oven. The coconut milk (even a light version) can be purchased in a can in most supermarkets.

4 chicken breast halves, boned and skinned
2 tablespoons vegetable oil
4 tablespoons butter
1 large onion, chopped
2 cloves garlic, minced
2 tablespoons freshly grated, peeled ginger root
1 cinnamon stick
1 bay leaf
1/4 teaspoon ground cardamom
Pinch of ground cloves
1/4 teaspoon dried red pepper flakes
1 teaspoon sweet paprika
1 teaspoon salt
1 teaspoon sugar
1 1/2 cups canned unsweetened coconut milk
4 tablespoons tomato paste

- Trim the chicken breasts of all excess fat.
- In a large sauté pan, heat the oil over low heat and sauté the chicken for just a minute on each side until the surface is opaque. Remove the chicken and reserve.
- Wipe out the pan and add the butter. Sauté the onion, garlic, and ginger for 5 minutes, stirring constantly, until very soft but not colored.
- Add the cinnamon stick, bay leaf, cardamom, cloves, red pepper flakes, paprika, salt, and sugar. Sauté for a few minutes, stirring. Whisk in the coconut milk and tomato paste until smooth. Add the chicken, turning to coat and bring to a simmer. Cover and simmer for 8 to 10 minutes until the chicken is cooked through and opaque in the middle.
- Remove the cinnamon stick and bay leaf and serve the chicken directly from the pan.
- If you like a smooth sauce, arrange the chicken on a serving platter and cover. Remove the cinnamon stick and bay leaf and purée the sauce in the blender until smooth. Pour over the chicken and serve.

Serves 4

MENU

Chicken in Indian Masala Sauce
Rice (page 250)
Sautéed zucchini rounds
Baked Apples (page 269)

Baked Berber Chicken

This North African–inspired marinade gives the chicken lots of flavor. I use boned and skinned chicken breasts since they're fast cooking, easy to eat, and our favorite part of the chicken. I've used this marinade and the same cooking technique with fish—bluefish, scrod, halibut, swordfish—and I think it's just as good. Canned tomatoes are ripe and flavorful in the winter, but in the summer, you could use three large garden tomatoes, peeled, seeded, and chopped.

6 chicken breast halves,
   boned and skinned

For the marinade:
1/4 cup olive oil
2 tablespoons fresh
   lemon juice
1 tablespoon peanut
   butter
1 small clove garlic,
   minced
1 teaspoon salt
1 teaspoon paprika
1/2 teaspoon cumin
1/2 teaspoon coriander
1/8 teaspoon cayenne
   pepper
1 teaspoon honey

1 cup chunky-style
   crushed tomatoes
3 tablespoons chopped
   cilantro or parsley

♦ Trim the chicken breasts of all excess fat.
♦ Place all the marinade ingredients in a shallow glass dish just large enough to hold the chicken in a single layer. Whisk the marinade together until smooth. Add the chicken, turning to coat all sides. Cover with plastic wrap and refrigerate for at least 1 hour.
♦ At dinnertime, preheat the oven to 425°F.
♦ Top the chicken with the crushed or chopped tomatoes and half the cilantro. Cover with foil and bake for about 25 minutes, basting a few times. The chicken should be cooked through and opaque. It should be firm to the touch but not hard.
♦ Season the sauce to taste, and serve the chicken over couscous and chick peas, garnished with the remaining cilantro or parsley for color.

Serves 4 to 6

MENU

Baked Berber Chicken
Couscous (page 250) and chick peas
Green salad with red onion, black olives, and orange sections
Pita Crisps (page 262)
Sugared mint tea

Chicken, Sweet Potato & Apple Bake

This dinner nearly cooks itself if you simply combine the three main ingredients in a roasting pan and put them in a hot oven. Chicken legs are used here since they're economical and full of flavor. Be sure to cut off all excess skin and any pockets of fat to make them low in fat as well. A maple syrup glaze finishes this seasonal New England favorite. For a small group or a large crowd, this is easy to manage.

2½ pounds chicken legs (about 24)

3 sweet potatoes (about 1½ pounds), peeled and cut into 1½-inch chunks

3 apples, peeled, cored and cut into eighths

2 tablespoons vegetable oil

Salt and pepper to taste

For the glaze:

1 tablespoon butter

2 tablespoons brown sugar

2 tablespoons maple syrup

Grating of nutmeg

♦ Preheat the oven to 425°F. Lightly oil a large roasting pan or baking dish.

♦ Trim the chicken legs of all excess fat and skin.

♦ Combine the sweet potatoes and apples in the pan or dish and drizzle with oil. Toss to coat evenly. Nestle the chicken legs into the potatoes. Sprinkle with salt and pepper.

♦ Bake in the middle of the oven for 30 minutes.

♦ Meanwhile, combine the glaze ingredients in a small saucepan. Heat until the butter and sugar melt. Set aside.

♦ Remove the chicken from the oven and carefully turn the chicken, apples, and sweet potatoes. Baste with any accumulated juices. Brush the chicken with the glaze and return to the oven for 25 to 30 more minutes. Baste occasionally with the pan juices until the chicken is browned and the potatoes are fork tender. Remove from the oven and serve.

Serves 6 to 8

MENU

Chicken, Sweet Potato & Apple Bake
Sautéed spinach or other greens
Cornbread (page 260)
Chocolate pudding

Braised Chicken Legs & Mushrooms Moutard

There is lots of hearty flavor in this braised dish. The chicken legs marry well with the strong flavors of the garlic, prosciutto, and mushrooms.

10 chicken legs
2 tablespoons vegetable oil
2 tablespoons butter
2 cloves garlic, minced
1/4 cup minced shallots
2 1/8-inch slices lean prosciutto, diced
1/2 pound brown, shitake, or portobella mushrooms, thinly sliced
2 cups chicken broth
2 tablespoons Dijon mustard
1 tablespoon flour
1/4 cup minced parsley
Pepper to taste

+ Trim the chicken legs of all excess fat and skin.
+ Heat the oil in a large sauté pan over medium-high heat. Add the legs and brown on all sides. Remove and set aside.
+ Wipe out any remaining oil in the pan, reduce the heat to low, and add the butter. Sauté the garlic and shallots, stirring, until softened but not colored. Add the prosciutto and sauté for 1 minute. Add the mushrooms and increase the heat to medium. Sauté, stirring, until the juices have evaporated, about 5 minutes.
+ Add the chicken broth and bring to a boil. Add the chicken legs, reduce the heat to low, cover well, and simmer for 45 minutes. Remove the chicken to a serving platter and keep warm. Remove any fat from the surface of the sauce.
+ In a small bowl, mix the mustard and flour until smooth. Whisk into the sauce. Heat until thickened. Add the parsley and season with pepper. Pour the sauce over the chicken and serve hot.

Serves 4 or 5

MENU

Braised Chicken Legs & Mushrooms Moutard
Cooked carrots
Polenta (page 253)
Chocolate-dipped dried fruit and glacéed apricots (page 269)

Grilled Tuscan Chicken Breasts on Vermicelli

*W*hen *winter cold makes you yearn for a summer Mediterranean meal of grilled chicken, sangria, and pasta, try this scrumptious chicken breast that's marinated in olive oil and spices. For winter grilling, spare the grill chef and use an indoor stove-top grill. This menu will satisfy your taste for summer flavors as you dream of warmer weather.*

4 chicken breast halves,
  boned and skinned
¹⁄₄ cup olive oil
1 clove garlic, split
  in half
³⁄₄ teaspoon salt
Thyme, rosemary, or
  oregano to taste,
  optional
Pepper to taste

For the pasta:
³⁄₄ pound vermicelli or
  thin spaghetti
¹⁄₄ cup olive oil
¹⁄₂ cup crumbled Feta
  cheese
12 small black, oil-
  cured olives
8 cherry tomatoes,
  halved
3 tablespoons chopped
  parsley
Salt and pepper to taste
1 lemon, cut into
  wedges

- Trim the chicken breasts of all excess fat.
- Combine the oil, garlic, salt, herbs, and pepper in a shallow glass or plastic container. Add the chicken and marinate for at least 1 hour, covered and refrigerated.
- When ready to cook the chicken, heat the grill or a large heavy sauté pan over medium heat.
- Turn the chicken to coat it with the marinade, and arrange it on the grill or in the pan. Cook for 8 to 10 minutes total, turning once, until the chicken is just opaque and cooked through.
- Cook the pasta in a large pot of boiling salted water according to the package directions until tender, and drain. Toss the pasta with the olive oil, Feta cheese, olives, cherry tomato halves, and chopped parsley. Season with salt and pepper. Transfer to a decorative serving platter.
- Arrange the chicken over the pasta and garnish with lemon wedges.

Serves 4

MENU

Grilled Tuscan Chicken Breasts on Vermicelli
Crusty French rolls
Fresh berries topped with vanilla yogurt

Spiced Chicken Sticks

Marinating fish, beef, or chicken early in the day gives them flavor, and makes the cook's work easy. All it takes is a hot grill at dinnertime and a few minutes of cooking. Peanut butter and tomato paste make this a thick marinade with ginger, cilantro, and cumin for added flavor.

4 chicken breasts
  halves, boned and
  skinned

For the marinade:
3 tablespoons fresh
  lemon juice
1/4 cup olive oil
1 clove garlic, crushed
3 tablespoons chopped
  cilantro
1 1/2 tablespoons peanut
  butter
1 tablespoon tomato
  paste
1 teaspoon paprika
3/4 teaspoon salt
3/4 teaspoon cumin
Pinch of cayenne pepper
Black pepper to taste

- Trim the chicken breasts of all excess fat and skin. Cut each chicken breast into 5 or 6 pieces and place in a large bowl.
- In a small bowl, combine the marinade ingredients. Whisk until smooth and pour over the chicken, tossing to coat on all sides. Cover and refrigerate for at least 2 hours, stirring a few times.
- Prepare the grill.
- When the grill is hot, remove the chicken from the marinade and skewer on metal skewers or bamboo sticks that have been soaked in water for 30 minutes to prevent them from burning.
- Grill the chicken 4 to 6 inches over the hot coals for 5 or 6 minutes total, turning often, until it is a little crusty on the outside and opaque throughout. Don't overcook.

Serves 4

MENU

Spiced Chicken Sticks
Brown Rice (page 251)
Caesar Salad (page 35)
Iced coffee and cookies

Grilled Marmalade Chicken

A marmalade and vinaigrette dressing combination was the favorite chicken marinade of my childhood and the inspiration for Marmalade Chicken. The marmalade adds a sweetness to the marinade that caramelizes when the chicken is grilled. The vinaigrette ingredients give the chicken flavor, tenderness, and fat to protect it as it cooks over the hot coals. I use vinaigrette dressings frequently for grill cooking—as a marinade for meat or chicken, brushed over skewered vegetables on the grill, or on thick slices of French bread to make grilled croûtes.

1 4-pound chicken, cut into 8 pieces, 6 chicken breast halves, or 4 pounds chicken wings, about 20

For the marinade:
¹⁄₄ cup marmalade (orange, citrus, or ginger)
1¹⁄₂ tablespoons brown sugar
2 teaspoons Dijon mustard
3 tablespoons Balsamic vinegar
2 tablespoons olive oil
1 clove garlic, minced
¹⁄₂ teaspoon salt
Pepper to taste

- Trim the chicken of all excess fat and skin. If you are using chicken wings, remove the wing tips. Place in a glass or plastic container.
- In a medium bowl, stir together the marinade ingredients. Pour over the chicken and turn to coat all sides. Cover and refrigerate for at least 2 hours.
- Prepare the grill.
- Grill the chicken 4 to 6 inches above hot coals until browned and crisp and cooked through. Turn them frequently and cover as necessary to keep the flames down. The breasts will be done before the dark meat.

Serves 4 to 6

MENU

Grilled Marmalade Chicken
Grilled vegetable skewers (mushrooms, onion, peppers, summer squash)
Grilled French bread rounds
Ice cream cones

Grilled Hawaiian Chicken Wings

Chicken wings are at their best when marinated and grilled. Much of the fat cooks away to a crispness, and the sweetened marinade gives the chicken a caramelized taste. Use the wing tips to make a quick chicken stock for cooking rice.

4–5 pounds chicken
wings (20–25)

For the marinade:
1/2 cup ketchup
1/4 cup vegetable oil
1/4 cup brown sugar
1/4 cup cider vinegar
2 tablespoons honey or
light corn syrup
1 tablespoon
Worcestershire sauce
1 teaspoon salt
1/4 teaspoon cayenne
pepper

+ Trim the chicken wings of any excess fat and skin and remove the wing tips. Place the chicken in a plastic or glass container.
+ In a small bowl, combine the marinade ingredients and mix thoroughly. Pour over the chicken, turning to coat all sides. Cover and refrigerate for at least 2 hours.
+ Prepare the grill.
+ Grill the wings 4 inches above the hot coals. Turn frequently to avoid burning. Cook for about 30 minutes until browned and crisp and cooked through. Cover the grill as necessary to keep the flames down.

Serves 6 to 8

MENU

Grilled Hawaiian Chicken Wings
Rice (page 250)
Pickled beets and assorted pickles
Fresh pineapple and frozen candy bars

Dad's Tabasco Chicken

*S*picy *grilled chicken is a good choice for a Father's Day dinner with potato salad, cherry tomatoes, and watermelon to round out a simple meal that kids can make for dad. Chicken legs and thighs have a more robust flavor than the breasts, and are especially suited to hot grill cooking and spicy marinades. Remember to marinate the chicken early in the morning if possible so it has time to develop lots of flavor. The measurements for the marinade ingredients are easy for anyone to remember.*

6 chicken legs
6 chicken thighs

For the marinade:
2 tablespoons soy sauce
2 tablespoons ketchup
2 tablespoons cider
  vinegar
2 tablespoons Tabasco
  sauce
2 tablespoons brown
  sugar

+ Trim the chicken of all excess fat and skin.
+ In a large glass or plastic container, combine the soy sauce, ketchup, vinegar, Tabasco, and sugar. Stir to combine.
+ Add the trimmed chicken and turn to coat each piece. Cover, refrigerate, and marinate for at least 2 hours, turning occasionally.
+ Prepare the grill.
+ Grill the chicken 4 inches over the coals for about 30 minutes until crisp and cooked through, turning often to brown on all sides. Cover as necessary to keep the flames down.

Serves 4 to 6

MENU

Dad's Tabasco Chicken
Potato Salad (page 244)
Cherry tomatoes
Garlic Bread (page 261)
Watermelon
Homemade ice cream sandwiches

Grilled Chicken with Dry-Rubbed Spice Blends

Before the outdoor grill is put away and you move on to cool-weather stews and soups, try one of these three spicy dry marinade blends for grilled chicken. Spice blends that are rubbed into meat, chicken, or fish are similar to liquid marinades but they add flavor in a more direct way. The dry-rub method works especially well for grilled chicken drumsticks or meats with a little fat on them (chops, steaks, or ribs). For indoor cooking, try quick-cooking chicken breasts, skirt steak, or fish in the Cajun style—rubbing them with spices and cooking them in a hot, heavy pan.

Red Hot Pepper Rub
1 teaspoon cayenne
 pepper
1 teaspoon cumin
1 teaspoon garlic
 powder
1 teaspoon paprika
1 teaspoon salt

Cajun Spice Rub
1 teaspoon salt
1 teaspoon paprika
1 teaspoon oregano
1 teaspoon thyme
1/2 teaspoon cayenne
 pepper

Moroccan Spice Rub
1 teaspoon salt
1 1/2 teaspoons cumin
1 teaspoon ginger
1 teaspoon garlic
 powder
1/2 teaspoon paprika
1/4 teaspoon tumeric
1/4 teaspoon cinnamon

+ In a small bowl, combine the spices for 1 of the dry-rub spice blends.
+ Allow 1 to 2 teaspoons of blended spices for each 1 pound of poultry or meat.
+ Measure the spice blend into your hand and rub it into the surface of the chicken or meat. Let it marinate for at least 2 hours.
+ Prepare the grill.
+ Grill the chicken or meat 4 to 6 inches over hot coals until browned and crisp and cooked through. Turn frequently and cover as necessary to keep the flames down.

MENU

Grilled Chicken with Dry-Rubbed Spice Blends
Coleslaw (page 243)
Corn-on-the-cob
Garlic bread
Frozen fruit juice bars

Beef, Lamb & Pork

Meat is still an important part of our diets, even if we're eating less of it. We're learning to eat smaller portions, trim the fat from the meat, and let the vegetables, starches, and bread fill us up. Try to stick with 1/4 pound of meat per person as a reasonable and healthy serving.

Roasts usually aren't part of quick dinner menus, unless you can put meat in the oven and walk away to do other things. If you have the time, roasts can make dinner hours easier, especially when you have leftovers for another night.

The meat recipes in the book use mostly quick-cooking chops, ground meat, or sirloin strips or tips for grilled kebobs and stir-fried dinners.

Beef has always been an American staple. There are so many cuts and grinds to choose from that it is as versatile as it is delicious.

Lamb has always had a following and it lends itself to many international flavors and dishes.

Today **pork** is better than ever and gaining in popularity. Bred to be leaner, pork is healthier for you and as quick-cooking as chicken. Try the lean chops, cutlets, and tenderloins, and cook them the same way you would boned and skinned chicken breasts—briefly, until cooked through, or it will toughen.

Get to know your butcher. Even in large supermarkets, the butcher will custom-cut or trim meats for you, help you choose the best cuts for the occasion, and suggest cooking techniques. For Middle Eastern Burgers (page 179) or Pan-Fried Peking Ravioli (page 94), choose a package of lean chops and ask your friendly butcher to trim and grind the meat for your recipe. You'll know what you're getting, and know it's the best.

Ground meat discolors readily because of the surface exposure to air, which also causes deterioration. Buy freshly ground meat the day you plan to cook and eat it.

Halloween Beef Ghoul-ash

*H*alloween *dinner means trick-or-treat interruptions, and excess candy for dessert. Why not make a double or triple recipe of Ghoul-ash and treat parents, as well as children, with a portable, hot cupful—and plastic fork—to go?*

1 pound ground beef (or a combination of beef and lamb)
1 onion, finely chopped
1 clove garlic, minced
1/2 teaspoon cinnamon
1/4 teaspoon allspice
1 tablespoon tomato paste
1 cup chicken broth
1 1-pound can whole tomatoes, drained and chopped
Salt and pepper to taste
6 ounces elbow macaroni
1/2 cup freshly grated Parmesan cheese

♦ Brown the beef, onion, and garlic in a sauté pan until the meat is no longer pink, breaking up the chunks. Drain off any accumulated fat. Stir in the spices, tomato paste, broth, and tomatoes. Simmer the sauce, stirring occasionally, until the liquid is reduced and the sauce is thickened, about 10 to 15 minutes. Season to taste with salt and pepper.

♦ While the ghoul-ash is simmering, cook the pasta in boiling salted water according to the package directions until tender. Drain well and add to the sauce. Stir in the Parmesan cheese and mix to combine.

♦ Heat thoroughly and serve in soup bowls, or for trick-or-treaters, in hot cups.

Serves 4 to 6

MENU

Halloween Beef Ghoul-ash
Raw vegetable platter
Trick-or-treat candy

Meatballs in Tomato Sauce

As winter approaches, I seem drawn back into my childhood and the simple, nostalgic flavors of home-cooking. One of those homey and versatile dishes that still provides comfort is meatballs and spaghetti. By updating the dish with more nutritious ingredients and baking the meatballs briefly before simmering them in sauce, this old-fashioned favorite is once more in fashion. I've doubled the recipe since the meatballs and sauce freeze well, and they make delicious meatball sandwiches on toasted rolls, topped with shredded cheese. Preparing the meatballs and sauce ahead of time enhances the flavors.

2 pounds lean ground beef

4 slices firm white bread, grated to crumbs

1/4 cup finely chopped onion

1/4 cup finely chopped parsley

1 10-ounce package frozen chopped spinach, defrosted and squeezed dry

1 cup finely chopped mushrooms

1/4 cup freshly grated Parmesan cheese

2 eggs

2 teaspoons salt, or more to taste

Pepper to taste

For the sauce:

2 28-ounce cans of chunky-style tomatoes

2 cloves garlic, minced

1/2 teaspoon oregano

1/4 cup olive oil

Salt to taste

+ Preheat the oven to 400°F. Lightly oil a jellyroll pan or roasting pan.

+ In a large bowl, combine the ground beef, bread crumbs, onion, parsley, spinach, mushrooms, Parmesan cheese, eggs, salt, and pepper. Mix lightly but thoroughly. Form into 24 large meatballs.

+ Arrange the meatballs in the pan and bake in the middle of the oven for about 25 minutes, turning once.

+ In a large sauce pan, heat the tomatoes, garlic, oregano, olive oil, and salt and pepper to taste. Simmer covered, for 10 minutes to blend the flavors.

+ Add the meatballs to the sauce and simmer uncovered, for about 15 minutes more, or until the sauce is as thick as you like it.

+ Serve immediately or cool and refrigerate. Or freeze it in labeled plastic contains for later use.

Serves 10

MENU

Meatballs in Tomato Sauce
Spaghetti
Mixed green salad vinaigrette
Spumoni or Italian ices

Beef au Poivre

Beef au Poivre is the classic Steak au Poivre or, less elegant, Hamburgers au Poivre that works well for fast dinners. This version has slimmed down from the original, with beef broth and mustard taking the place of some of the cream. The optional Cognac adds an authentic flavor that complements the pepper, and the finishing cream mellows the sauce. I've used boneless top loin steaks, sirloin tip/strips, or skirt steaks, all about 3/4-inch thick and cut into individual 1/3 to 1/2 pound portions. Be sure to trim the steaks of all fat, or use extra-lean ground beef for the patties. Small portions of good things make them seem like treasures, and keep us healthier as well. Fill out the meal with simple vegetables, potatoes, and French bread.

1½–2 pounds boneless top loin steaks, cut into 4 medallions, or extra-lean ground beef formed into 4 patties

1 tablespoon cracked black peppercorns

Salt to taste

2 tablespoons butter or vegetable oil

3 tablespoons Cognac or other brandy, optional

½ cup beef broth

1 rounded tablespoon Dijon mustard

1 clove garlic, peeled and skewered with a toothpick

⅓ cup heavy or whipping cream

Snipped chives or chopped parsley for garnish

♦ Sprinkle each side of the steaks or burgers with the pepper and press into the meat. Set aside and refrigerate for at least 15 minutes. Season the meat with salt.

♦ Heat a heavy sauté pan or skillet over medium heat until very hot. Add the meat and cook for about 3 minutes on each side until browned on the outside and still quite pink on the inside, or any way you like it cooked. Remove the meat to a platter.

♦ Add the Cognac and whisk to scrape the bottom. Carefully ignite and shake the pan until the flames die out. Add the broth, mustard, garlic, and cream, whisk together, and cook down over medium-high heat until thickened. Remove the garlic and adjust the seasoning.

♦ Spoon the sauce over the meat and serve hot, garnished with chives or parsley.

Serves 4

MENU

Beef au Poivre
Sautéed julienned summer squash, peppers, and carrots
Baked potatoes (page 254)
French bread
Iced coffee

German Pot Roast

Chilly nights need familiar comforting foods. Pot roast is easy to make, and it provides delicious gravy and great leftovers for another night or for sandwiches. It's best made the night before so the flavors can develop. This is a German version, with spices and tomatoes, that works well with noodles.

3½–4 pounds flat-cut brisket
¼ cup flour
1 teaspoon salt
3 tablespoons vegetable oil
2 onions, sliced
1 teaspoon powdered ginger
⅛ teaspoon allspice
Pepper to taste
1 1-pound can of whole tomatoes, drained and chopped
2 tablespoons tomato paste
1 cup water
3 tablespoons cider vinegar
2 tablespoons brown sugar
1 bay leaf

+ Trim the meat of excess fat and pat dry. Combine the flour and salt and dust the meat on all sides, reserving any extra.
+ Heat 2 tablespoons of oil in a large, heavy pot. Brown the meat over medium-high heat. Remove the meat and reduce the heat to low.
+ Add the remaining tablespoon of oil and sauté the onions, stirring frequently, until the onions are soft but not colored, about 5 minutes.
+ Add any remaining flour and the remaining ingredients. Stir to combine well. Bring to a simmer and add the meat with any accumulated juices. Cover with foil and then with the cover. Simmer for about 2 hours, turning once, until fork-tender. Cool and refrigerate.
+ Skim off any accumulated fat from the sauce. Warm it slightly so you can remove the meat from the pot. Cut the pot roast against the grain into thin, diagonal slices. Return the meat to the pot with the sauce and heat to serve.

Serves 6 to 8

MENU

German Pot Roast
Bowtie noodles
Creamy coleslaw (page 243)
Spice cake

Korean Beef Stir-Fry with Mushrooms & Spinach

*L*ong-cooking beef stews may not be possible for quick dinners unless you make them ahead and simply reheat them. Instead, you could make a stir-fry stew using flavorful and tender skirt steak, flank steak, or sirloin strips or tips. This dish is similar in flavor to a beef stew my Korean cousin made years ago. It's best to have all the ingredients cut and prepared before you start since stir-frying takes just a few minutes to cook. Kim Chee is the popular Korean condiment of very spicy pickled cabbage. It's available in Asian groceries or in many supermarket produce departments.

3 tablespoons vegetable oil

2 cloves garlic, minced

2 tablespoons minced fresh peeled ginger root

1/2 pound white mush-rooms, sliced

1 1/2 pounds skirt steak, flank steak, or sirloin strips, cut into very thin diagonal slices

1 8-ounce can sliced water chestnuts, drained

1 cup beef broth

1/4 cup soy sauce

1 tablespoon sugar

3 tablespoons water

1 tablespoon cornstarch

2 cups packed fresh spinach leaves, stems removed and coarsely chopped

♦ Heat the oil in a large sauté pan. Sauté the garlic and ginger over low heat, stirring constantly, until softened. Don't let them color or burn.

♦ Add the mushrooms and increase the heat to medium. Sauté for 1 minute.

♦ Add the beef and sauté for another minute, stirring constantly.

♦ Stir in the water chestnuts.

♦ In a small bowl, combine the broth, soy sauce, and sugar and add to the beef. Simmer for 1 or 2 minutes.

♦ In another small bowl, combine the water and cornstarch, stirring to dissolve. Add to the pan and heat until the sauce thickens.

♦ Add the spinach leaves and stir to mix.

♦ Serve hot.

Serves 4 to 6

MENU

Korean Beef Stir-Fry with Mushrooms & Spinach
Rice (page 250)
Kim Chee
Fresh orange and grapefruit sections

Spicy Beef Satay on Skewers

One of the most popular, and most familiar, Indonesian dishes in this country is satay, a spicy peanut butter marinade/sauce that works equally well with beef, chicken, or shimp. Marinated strips of well-trimmed beef sirloin tips, skewered with metal skewers or water-soaked bamboo sticks, can be cooked under the broiler in winter or on the grill in summer.

1½ pounds beef sirloin strips or tips, trimmed and cut into thin strips

For the marinade:
2 tablespoons peanut or vegetable oil
4 tablespoons peanut butter
3 tablespoons soy sauce
1 teaspoon brown sugar
1 clove garlic, minced
3 tablespoons lemon juice
2 teaspoons minced fresh ginger root
1 teaspoon curry powder
⅛ teaspoon cayenne pepper

- Pile the beef strips in a large bowl.
- In a small bowl, combine the marinade ingredients and mix until smooth. Add the marinade to the beef and toss to coat well. Cover and refrigerate for at least 2 hours.
- Thread the marinated beef on metal skewers, or bamboo skicks that have been soaked in water for 30 minutes to prevent them from burning.
- Prepare the grill or preheat the broiler.
- Grill the meat over hot coals, or close under a broiler, until crusted on the outside and still slightly pink on the inside. Any leftovers make great sandwiches packed in pita bread halves, and topped with chopped cucumber and tomato and a drizzle of seasoned rice wine vinegar.

Serves 4 to 6

MENU

Spicy Beef Satay on Skewers
Chinese egg noodles with sesame oil, scallions, soy sauce, and a pinch of sugar
Stir-fried Chinese vegetables (bok choy, cabbage, broccoli, or snow peas)
Grapes and gingerbread cookies

Teriyaki Beef Sticks

Hooray for the grill! Dinners seem easier and more fun when the grill chef becomes involved and there's less to do in the kitchen. This marinade works with beef, chicken, or pork, or as a seasoning for rice. Marinate the meat early in the day for maximum flavor.

For the marinade:
1/3 cup soy sauce
2 tablespoons Balsamic
    vinegar
1 tablespoon water
2 tablespoons vegetable
    oil
1 1/2 tablespoons sugar
1 wedge fresh peeled
    ginger root
1 clove garlic, minced
1 scallion, chopped

1 1/2 pounds skirt or flank
    steak, or sirloin tips or
    strips, cut into very
    thin diagonal slices

- Combine the marinade ingredients in a small bowl and stir together.
- Refrigerate in a glass jar until ready to use as a marinade or flavoring sauce. It will keep for a week.
- Place the beef slices in a large glass or plastic bowl. Add the marinade, tossing to coat the meat well. Cover and refrigerate for at least 1 hour.
- Prepare the grill or heat the broiler.
- Thread the marinated beef on metal skewers or on bamboo sticks that have been soaked in water for 30 minutes to prevent them from burning.
- Grill the meat 4 inches over the hot coals or close under a broiler until browned on the outside and still juicy on the inside.
- Serve hot.

Serves 6

MENU

Teriyaki Beef Sticks
Sticky rice balls (page 250)
Cucumber salad with pickled ginger
Fresh fruit platter and fortune cookies

Pan-Fried Peking Ravioli

Family dinners can be family entertainment if you make a dish that needs everyone's participation in assembly and cooking. Pan-Fried Peking Ravioli are fun for week-end hors d'oeuvres as well. For the leanest and freshest ground meat—especially fattier meats like pork or lamb—choose lean chops or roasts and have your butcher trim and grind them. For the best results, make these ravioli, or "pot stickers," in a nonstick pan where they'll never stick.

1 tablespoon cornstarch
1 tablespoon Balsamic vinegar or sherry
3/4 pound lean ground pork, from about 1 pound of boneless, center-cut pork chops
1/3 cup finely chopped scallions, white and some green parts
1 8 1/2-ounce can water chestnuts, drained and finely chopped
1 clove garlic, minced
2 tablespoons grated fresh ginger root
2 tablespoons soy sauce
2 tablespoons sesame seeds
1 tablespoon sesame oil
1/2 teaspoon salt
Pepper to taste
1 12-ounce package (about 60) 3-inch round Chinese pasta wrappers
4 tablespoons vegetable oil
Water for steaming

+ In a small bowl, combine the cornstarch and Balsamic vinegar.
+ In a large bowl, combine the pork, scallions, water chestnuts, garlic, ginger, soy sauce, sesame seeds, sesame oil, salt, pepper, and cornstarch mixture.
+ Place 1 rounded teaspoon of the filling in the center of the wrappers. Moisten the edge with water and fold over to make a half circle, sealing the edge. Stand up with the pinched edges on top, flattening the smooth bottom, and pinching the ends to seal. (They look like an army of miniature stegosaurus dinosaurs.) Repeat until the filling is used up.
+ The ravioli can be frozen at this point in a single layer on a wax paper-lined cookie sheet. When they're frozen, transfer the ravioli to a plastic bag.
+ Cook the ravioli in 2 batches. Add 2 tablespoons of oil to a large, nonstick sauté pan and heat. Add half the ravioli close together and brown on the bottom, shaking the pan to keep the ravioli from sticking.
+ When browned, add 1/2 cup of water and cover immediately. Steam over low heat for about 12 minutes until the water evaporates. Remove with a slotted spatula.
+ Repeat with the remaining ravioli.

Yields about 40 ravioli, to serve 6 to 8

MENU

Pan-Fried Peking Ravioli
Rice (page 250)
Raw vegetable sticks with a dressing/dip (page 259)
Orange sherbet and fortune cookies

Lemon Mustard Pork Chops

*Today's leaner pork chops can and should be cooked briefly, like steaks and burgers, so that they remain tender and juicy on the inside. Without the fat of yesteryear, pork can become dry and tough if cooked too long. The boneless pork chops absorb the flavors of the marinade in this simple recipe with a reduced marinade sauce. You can grill or pan fry the chops for summer or winter dinners. Whenever you use a marinade to make a sauce, it **must** be boiled to kill any bacteria from the raw meat, chicken, or fish.*

4 loin pork chops,
   3/4-inch thick

For the marinade/sauce:
1/4 cup fresh lemon juice
   (about 1 large lemon)
Grated zest of 1 lemon
2 tablespoons olive oil
2 tablespoons Dijon
   mustard
1 clove garlic
1 teaspoon brown sugar
1/2 teaspoon salt
Pepper to taste
Sprig of fresh rosemary,
   tarragon, or herb of
   your choice

Fresh chopped herbs of
   your choice for garnish

- Trim the pork chops of all excess fat.
- In a small bowl, combine the marinade ingredients and whisk together until smooth.
- Place the chops in a shallow glass or plastic container large enough to hold them in a single layer. Pour the marinade over the chops. Turn to coat them on all sides. Cover and refrigerate for at least 2 hours.
- Prepare the grill (outdoors or cooktop) or heat a large sauté pan or skillet.
- Remove the chops from the marinade and transfer the marinade to a small saucepan.
- Cook the chops for about 4 minutes on each side until cooked through—past pink but still juicy.
- While the chops are cooking, heat the marinade and cook down by almost half to about 3 tablespoons. Remove the herbs. Spoon a little sauce over each cooked chop and top with fresh herbs.

Serves 4

MENU

Lemon Mustard Pork Chops
Baked sweet potatoes
Broccoli (page 242)
Gingerbread cake (page 209) with fresh berries

Pork Chops with Orange Sauce & Cranberries

When the season's first cranberries appear in the markets, it's a reminder of holidays ahead. The tart cranberry flavor does more than make a good relish for turkey. It's a great addition to pork and chicken dishes. Buy a few extra bags of cranberries when they are in season and freeze them for an out-of-season treat.

4 pork chops, 1-inch thick
2 tablespoons vegetable oil
2 tablespoons butter
1/4 cup minced shallots
1 tablespoon minced fresh peeled ginger root
1 tablespoon flour
1/2 cup orange juice
Grated zest of 1 orange
1/2 cup chicken broth
1 teaspoon sugar, or to taste
Salt and pepper to taste
1 cup fresh cranberries
1/4 cup sour cream, optional

- Trim the pork chops of all excess fat.
- In a large heavy sauté pan, heat the oil and sear the pork chops for 1 minute on each side. Remove from the pan and pour off any excess oil.
- Melt the butter in the pan over low heat and sauté the shallots and ginger for about 5 minutes, stirring often until soft but not colored. Whisk in the flour and cook for 1 minute. Whisk in the orange juice, zest, chicken broth, and sugar. The sauce will thicken as it comes to a simmer. Season with salt and pepper.
- Add the pork chops back to the sauce, cover, and simmer for 5 minutes. Turn the pork chops, add the cranberries, cover, and simmer for about 5 to 10 more minutes until the pork is tender and cooked through and the cranberries have popped.
- Serve the pork chops with a spoonful of the sauce and cranberries. Top with sour cream if you like.

Serves 4

MENU

Pork Chops with Orange Sauce & Cranberries
Polenta (page 253)
Steamed broccoli
Banana slices dipped in melted chocolate—use toothpicks (page 269)

Grilled Indian Lamb

Don't overlook lamb in the summer months. It's a real treat for a backyard barbeque. Find an accommodating butcher who will butterfly a leg of lamb, then take it home and marinate it overnight in yogurt with Indian spices. Serve it with pilaf and a refreshing salad, or with grilled vegetables basted with aïoli, a garlic mayonnaise.

5–6 pound leg of lamb, boned, butterflied, and trimmed of all fat

For the marinade:
1 cup plain yogurt
2 cloves garlic, minced
Juice of 1 lemon
2 tablespoons olive oil
1/2 teaspoon crushed red pepper flakes
1 teaspoon tumeric
1 1/2 teaspoons cumin
1/2 teaspoon coriander
Pinch of allspice
Pinch of cinnamon
2 tablespoons chopped fresh ginger root

♦ Place the lamb in a glass or plastic container large enough to hold the butterflied meat. Make small incisions where the meat is very thick.
♦ Combine the marinade ingredients in a small bowl and brush each side of the meat with the mixture. Cover with plastic wrap and refrigerate overnight or up to 2 days. Longer marinating time will let the flavors permeate the meat.
♦ Prepare the grill.
♦ Sear the meat on both sides for 1 minute. Cover the grill and open the vent holes in the lid. Grill for about 10 minutes on each side or until the meat is done the way you like it. Grilling time will vary according to the thickness of the meat.
♦ Let the lamb rest for 5 minutes before sprinkling with salt and pepper. Slice across the grain and serve warm.
♦ Leftovers make great pita bread sandwiches.

Serves 6 to 8

MENU

Grilled Indian Lamb
Rice Pilaf (page 252)
Chopped cucumbers and tomatoes with mint, parsley, scallion and lemon
Fruit chutney (page 166–167)
Ice cream pie

Lamb Stew with White Beans & Tomatoes

When busy schedules make long-cooking lamb stews impossible, this quick dinner will give you the same flavors in no time, and transport you to Southwest France, too! Ask your butcher to grind a piece of fresh lean lamb for less fat and the best flavor.

1 pound lean ground beef
1/2 pound lean ground lamb
1 clove garlic, minced
1 tablespoon tomato paste
2 tablespoons water
1/2 cup fresh bread crumbs from 1 slice of bread
1/4 teaspoon thyme
1 teaspoon salt
Pepper to taste
2 tablespoons olive oil
2 cups cooked small white beans (1 1-pound can), drained
2 cups chunky-style crushed tomatoes
1/4 cup minced parsley

♦ In a large bowl, combine the ground beef, lamb, garlic, tomato paste, water, bread crumbs, and seasoning. Mix gently but thoroughly and form into 8 patties.

♦ Heat the olive oil in a large sauté pan. Add the meat patties and cook over medium heat for a few minutes on each side until browned on both sides but pink in the center. Remove the meat and pour off any accumulated fat in the pan.

♦ Add the drained beans and tomatoes, stirring to combine. Return the meat to the pan, cover, and heat for a few minutes until hot and bubbly and cooked through.

♦ Top with the parsley, season with salt or pepper, and serve hot with crusty bread.

Serves 6

MENU

Lamb Stew with White Beans & Tomatoes
Crusty French bread
Artichokes vinaigrette
Baked Apples (page 269)

Seafood

S eafood is unsurpassed in taste when it's fresh and properly cooked. With cholesterol-fighting omega-3 acids, seafood is truly good for you and quick cooking as well. It's always best to plan seafood dinners the day you go to the fish store, and at the time when there is a fresh shipment of fish. At the seafood counter, what you see—and smell—is what you get. Fish should look fresh, shiny, alive, and almost translucent, not dull. There should be a sweet, mild smell to the fish—not an off, fishy, ammonia smell. Shopping for seafood requires more flexibility than in any other food department. If the fish you want to buy looks as if it has been sitting around for a week, or it's only available frozen or previously frozen, buy another variety that **is** fresh. Don't be afraid to ask how fresh, when it came in, or if you can look at it more closely. With the price of fish today, you're entitled to ask. It's worth a small added cost to patronize a fish store that handles fish well and gets fresh shipments frequently.

Although some kinds of fish are threatened, endangered, in short supply, or out of season, other species are taking their place and finding a niche. Farm-raised fish is making some species more readily available and healthier to eat. Luckily, salmon is with us year-round. I'm reluctant in some recipes to specify species of fish, but will suggest a *firm white fish fillet* and assume you will choose scrod, cod, cusk, hake, haddock, or whichever looks freshest at the fish counter the day you buy it.

In buying fish, the general rule is to buy 1/3 to 1/2 pound per person.

Fish steaks are cut in cross sections from a large fish, usually with the skin on the steak, and sometimes with the backbone intact.

Fish fillets are the sides of the fish cut from the backbone. They're mostly boneless and skinless. Rub your finger along the flesh to feel for small bones and pluck them out with your fingers, tweezers, or pliers.

Chunks of fish trimmings are often sold for fish stews and chowders, and at a lower cost.

When broiling, high-temperature baking, or grilling, the rule is generally to cook the fish for about 10 minutes per inch of fish. It should be cooked until no longer squishy and opaque throughout, or beginning to flake if it's a flaky fish rather than a denser fish steak.

Shellfish

Shrimp, except in the Northwest and the Gulf area, is nearly always previously frozen and defrosted at the fish counter. The magic of shrimp is not only its delightful flavor and texture, but the beautiful color it becomes when it's cooked. From a pale grey, tan, or pink, comes a bright pink-orange as it begins to curl into a crescent. If shrimp cooks too long, it tightens into a spiral and becomes tough, so cook shrimp just until it is opaque throughout and firm to the touch. The shells are easy to peel before cooking, and the intestinal vein should be removed (page 248). If you're cooking shrimp for cocktails or salads, the shells add flavor as they cook. You can just as easily peel the shells after cooking.

Lobsters are one of summer's joys—a great, messy finger-food dinner with corn-on-the-cob and watermelon. There are times of the year when the shells are harder or softer, but lobsters should always be lively, active, and resist the grabber. For cooking information, see page 249.

Scallops are so perfect when they're fresh, that all they need is a quick sauté in butter, some fresh herbs, and a bed of angel hair pasta to make dinner a hit. Whether cape or sea varieties, they should be a bright, shiny, opalescent white color. It's better to buy fewer sea scallops that are beauties, and perhaps more expensive per pound, than it is to buy a larger quantity of old or previously frozen cape scallops that have lost their lustre and flavor. Some scallops still have their *feet* attached, the small opaque muscle that holds the scallop to the shell. If it's still attached, it's easy to peel off. When cooked, the *feet* can have the consistency of rubber bands, so remove them beforehand.

Squid, or **calamari**, is sold as fish bait, so it's hard to sell as the scrumptious gift from the sea that it is. If squid is cooked properly it stays tender and sweet. The first step is to find it, sometimes in the fresh seafood case, and hopefully already cleaned. Squid will most likely be in the frozen seafood section, and you will have to defrost and clean it (page 249). It is sensational when briefly sautéed in olive oil and garlic and served over pasta, dipped in batter and fried, or added to a seafood stew.

Scallop & Snow Pea Stir-Fry with Hoisin or Peanut Sauce

Seafood and stir-fry are words that mean fast and easy dinner. Scallops (or shrimp) and colorful vegetables are matched well with these easy cornstarch-thickened sauces.

Hoisin Sauce:
1/2 cup chicken broth
2 teaspoons cornstarch
2 tablespoons soy sauce
1/2 cup hoisin sauce

Peanut Sauce:
1/2 cup chicken broth
1 teaspoon cornstarch
2 tablespoons vinegar
2 tablespoons soy sauce
1 teaspoon sugar
1/4 cup peanut butter

3 tablespoons vegetable
  or peanut oil
2 slices fresh ginger root
1 clove garlic, smashed
1 pound sea scallops, cut
  in half horizontally if
  very large
1/4 pound snow peas,
  strings removed
1 red pepper, seeded and
  cut into 1-inch pieces
3 scallions, cut into
  1-inch diagonal pieces

* In a small bowl, combine the hoisin or peanut sauce ingredients. Whisk until smooth, and set aside.
* In a large sauté pan, heat the oil, and add the ginger and garlic. Over medium heat, sauté the scallops for about 2 minutes, stirring, until mostly opaque but not quite done. Add the snow peas, peppers, and scallions, and continue to sauté, stirring, for 1 minute.
* Remove the ginger and garlic. Add the sauce and bring to a simmer. It will thicken as it heats. Serve immediately over rice.

Serves 4

MENU

Scallop & Snow Pea Stir-Fry with Hoisin or Peanut Sauce
Rice (page 250)
Sponge cake topped with sweetened berries and whipped cream

Carmelita's Scallops Florentine

*F*resh sea scallops, angel hair pasta (capellini), and fresh spinach each take about three minutes to cook, so this dish is done in no time once the cooking begins. Preparation time is in boiling the water, washing, drying, and removing the tough stems from the spinach, and removing the tough opaque muscle from the sides of the scallops if it's still intact. The lesson here is that quality ingredients, simply cooked, make the best dishes.

1/4 cup olive oil
1 pound fresh sea
  scallops
3 cloves garlic, minced
1/2 pound fresh spinach,
  washed, dried and
  tough stems removed
Salt and pepper to taste
3/4 pound angel hair pasta
1/2 cup freshly grated
  Parmesan cheese

♦ In a sauté pan, heat half the oil and sauté the scallops for only 1 or 2 minutes on each side until nearly opaque throughout and no longer squishy. Remove from the pan and cover.

♦ Add the remaining oil and sauté the garlic briefly until soft but not colored (burned garlic will ruin a dish). Add the spinach and sauté just until wilted, stirring often. Return the scallops to the spinach just to warm. Season well with salt and pepper.

♦ Cook the angel hair pasta in boiling salted water according to the package directions until tender. Drain. Toss with additional olive oil or butter if you can afford the calories and fat.

♦ Transfer to a decorative serving platter and top with the scallops and spinach. Season with salt and pepper and sprinkle with Parmesan cheese.

Serves 4

MENU

Carmelita's Scallops Florentine
Red pepper and carrot sticks
Crusty rolls
Cheesecake and fresh berries (page 267)

Summer Scallop & Corn Sauté

*S*ea *scallops and seasonal corn complement each other in this super summer one-dish dinner. Add more color from your garden with tomatoes, peppers, parsley, and scallions. Dinner is cooked in just ten minutes.*

3 tablespoons butter
1 red or green pepper, seeded and chopped
2 cups corn kernels cut from 4 ears of corn
1/2 cup heavy or whipping cream
1 pound fresh sea scallops
Salt and pepper to taste
1/4 cup minced parsley
2 scallions, thinly sliced on a diagonal
1 large garden tomato, peeled, seeded, and chopped
1/2 cup crisp-cooked, crumbled bacon

♦ In a large sauté pan, melt the butter over medium heat. Add the pepper and sauté for 1 minute, stirring.

♦ Add the corn kernels and cream, and sauté for a few minutes until the corn is mostly cooked and the cream is reduced by 1/2.

♦ Add the scallops and cook for about 4 minutes, stirring often, until the scallops are opaque throughout and no longer squishy. Season generously with salt and pepper. Stir in the parsley and scallions. Drain the tomatoes of excess juice and add to the scallops.

♦ Heat briefly and serve immediately in wide soup bowls with crusty rolls to soak up the juices. Top with the bacon.

Serves 4

MENU

Summer Scallop & Corn Sauté
Crusty rolls
Mixed green salad vinaigrette with toasted pine nuts
Watermelon

Crab Cakes Dijon

Asparagus and crab cakes make a quick, luxurious spring dinner. You may use fresh crabmeat—costly and delicious—pasteurized and frozen crabmeat, or even the imitation crab, which is a bit harder to form into cakes but still tastes great. The crab cakes are very rich, so skip the butter on the noodles and asparagus. Set the cakes on a nest of noodles, and arrange the colorful vegetables around the centerpiece.

½ pound crabmeat
3 tablespoons Dijon
   mustard
3 tablespoons mayonnaise
⅓ cup + ⅔ cup
   unseasoned dry
   bread crumbs
3 tablespoons finely
   chopped parsley
1 scallion, minced
1 teaspoon fresh lemon
   juice
2 tablespoons vegetable
   oil
½ pound fine egg
   noodles
Lemon wedges for
   garnish

- In a large bowl, combine the crabmeat, mustard, mayonnaise, ⅓ cup bread crumbs, parsley, scallion, and lemon juice. Stir to combine. Put the remaining ⅔ cup bread crumbs on a piece of wax paper.
- Form the crabmeat into 4 patties, pressing gently to hold them together. Dip each side into the bread crumbs and set on a platter. Refrigerate, loosely covered, for 30 minutes.
- Cook the noodles in a large pot of boiling salted water according to the package directions until tender. Drain.
- While the noodles are cooking, heat the oil in a wide nonstick sauté pan and cook the crab cakes over medium heat until browned and heated through. Serve on the cooked egg noodles and garnish with a wedge of lemon.

Serves 4

MENU

Crab Cakes Dijon *on egg noodles*
Asparagus
Sliced tomatoes
Vanilla layer cake (page 265)

Fisherman's Stew

Although seafood is delicious and healthy at any time of year, this seafood stew is especially good for cold nights and company dinners. The seafood can be as economical or as extravagant as you like. Calamari rings are a great addition.

4 tablespoons olive oil
1 large onion, finely chopped
1 large clove garlic, minced
1 teaspoon anchovy paste
1/2 teaspoon fennel seeds, crushed
1 28-ounce can chunky-style crushed tomatoes
2 tablespoons red wine vinegar
1 pound scrod (cod) or other mild white fish fillets, cut into large pieces
6–8 sea scallops
1/2 pound large shrimp, peeled and deveined
1/4 cup chopped parsley
Salt and pepper to taste

♦ In a large sauté pan, heat the oil over low heat and add the onion and garlic. Sauté for about 5 minutes, stirring constantly, until the onion is soft. Stir in the anchovy paste and fennel seeds, and sauté for 1 minute.

♦ Add the tomatoes and vinegar to the pan, stir well, and bring to a boil. Add the fish, scallops, and shrimp and simmer for 3 minutes, or just until cooked through.

♦ Sprinkle with parsley and season with salt and pepper to taste. Serve hot over mashed potatoes, polenta, or rice.

Serves 4 to 6

MENU

Fisherman's Stew
Mashed Potatoes (page 254), Polenta (page 253), or Rice (page 250)
Raw cauliflower and radish salad
Butterscotch pudding

Baked Fish Provençale

For spring diets and delicious dinners, fish and vegetables are a natural. Fish fillets can be baked on a bed of julienned Provençale vegetables (similar to a ratatouille) for a colorful 20-minute dinner that's low in cholesterol and high in nutrition. Be sure the fish steaks or fillets are about 1-inch thick so they don't overcook in the hot oven as they cook with the vegetables.

¼ cup olive oil.
1 small onion, sliced
1 red pepper, julienned
1 green pepper, julienned
2 small zucchini, cut into
  thin diagonal slices
1 large tomato, peeled,
  seeded, and chopped
Salt, pepper, and dried
  oregano to taste
½ bay leaf
1½ pounds mild, white
  fish fillets, skinned
  and boned, or salmon
  or swordfish steaks, all
  1-inch thick
1 lemon, very thinly
  sliced
¼ cup dry white wine
8 small black oil-cured
  olives
Minced parsley for
  garnish

♦ Preheat the oven to 450°F. Oil the bottom of an 8 x 12-inch glass baking dish.
♦ Scatter the vegetables over the bottom of the dish and season with salt, pepper, and oregano. Lay the fish on top, skin side down. Season with salt and pepper, and drizzle the remaining oil over the fish, rubbing the surface to coat it completely. Season again with salt and pepper. Lay the lemon slices over the fish and pour the wine in the bottom of the dish.
♦ Bake in the middle of the oven for about 15 minutes until the fish tests done (opaque throughout or flaky) and the vegetables are crisp-tender.
♦ Remove the lemon slices and bay leaf from the baking dish and top the fish with black olives and parsley. Serve hot from the dish with garlic bread to soak up the delicious juices.

Serves 4 to 6

MENU

Baked Fish Provençale
Garlic Bread (page 261)
Stewed rhubarb and cream

Salmon with Tomatoes & Saffron Sauce

For cooler months, oven-poaching is a wonderful way to cook fish. Here the fish cooks in a small amount of liquid with shallots, tomatoes, onions, herbs, and spices. A parchment paper cover protects the fish from the high heat, and the fish will be perfectly cooked in just minutes. The reduced cooking juices make a delicious sauce. Use this technique and experiment with other flavors that you like. In this recipe, don't substitute half-and-half or even light cream for the heavy or whipping cream or the sauce will curdle when it's boiled and reduced.

1 tablespoon butter
1½–2 pounds salmon fillet, all bones removed
Salt and black pepper to taste
2 ripe tomatoes, peeled, seeded, and chopped
2 tablespoons minced shallots or white part of scallion
½ cup heavy or whipping cream
½ teaspoon honey
½ teaspoon coriander
½ teaspoon saffron
Pinch of cayenne pepper
2 tablespoons minced parsley

* Preheat the oven to 450°F. Grease a shallow glass baking dish with half the butter.
* Place the salmon, skin side down, in the dish. Season with salt and pepper. Sprinkle the tomatoes and shallots around the fish. Pour the cream into the bottom of the baking dish.
* Grease a piece of parchment paper with the remaining butter and place it, buttered-side down, over the fish to cover completely.
* Bake in the middle of the oven for about 15 minutes until the fish is opaque throughout and begins to flake. Carefully remove the fish with two spatulas and arrange it on a serving platter. Cover the fish with the parchment paper to keep it warm.
* Pour the cooking juices into a shallow sauté pan and reduce over medium-high heat until slightly thickened. Stir in the honey, coriander, saffron, and cayenne, and let it simmer for 1 minute. Taste, and season with salt and pepper. Pour over the fish and sprinkle with parsley.

Serves 4 to 6

MENU

Salmon with Tomatoes & Saffron Sauce
Noodles
Mixed green salad vinaigrette
Crusty French rolls
Chocolate Cake (page 265)

Braised Scrod Marakkech

Some exotic spices can make a simple piece of fish take center stage at the dinner table. Just rub the spices into the fish, top with tomatoes and wine, and bake in a hot oven. Dinner couldn't be much simpler. Use scrod, cod, hake, cusk, halibut, or any mild, white fish.

3 tablespoons butter
1/4 cup minced shallots
1 1/2 pounds scrod fillets
　　or other mild, white
　　fish about 1-inch thick
1 teaspoon cumin
1/2 teaspoon paprika
1/2 teaspoon salt
1/2 teaspoon tumeric
Pinch of cayenne pepper
Black pepper to taste
1 1-pound can peeled
　　tomatoes, drained
　　and chopped
1/2 cup dry white wine
2 tablespoons minced
　　cilantro or flat leaf
　　parsley

♦ Preheat the oven to 425°F. With a teaspoon of butter, grease the bottom of a glass baking dish large enough to hold the fish.
♦ Sprinkle the shallots in the bottom of the dish and lay the fish on top, skin side down.
♦ In a small bowl, combine the spices and rub into the fish.
♦ Scatter the tomatoes over the fish and pour the wine on top. Cover lightly with buttered parchment paper and bake for 10 to 15 minutes, until the fish is opaque and cooked through. Remove the fish to a serving platter and cover with parchment paper to keep warm.
♦ Pour the vegetables and liquid into a sauté pan and reduce the cooking juices by 1/2 over high heat. Remove from the heat and whisk in the remaining butter, a little at a time. Stir in the cilantro, taste, and adjust the seasoning. Spoon the sauce over the fish and serve immediately.

Serves 4

MENU

Braised Scrod Marakkech
Couscous (page 250)
Green peas
Frozen yogurt sundaes

Nested Oriental Scrod

Thin spaghetti makes perfect nests for individual portions of fish. Marinated fish is put in the nest of cooked pasta and baked in a hot oven to cook through. It's a nice presentation that works for weekday meals and even for company. The critical factor is that the fish be absolutely fresh. For this dish, use any mild, white fish, boned and skinned and about ³/₄-inch thick.

2 pounds fresh scrod
  or cod fillets, ³/₄-inch
  thick

For the marinade:
¹/₄ cup soy sauce
2 tablespoons Balsamic
  vinegar
2 tablespoons vegetable
  oil
2 teaspoons sugar
1 tablespoon coarsely
  chopped fresh peeled
  ginger root
¹/₄ teaspoon hot oil or
  a pinch of cayenne
  pepper

³/₄ pound angel hair pasta
3 tablespoons vegetable
  oil
1 tablespoon roasted
  sesame oil
1 teaspoon salt, or to taste
2 tablespoons sesame
  seeds
4 scallions cut into thin
  diagonal slices

+ Cut the fish into 6 even portions. In a large glass or plastic container, combine the soy sauce, vinegar, oil, sugar, ginger, and hot oil. Stir well to mix. Add the fish, turning to coat all sides. Cover and refrigerate for 30 minutes.
+ Preheat the oven to 400°F. Lightly oil a large shallow baking dish or roasting pan.
+ Cook the pasta in a large pot of boiling salted water according to the package directions until tender. Drain well and toss with the vegetable oil, sesame oil, and salt. With a large serving fork, scoop up individual portions of pasta and make 6 nests on the baking dish.
+ Remove the fish from the marinade and arrange on top of the pasta. Sprinkle the fish with the sesame seeds.
+ Bake in the middle of the hot oven for about 20 minutes (less if the fish is thinner, more if it is thicker) until the fish is opaque and the pasta is a little crunchy. Remove, sprinkle with the scallions, and serve immediately.

Serves 6

MENU

Nested Oriental Scrod
Snow peas, peppers, and bok choy, stir-fried
Rice cakes
Frozen fruit juice bars

Gremolata Fish

Gremolata is the favorite Italian combination of fresh parsley, garlic, and lemon zest that's used to finish a sauce. It's a perfect way to add flavor but few calories to fish. You might even add a handful of fresh mint leaves to make a Mint Gremolata. Use any fresh fish that you like: sole, haddock, bluefish, snapper, etc.

1½ pounds fresh fish fillets, skinned, 1-inch thick
Salt and pepper to taste
3 tablespoons olive oil
⅓ cup coarsely chopped parsley
Grated zest from 1 large lemon
1 clove garlic, peeled and chopped

+ Preheat the oven to 425°F. Use 1 tablespoon of the oil to lightly grease a baking dish large enough to hold the fish in one layer.
+ Place the fish in the baking dish, skin side down and season with salt and pepper. Rub the remaining oil completely over the fish.
+ Bake for about 10 minutes (10 minutes per inch of fish), until opaque throughout and beginning to flake.
+ To prepare the gremolata, combine the parsley, lemon zest (just the yellow part), and garlic, and chop together until fine.
+ Serve the fish topped with any accumulated pan juices, and sprinkled on top with the gremolata.

Serves 4

MENU

Gremolata Fish
Rice (page 250)
Lettuce wedges with Russian Dressing (page 259)
Carrot cake (page 212)

Baked Bluefish Dijon

*M*ustard *and garlic make this assertive sauce a good match for bluefish or any strong-flavored fish. The sauce acts as a protective coating for high-temperature baking. The suggested cooking time is 10 minutes per inch of fish.*

2 pounds fresh bluefish
  fillets, 1-inch thick
½ cup mayonnaise
1 tablespoon Dijon
  mustard
1 tablespoon lemon juice
1 clove garlic, minced
1 teaspoon prepared
  white horseradish,
  drained
Pepper to taste
Lemon wedges for
  garnish

+ Preheat the oven to 450°F. Line a baking dish with foil.
+ Run your finger along the middle of the fish to check for any bones. Remove them by hand or with tweezers or needlenose pliers.
+ Place the fish on the foil, skin side down.
+ Combine the mayonnaise, mustard, lemon juice, garlic, horseradish, and pepper in a small bowl. Spread half of the sauce evenly over the fish to make a protective coating from the high heat. Be sure the surface is completely covered.
+ Bake in the upper half of the oven for 10 to 12 minutes, or until the fish is firm to the touch, opaque throughout, and flaky.
+ Drain off any excess liquid and serve the fish hot with a wedge of lemon. Serve the remaining sauce on the side.

Serves 4 to 6

MENU

Baked Bluefish Dijon
Baked potatoes
Coleslaw vinaigrette
Fruit cobbler (page 228) with ice cream

Baked Scrod with Dill Sauce

Similar to Bluefish Dijon, this is another high-temperature baked fish protected with a flavorful coating that also acts like a sauce. Mustard, lemon, and dill complement the scrod but you could also use cod, haddock, hake, halibut, or any fresh mild white fish.

2 pounds fresh scrod fillets, 1-inch thick

1/3 cup mayonnaise

1 tablespoon Dijon mustard

2 teaspoons lemon or lime juice

2 teaspoons prepared white horseradish, drained

2 tablespoons snipped fresh dill

+ Preheat the oven to 450°F. Line a baking dish with foil.

+ Run your finger along the center of the fish to check for any bones, and remove them by hand with tweezers, or needlenose pliers.

+ Place the fish on the foil, skin side down.

+ In a small bowl, combine the mayonnaise, mustard, and lemon juice. Brush about half this sauce over the surface of the fish to cover it lightly but completely to protect it from the high heat.

+ Bake the fish in the upper half of the oven for 10 to 12 minutes until it is firm to the touch, opaque throughout, and flaky.

+ Add the horseradish and dill to the remaining sauce and serve with the fish.

Serves 4 to 6

MENU

Baked Scrod with Dill Sauce
Cooked julienned carrots
Brown Rice (page 251)
Cheesecake (page 267) glazed with warmed apricot jam

Baked Scrod with Cream Sauce & Tropical Fruit

*F*ish and fruit complement each other in this quick baked dish. The fish is
cooked in cream and wine that is reduced to a subtly-seasoned sauce. Tropical
fruit garnishes the top along with a sprinkling of fresh mint. Peel and slice the fruit
while the fish is baking so the fish doesn't get cold while you assemble the dish. Use any
mild white fish that's fresh.

1 tablespoon butter
2 tablespoons minced
   shallots
2 tablespoons minced
   fresh peeled ginger root
1 1/2 pounds scrod or cod
   fillets, 1-inch thick
1/2 cup heavy or whipping
   cream
1/3 cup dry white wine
Salt and black pepper to
   taste
Pinch of cayenne pepper
Pinch of cinnamon
1 large ripe mango,
   peeled and cut into
   thin slices
2 ripe kiwis, peeled and
   cut into thin rounds
2 tablespoons chopped
   fresh mint

+ Preheat the oven to 450°F. Butter a shallow glass
  baking dish large enough to hold the fish. Butter
  a piece of parchment paper large enough to cover
  the fish.
+ Sprinkle the bottom of the dish with the shallots
  and ginger. Arrange the fish, skin side down, and
  pour the cream and wine over the fish. Season
  with salt and pepper. Cover with the prepared
  parchment paper, buttered side down, and bake
  in the middle of the oven for 10 to 12 minutes,
  until the fish is firm, opaque throughout and
  begins to flake. Remove the fish carefully with
  spatulas to a serving platter and cover with the
  parchment paper to keep warm.
+ Pour the cooking juices in a sauté pan and add
  the cayenne and cinnamon. Reduce by 1/2 over
  high heat, whisking until thickened. Add any
  accumulated juices from under the fish. Taste and
  season with salt and pepper. Strain the sauce over
  the fish.
+ Arrange the mango slices and kiwi rounds over
  the fish and sprinkle with the mint.

Serves 4

MENU

Baked Scrod with Cream Sauce & Tropical Fruit
Wild rice
Watercress, endive, and arugula salad vinaigrette
Dinner rolls
Cookies and iced tea

Grilled Tandoori Swordfish

There is nothing as luxurious in the summer months as fresh grilled swordfish steaks. Marinating them in Indian spices and yogurt only adds to their goodness. This tandoori marinade works wonders for grilled chicken, too.

For the marinade:

1/2 cup plain yogurt

2 tablespoons fresh lemon juice

1 small clove garlic, minced

1 tablespoon vegetable oil

1/2 teaspoon cumin

1/4 teaspoon coriander

1/4 teaspoon tumeric

1/4 teaspoon paprika

1/4 teaspoon salt

1/8 teaspoon crushed red pepper flakes

1 teaspoon minced fresh peeled ginger root

2 pounds fresh swordfish steaks, 1-inch thick

♦ In a shallow glass baking dish, combine the marinade ingredients. Stir thoroughly to combine.

♦ Add the swordfish to the dish in a single layer, turning to coat both sides. Cover with plastic wrap, refrigerate, and marinate for 30 minutes to 1 hour.

♦ Prepare the grill.

♦ Grill the fish, 4 to 6 inches over the hot coals, for about 8 minutes on each side, until opaque throughout and still moist.

Serves 4 to 6

MENU

Grilled Tandoori Swordfish
Chopped cucumbers and yogurt flavored with salt and mint
Orzo with sautéed pine nuts
Lemonade (page 271)

Grilled Lemon-Pepper Swordfish

The dense, meaty texture and mild flavor of swordfish makes it appealing even to those who claim not to like fish. Be sure to buy it when it's fresh. You can grill it outside or on a stove-top grill indoors when the weather doesn't cooperate. The lemon marinade is cooked down to a glaze for the cooked fish which is finished with minced tomatoes and fresh herbs of your choice. The lemon flavor works well with basil, tarragon, dill, mint, chives, or even parsley. Be generous with the pepper.

For the marinade:
1/4 cup fresh lemon juice from 1 large lemon
2 tablespoons olive oil
1/2 teaspoon salt
Pepper to taste
1 clove garlic, minced

1 1/2 pounds swordfish, 1-inch thick
2 plum tomatoes, finely diced
2 tablespoons chopped fresh herbs (basil, tarragon, mint, dill, parsley)
Lemon rounds for garnish

+ In a shallow glass or plastic dish, combine the lemon juice, oil, salt, pepper, and garlic. Add the swordfish, cover, and refrigerate for 30 minutes to 1 hour, turning once.
+ Prepare the grill.
+ Remove the swordfish and reserve the marinade.
+ Grill the fish, 4 to 6 inches over the coals, for about 8 minutes on each side until opaque and white throughout.
+ In a small saucepan, boil the reserved marinade until it is reduced by 1/2 to make a glaze. Brush it over the grilled fish and top with the tomatoes and fresh herbs. Garnish with lemon rounds. Serve immediately.

Serves 4

MENU

Grilled Lemon-Pepper Swordfish
Boiled new potatoes
Mixed green salad with arugula and radicchio
Breadsticks
Tropical fruit platter (mango slices, kiwis, pineapple)

Grilled Shrimp Adobo

In the heat of the summer, it's good to have a large repertoire of marinades for seafood, beef, chicken, fish, and pork. Let the marinade work its magic while you prepare the grill. To prevent shrimp from falling through the grill, thread them on metal skewers or bamboo sticks that you've soaked in water for 30 minutes.

1½ pounds extra-large shrimp, peeled and deveined

For the marinade:
Juice from 1 orange
Juice from 1 lime
¼ cup medium or hot prepared salsa
2 tablespoons olive oil
2 tablespoons tomato paste
1 large clove garlic, minced
½ teaspoon oregano
½ teaspoon cumin
½ teaspoon salt
Pepper to taste

♦ Pile the shrimp in a glass or plastic container.
♦ Combine the marinade ingredients in a processor bowl and process to a paste, or whisk together in a small bowl. Cover the shrimp with the marinade, turning to coat all sides. Cover and refrigerate for at least 30 minutes.
♦ Prepare the grill.
♦ Cook the shrimp, 4 inches over the hot coals, for about 5 minutes total, turning a few times until they are pink and opaque throughout. Don't overcook them.

Serves 4

MENU

Grilled Shrimp Adobo
Rice Pilaf (page 252)
Chopped tomatoes vinaigrette
Melon wedges
Brownies (page 233)

Pasta

hen I walk into the house with no advance preparation for dinner, and everyone is hungry, I turn to our favorite—pasta.

It comes in a multitude of shapes and colors, and is available dried, fresh, and frozen. It comes filled with meat, cheese, and spinach. Tossed with butter or oil, it's happy all by itself. Serve it as a side dish with a sauce or turn it into a main course with the addition of vegetables, seafood, chicken, or meats and a topping of cheese. Few foods are as adaptable and universally loved.

Pasta is made with flour or semolina (durham wheat), water, and sometimes eggs. Tomato and spinach may be used to flavor and color it. Pasta comes in long strands that may be thin (capellini or angel hair, vermicelli, thin spaghetti), thicker (spaghetti), or flat (linguini or fettuccine). Or it may be in stubbier shapes that work well with chunky sauces: elbows, ziti or penne, fuscelli or twists, shells, farfalle or bowties, ruffles. . . . Dried pasta keeps well on a pantry shelf, so keep a good supply on hand.

Orzo is a rice-shaped pasta, delicious hot, or as the basis of a cold summer salad. **Couscous** has been described as Moroccan pasta in a grain-like shape and made from semolina flour. It's a perfect quick-dinner starch because it's precooked and needs only 5 minutes in boiling liquid to cook.

Pineapple Kugel

Kugel is a noodle pudding that has so many variations—with eggs or without, with cheese and sour cream or without, and some with fruit and spices. Kugel is invariably baked, although you can add cottage cheese, sour cream, and a bit of sugar to buttered noodles and you have a cooktop kugel. Applesauce is a good alternative to pineapple, or add a few spoonfuls of marmalade. This is a well-loved and comforting dish that easily allows the cook to use his or her imagination. You can make the kugel in two smaller batches, cool, and freeze one for another dinner.

1 pound broad egg
  noodles
8 tablespoons butter
1 cup sour cream
1 pound cottage cheese
1 cup milk
1 8-ounce can crushed
  pineapple in natural
  juice
1/4 cup sugar, or to taste
2 teaspoons salt
1/4 teaspoon cinnamon
1/2 teaspoon powdered
  ginger
6 tablespoons unseasoned
  bread crumbs

+ Preheat the oven to 375°F. Butter a 9 x 13-inch baking dish or 2 shallow, 2-quart baking dishes.
+ Cook the noodles in a large pot of boiling salted water according to the package directions until tender. Drain well and return to the pot.
+ Stir in 6 tablespoons of the butter. Add the sour cream, cottage cheese, milk, pineapple with juice, sugar, salt, cinnamon, and ginger. Stir well to combine. Taste and adjust the flavoring.
+ Transfer to the prepared baking dish or dishes. Sprinkle the top evenly with bread crumbs. Dot with the remaining 2 tablespoons of butter.
+ Bake in the middle of the oven for about 1 hour until golden brown and bubbly. Cut into squares and serve warm.

Serves 8 to 10

MENU

Baked chicken (page 245)
Pineapple Kugel
Artichokes (page 241)
Chocolate Cake (page 265)

Orzo-Spinach Pilaf

Orzo is a rice shaped pasta that needs just a few ingredients to turn it into a delicious pilaf. You could also add artichoke hearts as well as the spinach, and chopped fresh dill for additional flavor.

8 ounces (1¼ cups) orzo
3 tablespoons butter
1 10-ounce package frozen, chopped spinach, defrosted and squeezed dry
2 scallions, thinly sliced
Grated zest of 1 lemon
¼ cup chicken broth, approximately
Salt and pepper to taste
¼ cup pine nuts

♦ Cook the orzo in a medium-size pot of boiling salted water according to the package directions until tender, about 9 minutes. Drain well and return to the pot.

♦ In a sauté pan, melt the butter and sauté the spinach and scallions for about 3 minutes, stirring. Add to the orzo with the lemon zest and chicken broth. Stir well and add salt and pepper to taste. Add more chicken broth if needed to moisten the pilaf.

♦ Add the pine nuts to a dry sauté pan and cook over medium heat until golden. Stir often to prevent them from burning. Stir into the pilaf.

Serves 6

MENU

Roast leg of lamb (Roasting Chart, page 247)
Orzo-Spinach Pilaf
Steamed asparagus
Strawberry shortcake (page 220)

Sunday Brunch Pasta

*O*ur favorite Sunday Brunch Pasta is fine for weekday dinners as well as for brunch since it's quick, easy, and delicious. The colors and flavors here are a great surprise.

3/4 pound thin spaghetti
    or vermicelli
3 tablespoons butter
3 ounces cream cheese,
    cut into small pieces
1/4 cup snipped chives or
    scallion greens
2 ounces smoked salmon,
    cut into 1/4-inch strips
1 tablespoon tiny, brined
    capers, drained
Salt and pepper to taste
1 hard-cooked egg
    (page 240), chopped

+ Cook the pasta in a large pot of boiling salted water according to the package directions until tender. Reserve 1/4 cup of the cooking water. Drain the pasta well and return to the pot.
+ Add the butter and stir to melt. Add the cream cheese, chives, salmon, capers, and the reserved cooking water to make a creamy consistency. Toss to mix well. Season with salt and pepper. Transfer to a serving platter and top with the chopped egg.

Serves 4 to 6

MENU

Sunday Brunch Pasta
Mixed green salad with fresh fruit
Crusty French rolls
Cupcakes

Sesame Noodles with Vegetables

*F*resh Oriental noodles have become the rage for cold salads as well as for stir-fried lo mein dishes. They can be served with a Thai peanut butter sauce or the popular sesame oil sauce. In this recipe, the noodles become the main ingredient in a colorful, one-dish dinner with vegetables. Cut-up and cook the vegetables ahead of time and assemble at the last minute. Serve the noodles at room temperature.

¼ cup sesame seeds
2 tablespoons peanut oil
2 tablespoons soy sauce
1 tablespoon Balsamic vinegar
1 tablespoon sugar
1 teaspoon salt
1 10-ounce package fresh Chinese noodles
2 scallions, cut into thin diagonal slices
Broccoli flowers from 1 bunch, steamed and rinsed in cold water
2 large carrots, peeled, cut into matchsticks, cooked, and chilled
1 red pepper, seeded and cut into julienne strips
1 6-ounce can sliced water chestnuts, drained

♦ Toast the sesame seeds in the oven or in a dry sauté pan until golden. Be careful and watch the seeds closely since they can burn easily. Set aside to cool.
♦ Combine the peanut oil, soy sauce, vinegar, sugar, and salt in a large bowl.
♦ Cook the noodles in boiling salted water for 2 minutes until tender. Drain, run under cold water to cool, and drain again.
♦ Add the noodles to the sauce, and toss, using your hands. Mix in the scallions, broccoli, carrots, pepper, and water chestnuts. Serve on a platter and top with the sesame seeds.

Serves 4 to 6

MENU

Grilled chicken breasts (page 246)
Sesame Noodles with Vegetables
Fresh pineapple and grapes
Ginger cookies

Pasta Primavera

*P*asta Primavera makes a healthy vegetarian dinner or a colorful addition to a fancy buffet dinner. Primavera usually indicates that a dish has lots of spring vegetables, but it used to have a heavy cream-laden sauce too. This one is light and refreshing and loaded with vegetables that are sautéed and simmered in chicken broth. Have all the vegetables cleaned and cut before you begin cooking since this goes very quickly once you start.

_{1/2} cup olive oil
1 onion, chopped
1 clove garlic, minced
³/₄ pound asparagus,
  tough ends broken off
  and cut into 1-inch
  diagonal slices
2 cups bite-size broccoli
  flowers, cauliflower, or
  green beans
1 carrot, peeled and cut
  into matchsticks
1 cup chicken broth
1 cup frozen petite peas
¹/₂ pound snow peas,
  strings removed
1 yellow or red pepper,
  seeded and cut into
  thin strips
2 tomatoes, peeled,
  seeded, and chopped
1 pound thin spaghetti
1 cup freshly grated
  Parmesan cheese
Salt and pepper to taste
2 tablespoons chopped
  fresh herbs

+ In a large, wide sauté pan over medium heat, add the oil and sauté the onion and garlic for about 2 minutes. Sauté, stirring, until the onion is soft, but not colored.
+ Add the asparagus, broccoli, and carrot and sauté over medium heat for 2 minutes. Add the chicken broth, cover, and cook for about 3 minutes. Stir in the peas, snow peas, and pepper, and cook for 1 more minute. Add the tomatoes and heat.
+ While the vegetables are cooking, cook the pasta in a large pot of boiling salted water according to the package directions until tender and drain.
+ Pour the vegetables over the cooked pasta. Add the cheese, and toss thoroughly.
+ Taste and adjust the seasoning with salt and pepper to taste. Add fresh herbs of your choice. Serve immediately.

Serves 8

MENU

Beef tenderloin (Roasting Chart, page 247)
Pasta Primavera
Green salad vinaigrette with radiccio and endive
Crusty rolls or French bread
Pecan tarts and brownies (page 233)
Chocolate-dipped strawberries (page 269)

Pasta & Vegetables Carbonara

This pasta dish is similar to the classic carbonara, but with sautéed vegetables as well as bacon or ham. Use any pasta you like— long and thin (broken in half) or short. The egg yolks and cream make a rich sauce to coat the pasta and vegetables. This is a wonderful indulgence.

2 tablespoons butter
1 small onion, chopped
1 green pepper, seeded
　and julienned
1 yellow, orange, or red
　pepper, seeded and
　julienned
1/2 cup frozen petite peas,
　defrosted under hot
　water
Salt, pepper, and dried
　oregano to taste
2 egg yolks
1 1/4 cups light cream,
　heated
1/2 cup freshly grated
　Parmesan cheese
1 pound pasta
1/2 cup crisp-cooked
　crumbled bacon or
　chopped smoked or
　boiled ham

◆ In a sauté pan, melt the butter over low heat and sauté the onion for 3 minutes, stirring often, until very soft but not colored. Add the peppers and sauté for a few more minutes until the peppers are soft. Stir in the peas and season with salt, pepper, and oregano.

◆ In a small bowl, whisk together the egg yolks and Parmesan cheese, then slowly mix in the heated cream.

◆ Cook the pasta in boiling salted water according to the package directions until tender. Reserve 1/2 cup of the cooking water. Drain the pasta and return to the pot.

◆ Immediately combine the pasta, vegetables, Parmesan cheese, reserved cooking water, and the cream mixture, tossing continuously. Everything must be hot so that the heat of the pasta and vegetables can cook the sauce until it is thickened and creamy. Toss until the pasta is coated. Season with salt and pepper. Transfer to a decorative platter. Top with the bacon or ham and serve hot.

Serves 6

MENU

Pasta & Vegetables Carbonara
Mixed green salad vinaigrette
Seasonal fresh fruit and chocolate bars

Valentine's Pasta

The color of this dish makes it just right for a Valentine's Day dinner. The roasted peppers can easily be cut into heart shapes with a paring knife or cookie cutter. Pimientos are a kind of red pepper, so use either one. They both come roasted, seeded, and peeled in a jar for convenience.

1 6–7½-ounce jar roasted red peppers or pimientos
2 tablespoons butter + additional for spaghetti
2 tablespoons olive oil
¼ cup minced shallots
3 tablespoons tomato paste
½ teaspoon salt
½ teaspoon paprika
½ teaspoon cumin
Pepper to taste
¾ cup chicken broth
1 pound thin spaghetti
6 cherry tomatoes, cut in half
Minced parsley for garnish

♦ Remove the peppers from the jar and reserve the juice. Cut 6 2-inch heart shapes from the peppers, if desired, and chop the rest.

♦ In a sauté pan, melt 2 tablespoons of butter with the olive oil and sauté the shallots over low heat, stirring often, until softened but not colored, about 4 minutes. Whisk in the tomato paste, spices, chicken broth, and any reserved juices from the peppers. Bring to a simmer, add the chopped peppers, and simmer for a few minutes to reduce the liquid a bit.

♦ Cook the spaghetti in a large pot of boiling salted water according to the package directions until tender. Drain and toss with a few tablespoons of butter if you like.

♦ Add the tomato halves to the sauce and heat. Top the spaghetti with the sauce and sprinkle with parsley. Season to taste with salt and pepper, and garnish with the pepper hearts.

Serves 6

MENU

Valentine's Pasta
Bibb, radiccio, and endive salad vinaigrette, with a few cooked shrimp
Heart-shaped Pita Crisps (page 262)
Decorated sugar cookie hearts (page 266) and fresh strawberries
Champagne

Moroccan Couscous & Vegetable Stew

This one-dish dinner is not only colorful, but it's fast and nutritious, too. The vegetables cook with the aromatic spices in the broth, the couscous is stirred in, and in 5 minutes, dinner is ready. When you remove the lid, you'll be delighted with the color and aroma—it's magic! When I have some leftover roast or rotisserie chicken, I add it with the chick peas for more substance.

4 tablespoons butter
1 small onion, chopped
1 small jalepeño pepper, seeded and finely chopped
1 pound butternut squash, seeded, peeled, and cut into 1-inch chunks
2 carrots, peeled and cut into ¼-inch slices
2 cups boiling water
1 cinnamon stick
½ teaspoon cumin
½ teaspoon paprika
¼ teaspoon tumeric
Pinch of saffron
Pinch of cayenne pepper
2 small zucchini, cut into ½-inch slices
1 cup cooked chick peas, drained
2 cups chicken broth
Salt and black pepper to taste
1½ cups couscous
¼ cup toasted whole almonds
¼ cup raisins
Chopped parsley for garnish

♦ In a large, deep sauté pan, melt the butter and sauté the onion over low heat, stirring, for 4 minutes. Add the jalepeño, squash, and carrots and sauté for 1 minute. Add the boiling water and spices and stir well. Cover and simmer for 15 minutes.

♦ Add the zucchini and continue to simmer for 5 minutes. Stir in the cooked and drained chick peas. Add the chicken broth and bring to a boil. Taste and season with salt and pepper.

♦ Stir in the couscous, cover, and remove from the heat. Let it sit for 5 minutes until the couscous has absorbed most of the liquid.

♦ With a large fork, transfer the couscous and vegetables to a pretty serving platter. Sprinkle the top with almonds, raisins, and parsley.

Serves 6

MENU

Moroccan Couscous & Vegetable Stew
French bread
Chocolate chip cookies (page 232)

Popeye's Lasagna

Popeye's Lasagna includes artichoke hearts as well as spinach to make a great alternative to the usual meaty lasagna. This is especially easy to make with the No-Boil, pre-cooked, and dried lasagna sheets. If you can't find them, traditional lasagna noodles can be used. Cook them according to the package directions before assembling the lasagna.

1 15-ounce can flavored or chunky-style tomato sauce of your choice

9 sheets No-Boil lasagna noodles, or traditional lasagna noodles, cooked according to the package directions

1 pound ricotta cheese

1 egg

1 10-ounce package frozen chopped spinach, thawed, and squeezed dry

1/4 cup freshly grated Parmesan cheese

1/2 teaspoon salt

1 6 1/2-ounce jar marinated artichoke hearts, drained well with any tough outer leaves removed

12 ounces grated mozzarella cheese (about 3 cups)

♦ Preheat the oven to 350°F.

♦ Spread 1/2 the tomato sauce in the bottom of a 9 x 13-inch baking dish. Lay 3 lasagna sheets side by side, leaving an inch around the edges to allow for expansion.

♦ Combine the ricotta cheese, egg, spinach, Parmesan, and salt in a large bowl and mix thoroughly. Spread 1/2 the ricotta mixture over the noodles. Press the drained artichoke hearts evenly over the cheese. Top with 1/3 of the grated mozzarella cheese. Lay 3 more lasagna noodles on top, add the remaining ricotta cheese, and cover with another 1/3 of the grated mozzarella. Top with the remaining 3 lasagna noodles and cover with the remaining tomato sauce. Top with the rest of the mozzarella.

♦ Cover loosely with a foil tent and bake for 35 to 40 minutes. Uncover for the last 5 or 10 minutes to let the cheese color slightly. Let stand for 5 minutes before cutting and serving.

Serves 6 to 9

MENU

Popeye's Lasagna
Mixed greens and cherry tomato salad vinaigrette
Crusty Italian bread
Fresh fruit skewers
Vanilla Cake (page 265)

Roasted Vegetable Lasagna

Roasting gives vegetables a rich, sweet flavor that works so well in a vegetable-cheese lasagna. This recipe was developed for a fund-raising dinner for 60. Preparing four pans of lasagna was done easily the day before the event. The vegetables can be roasted ahead of time and refrigerated. Flavored, canned, crushed tomatoes make up the sauce, and No-Boil lasagna sheets are the noodles. If you can't find them, traditional lasagna noodles work well, too.

To prepare the vegetables:

2 large sweet onions, cut into eighths

1 butternut squash, peeled, seeded, and cut into bite-size chunks

2 red peppers, seeded and cut into large chunks

2 green peppers, seeded and cut into large chunks

4 large carrots, peeled and cut into $1/2$-inch slices

2 small zucchini, cut into $1/2$-inch slices

1 medium eggplant, cut into $1/2$-inch squares

$1/2$ cup olive oil

Salt and pepper to taste

♦ Preheat the oven to 425°F.

♦ Cut up the vegetables and divide them between 2 large roasting pans or heavy jellyroll pans. Don't crowd or mound the vegetables in the pan. You want them to roast, not steam. Drizzle the vegetables with the olive oil. Toss to coat well. Sprinkle generously with salt and pepper.

♦ Place in the hot oven and roast for 45 minutes to 1 hour, tossing the vegetables and reversing the pans half way through. The vegetables should be tender and somewhat caramelized. If the vegetables are browning too quickly, turn the oven down to 400°F. Taste, adjust the seasoning and cool before assembling in the lasagna. These can be made ahead, cooled, and refrigerated.

For the lasagna:

1 28-ounce can chunky-
  style crushed tomatoes
2 tablespoons olive oil
Salt, pepper, and oregano
  to taste
1 box (18–24) lasagna
  noodles or No-Boil
  lasagna sheets
1 pound ricotta cheese
$1/2$ cup heavy cream
1 egg
$1/2$ cup freshly grated
  Parmesan cheese
$11/2$ pounds mozzarella
  cheese, grated
18 paper-thin slices pro-
  sciutto ham, optional

- Preheat the oven to 375°F.
- Season the crushed tomatoes with the olive oil, salt, pepper, and oregano.
- Prepare 2 9 x 13-inch lasagna pans by spreading $3/4$ cup of the seasoned tomato sauce in the bottom of each—spread to the edges. Arrange 3 lasagna noodles over the tomato sauce in each pan.
- In a large bowl, combine the ricotta, cream, egg, Parmesan, and salt and pepper to taste. Stir well to combine.
- Spread $1/2$ the cheese mixture over the noodles in each pan. Spread $1/4$ of the mozzarella over the ricotta. Arrange the prosciutto over the mozzarella. Top with another layer of lasagna noodles. Use $1/2$ the cooled roasted vegetables for each lasagna in the next layer. Season with salt and pepper. Top with the remaining noodles. Spread 1 cup of tomato sauce over the top of each lasagna and sprinkle with the remaining mozzarella.
- Cover very loosely with foil and bake for 25 minutes. Remove the foil, reverse the pans in the oven, and continue to bake for 15 minutes more until very hot and bubbly.
- Allow the lasagna to sit for 10 minutes before cutting and serving.
- To freeze, allow the lasagna to cool completely before wrapping well and freezing.

Yields 2 lasagna to serve 20 to 24

MENU

Roasted Vegetable Lasagna
Crusty French rolls
Mixed green salad vinaigrette
Brownies (page 233) and strawberries

Antipasto Pasta

This quick and easy pasta dish was developed for my college-cooking son. Dinner is on the table in the time it takes to cook the pasta. Use any pasta you like, long or stubby.

1 pound pasta
1/3 cup olive oil
2 tablespoons red wine
  vinegar
2 large ripe tomatoes,
  peeled, seeded and
  chopped
1 6½-ounce jar mari-
  nated artichoke hearts,
  drained and cut
  in half
1 cup small pitted black
  olives
1 6- or 7½-ounce jar
  roasted peppers or
  pimientos, drained
  and cut into strips
½ cup freshly grated
  Parmesan cheese
¼ cup chopped fresh
  parsley
Salt and lots of pepper
  to taste

♦ Cook the pasta in a large pot of boiling salted water according to the package directions until tender.
♦ Drain and toss with the remaining ingredients. Serve warm or at room temperature. Pass additional Parmesan cheese.

Serves 4 to 6

MENU

Antipasto Pasta
Garlic Bread (page 261)
Ice cream sandwiches

Clam-ato Pasta

A wonderful combination for winter or summer—with canned or fresh minced clams.

3 tablespoons olive oil
3 tablespoons minced shallots
2 large cloves garlic, minced
1 10½-ounce can minced clams in juice
3 tablespoons tomato paste
½ teaspoon oregano
1 6-ounce jar roasted pimientos, sliced
12 fresh littleneck clams (steamers)
1 pound thin spaghetti or vermicelli
Parsley for garnish
Pepper to taste

♦ Heat the olive oil in a large sauté pan. Sauté the shallots and garlic over low heat, stirring, until softened but not colored, about 4 minutes. Add the minced clams and juice, tomato paste, and oregano. Whisk until smooth and simmer for about 5 minutes.
♦ Add the pimientos and whole clams, cover, and steam for just a few minutes until the clams open. Remove the whole clams and reserve.
♦ While the sauce is cooking, cook the pasta in a large pot of boiling salted water according to the package directions until tender. Drain the pasta and transfer to a pretty serving platter.
♦ Pour the sauce over the pasta, toss, and garnish with the reserved clams. Sprinkle with parsley and top with lots of pepper.

Serves 4

MENU

Clam-ato Pasta
Mixed green salad vinaigrette
Pudding pie (page 263)

Fettuccine & Shrimp with Spinach Pesto

Pesto now comes in many contemporary flavors, but it was originally based on garlic, olive oil, Parmesan cheese, pine nuts, and basil. Just a little of this intensely flavored treasure will go a long way on pasta, grilled fish, or baked potatoes. Pesto is also wonderful brushed on pizza with fresh tomatoes and cheese. The green color stays beautiful and vivid, and it even keeps well in the refrigerator or freezer. In the summer, brush basil or mint pesto on garden tomatoes and grilled chicken. Combine pesto with mayonnaise to make a sauce for cold shrimp or lobster. Buy small quantities of pine nuts—they're expensive—and taste them to be sure they're fresh and tasty. Store them in the freezer so they don't become rancid.

2–3 cloves garlic
1 10-ounce package frozen chopped spinach, defrosted and squeezed dry
1 cup chopped parsley
1/2 cup fresh pine nuts
1 cup freshly grated Parmesan cheese + additional for garnish
1 teaspoon salt
1 cup olive oil

1 pound fettuccine or thin spaghetti
1 pound large shrimp, cooked, shelled, and deveined
Pepper to taste

+ In a food processor with the motor running, drop the garlic through the feed tube to chop, stopping to scrape the sides a few times. Add the spinach, parsley, pine nuts, Parmesan, and salt, and continue to process briefly. Slowly add the olive oil through the feed tube with the motor running and process until nearly smooth and paste-like.

+ Cook the pasta in a large pot of boiling salted water according to the package directions until tender. Reserve 1/4 cup of the cooking water. Drain the pasta well and place in a large bowl with the cooked shrimp, 3/4 cup of pesto, and the reserved cooking water. Toss well to mix. Serve on a decorative serving platter. Pass additional Parmesan and a pepper grinder.

+ Store the extra pesto in a jar in the refrigerator or freeze in 1-cup plastic containers.

Serves 6
yields 2 1/4 cups pesto

MENU

Fettuccine & Shrimp with Spinach Pesto
Italian bread
Boston lettuce and sliced mushrooms salad vinaigrette
Seasonal fresh fruit

Ramen Stir-Fry with Chicken & Vegetables

I've always admired the convenience of the Ramen noodles, and wondered how to turn those packets of dry noodles with seasoning into fast, nutritious meals. It's easy if you stir-fry lots of vegetables, chicken, and add just a little of the salty seasoning in the packet. Cut up the chicken and vegetables before cooking since this dish takes just five minutes to cook. If you're really short on time, a good super-market salad bar has cleaned and cut-up broccoli and peppers, plus bean sprouts or other vegetables you might like. Add the vegetables according to their cooking time.

3 tablespoons peanut or vegetable oil

1 onion, coarsely chopped

2 boned and skinned chicken breast halves, each cut into 5 pieces

$1/4$ pound cultivated mushrooms, sliced

1 small zucchini, diagonally sliced

1 red pepper, cut into chunks or julienned

$1^1/2$ cups hot water

2 3-ounce packets of Ramen noodles

1 chicken seasoning packet from Ramen noodles, or to taste

$1/4$ pound fresh snow peas, strings removed

♦ Heat the oil in a wok or large sauté pan over medium heat. Add the onion, chicken, mushrooms, zucchini, and pepper, and stir-fry for about 5 minutes, until the chicken is opaque throughout and the vegetables are still a bit crisp. Transfer to a bowl and reserve.

♦ Add the water to the wok or pan. Break the noodles into 4 pieces and add to the water with the contents of 1 seasoning packet. Cook over low heat for a few minutes, stirring as the noodles soften and absorb the water.

♦ Return the chicken and vegetables to the noodles and add the snow peas, Stir and cook a minute to heat thoroughly. Serve immediately.

Serves 4

MENU

Ramen Stir-Fry with Chicken & Vegetables
Fresh or canned pineapple chunks, chilled
Fortune, almond, or pecan cookies

Fettuccine with Dilled Shrimp

Summer or winter, it's hard to get enough pasta, so here is a recipe that can be served all year-round. The sauce is velvety-smooth and delicious but be sure to use heavy cream. Substituting light cream, half-and-half, or yogurt will cause the sauce to curdle. Eat in moderation and consider this a well-deserved treat.

3/4 pound fettuccine or thin spaghetti
2 tablespoons butter

For the sauce:
1 8-ounce bottle clam broth
1/4 cup dry white wine or juice of 1 lemon
1/2 cup heavy or whipping cream
2 tablespoons fresh snipped dill + additional for garnish
1 pound large shrimp, shelled and deveined
Salt and pepper to taste
12 oil-cured black olives
1/2 cup crumbled Feta cheese

♦ Cook the fettuccine in a large pot of boiling salted water according to the package directions until tender. Drain the pasta well, toss with the butter, and transfer to a decorative serving platter.

♦ While the fettuccine is cooking, prepare the sauce. In a wide sauté pan, combine the clam broth and wine. Bring to a boil and simmer for a few minutes. Whisk in the cream and increase the heat to high. Reduce the liquid by 1/2. Stir in the dill. Add the shrimp to the sauce and simmer for 2 minutes, turning a few times, to cook the shrimp. They should be firm, pink, and curve into a crescent shape. Taste the sauce and season with salt and pepper.

♦ Spoon the sauce over the cooked fettuccine and garnish with olives, Feta cheese, and additional dill sprigs.

Serves 4

MENU

Fettuccine with Dilled Shrimp
Crusty Italian bread
Greens and watercress salad vinaigrette
Poached fruit salad (page 268) with custard sauce (page 264)

Fuscelli with Clams, Shrimp & Broccoli

Shellfish, broccoli, and garlic are naturals together and make a great topping for fuscelli (twists) or any pasta you like. Usually a sauce this chunky is best on a stubbier pasta.

1 bunch broccoli,
   cleaned, peeled, and
   cut into bite-size pieces
1 pound fuscelli or twist
   pasta
1/3 cup olive oil
3 cloves garlic, minced
2 6½-ounce cans minced
   clams in juice
1/4 pound shrimp, peeled
   and deveined
1/2 cup freshly grated
   Parmesan cheese
Salt and pepper to taste

- Cook the broccoli in boiling salted water until crisp-tender, rinse in ice water, and drain to retain the bright green color. Set aside.
- Cook the pasta in a large pot of boiling salted water according to the package directions until tender and drain. Toss with 2 tablespoons of the oil.
- In a large sauté pan, heat the remaining oil and add the garlic, cooking gently over low heat for about 3 minutes, stirring to prevent the garlic from coloring. Add the clams with their juice and the shrimp and heat to bubbling and the shrimp are pink. Toss with the pasta and broccoli and simmer for a few minutes until everything is hot. Season to taste with salt and pepper.
- Serve on a warmed platter and sprinkle with Parmesan cheese and pepper.

Serves 6 to 8

MENU

Fuscelli with Clams, Shrimp & Broccoli
Mixed green salad vinaigrette
Italian bread
Italian ices and almond macaroon cookies

Ziti with Sausage, Mushrooms & Tomatoes

Here's a hearty flavor-filled dinner for a chilly night. Serve the ziti with a sprinkle of Parmesan and crusty rolls. Sausage, mushrooms, and tomatoes make a great combination on pasta as well as on pizza.

3 tablespoons olive oil
1/2 pound kielbasa sausage cut into 1/2-inch cubes
1 large onion, coarsely chopped
2 cloves garlic, minced
1/2 teaspoon fennel seeds
1/2 pound white mushrooms, thinly sliced
4 tomatoes, peeled, seeded, and chopped (or 1 1-pound can whole peeled tomatoes, drained and chopped)
1/4 cup minced parsley
Salt and pepper to taste
1/2 pound ziti
1/2 cup chicken broth
1/3 cup heavy or whipping cream
Parmesan cheese for the top

♦ Heat the oil in a large sauté pan, and sauté the sausage until slightly browned. Remove and set aside.

♦ In the same pan, sauté the onion, garlic, and fennel seeds for about 5 minutes until the onion is soft but not colored. Add the mushrooms, increase the heat, and sauté until the mushrooms exude their juices and the liquid cooks off. Stir often. Add the tomatoes and half the parsley and simmer until thickened, about 10 minutes. Season with pepper.

♦ Cook the ziti in boiling salted water according to the package directions until tender. Drain the ziti well and add to the sauce. Stir in the chicken broth, cream, and remaining parsley, and heat thoroughly. Taste and adjust the seasoning with salt and pepper. Serve hot with a topping of Parmesan cheese.

Serves 6

MENU

Ziti with Sausage, Mushrooms & Tomatoes
Italian bread
Lettuce wedges with Russian Dressing (page 259)
Warm applesauce (page 269) with cinnamon red-hot candies

Peppery Shrimp & Corn Pasta

This one-dish dinner has everything going for it—quick-cooking shrimp and pasta, beautiful color, and a bit of spice and intrigue. Use 3/4 pound of pasta if you like lots of sauce and 1 pound if you prefer pasta with less sauce.

3/4–1 pound thin spaghetti
2 tablespoons butter
1/4 cup minced shallots
1 jalepeño pepper, seeded and finely chopped
1 red pepper, seeded and finely chopped
2 teaspoons flour
1/2 teaspoon ground cumin
1 8-ounce bottle clam broth
1/2 cup heavy or whipping cream
3/4 pound shrimp, shelled and deveined
1 cup corn kernels, cut from 2 ears of corn
3 tablespoons chopped cilantro
Salt and pepper to taste

♦ Cook the pasta in a large pot of boiling salted water according to the package directions until tender.
♦ While the pasta is cooking, prepare the sauce. In a large sauté pan, melt the butter over low heat and add the shallots. Sauté for a few minutes until soft. Add the peppers and sauté, stirring until soft. Stir in the flour and cumin and sauté for another minute. Whisk in the clam broth and cream and heat, stirring, until thickened.
♦ Add the shrimp and simmer until pink and nearly done, turning them to cook evenly. They will cook in just a few minutes. Add the corn and cilantro and heat through. Taste and adjust the seasoning with salt and pepper.
♦ Drain the pasta and arrange on a pretty serving platter. Spoon the sauce and shrimp over the pasta and serve hot.

Serves 4 to 6

Grains, Potatoes
& Beans

rains include many dinnertime favorites that add diversity as well as nutrition to cooking. Some of these are:

Rice comes in many varieties: **long-grain brown**, and **white** (all-purpose for most pilafs, side dishes, salads, and casseroles), **sweet and sticky** (for sushi), short-grain Italian **Arborio** (for risotto), nutty-flavored-and-colored **Basmati** (for Indian dishes), and **wild** rice that comes from native grasses.

Wheat is quick-cooking if the grain is cracked, or cut into coarse, medium, or fine bulgur. Fine-cut is best for cold tabouleh (page 38), coarse-cut is better for wheat pilafs (page 252), and medium-cut works for both. If you only buy one, make it medium-cut.

Rolled oats (quick or old-fashioned) are used mostly for cereal and baking, although I sometimes throw a handful into a pot of bubbling soup to thicken it.

Cornmeal (yellow) and **hominy** (white) are the basis of the popular polenta (page 253) and grits. Both are like a mush that takes on new dimensions with the addition of butter, cheese, and some flavoring in the cooking liquid. Polenta and grits are bland in flavor, and comforting in their texture, so they make a nice base for strong-flavored foods. Polenta can be turned into a jellyroll pan to cool and solidify before it is cut into shapes and baked or fried, or used as the starch layer in lasagna or Mexican meat pies.

Barley is an old-time favorite that works well in soups and casseroles. **Pearl** barley takes nearly 45 minutes to cook, but **pressed** barley takes less than half that time. It looks a little like rolled oats and it cooks like bulgur in just 15 minutes. You can cook it like rice or with rice, or in a pilaf (page 146).

Potatoes

We love potatoes in any form—mashed, boiled, roasted, fried—in salads (pages 44–45), in pies (page 149), in soups, as a side dish with fancy foods, or with simple hamburgers. Without lots of butter or sour cream, and with the nutrient-rich skin, potatoes are a nutritious complex carbohydrate, high in fiber and vitamin C too. There are more and more varieties to choose from. Mature, starchier **russets** or **Idahos** have a dry texture that work best for baking and frying. I usually use these for mashed potatoes since they readily absorb butter and cream (or milk) when they're hot.

The **red** or **white** all-purpose potatoes have a moist, waxier texture. These work well for potato salads when you want the slices and cubes to hold together. The new potatoes—**red** or **bliss**—are the first of the potato harvest, available from early spring through summer. These young potatoes are sweet, low in starch, and moist. Buy them small, and enjoy them boiled, steamed, or grilled.

Yukon gold potatoes are an increasingly popular variety because of the rich, creamy, moist flesh that's so tasty in mashed potatoes and in potato salad and needs very little butter. I've even discovered **purple** potatoes—inside as well as out—that make lavender-colored mashed potatoes!

Sweet potatoes and **yams** needn't only be turned into sweetened casseroles for Thanksgiving and other turkey dinners. Baked sweet potatoes are a real treat with just a little butter and salt, and they're rich in beta carotene (vitamin A), potassium, and fiber.

Buy potatoes without cracks, dark spots, eyes, or discolored skin. Potatoes should be stored in a dry, dark place, in a paper bag, or in a well-ventilated net bag to keep any moisture from causing growth or mold. Once potatoes have grown eyes and the skin begins to turn green, they're past their prime. As tempting as it is to buy a large bag of potatoes on sale, it's best to buy only what you realistically will eat, or you'll end up throwing the savings away. Sweet potatoes are much more perishable than the others, so buy them as you need them.

When you're cooking with potatoes, be sure to keep peeled and cut potatoes in a bowl of cold water to cover. Otherwise, the air will oxidize the potatoes and turn them brown. This happens to cut apples, pears, and avocados too, and is the reason that they need a bit of lemon juice on the cut surface to prevent browning.

Beans

Beans are becoming a more important and nutritionally recognized part of a healthy diet. Beans and rice together are a complete source of low-fat plant protein. Combined with cheese, meat, or poultry, beans also make a complete source of protein, and are high in fiber as well.

Beans are available in cans in so many varieties, but dried beans can easily be cooked, and stored in 2-cup plastic containers to be used as you need them (page 255). **Black** beans, or **turtle** beans, are the rage in soups, fruit salsas, and salads; **kidney** and **pinto** beans work well with rice in Mexican dishes; **chick peas,** also known as **garbanzo** beans or **ceci,** are essential to Middle Eastern cooking; and small **white** and **cannellini** beans are favorites in Italian soups and casseroles.

Spiced Indian Rice

Indian spices and interesting add-ins can make ordinary rice extra-ordinary. Try this dish with roast chicken, lamb chops, or even fish. A heat diffuser works well when simmering the rice to keep it from sticking to the bottom of the pot.

1/3 cup vegetable oil
1/2 medium onion, finely chopped
5 whole cloves
1 cinnamon stick
5 cardamom pods, pinched to expose the seeds
1/2 teaspoon coriander
1 cup Basmati or long-grain white rice
2 cups boiling water
1/2 teaspoon salt
1 tablespoon butter
1/4 cup currants
1/4 cup sliced almonds or cashew halves

♦ In a heavy saucepan, heat the oil and sauté the onion over low heat until softened but not colored. Add the cloves, cinnamon stick, cardamom pods, and coriander and sauté for another minute. Add the rice and sauté, stirring, until the rice is hot. Add the boiling water and salt, stir well, and bring to a boil. Cover and simmer for 15 to 17 minutes until the rice is tender and the liquid is absorbed. Remove the cinnamon stick and the cardamom pods that have floated to the top.

♦ In a sauté pan, melt the butter and sauté the currants and nuts for a few minutes. Fluff the rice with a fork and mix in the currants and nuts. Serve hot.

Serves 4 to 6

MENU

Broiled lamb chops (page 247)
Spiced Indian Rice
Spinach salad vinaigrette
Baked Apples (page 269) and cream

Confetti Rice Pilaf

Pilaf—rice or wheat—should be part of any basic cooking repertoire. The technique is simple and the creative possibilities are endless. Here, diced, colorful vegetables are sautéed with the onion to give the rice pilaf a sprinkle of color and added flavor.

5 tablespoons butter
1/4 cup finely chopped onion
1 large carrot, finely chopped
1 red pepper, seeded and finely chopped
1/2 cup thin spaghetti, broken into 1/2-inch pieces
1 1/2 cups rice
3 cups boiling chicken broth
1/4 cup minced parsley
Salt and pepper to taste

♦ Melt the butter in a heavy saucepan. Add the onion and carrot and sauté for 5 minutes over low heat, stirring to prevent the onion from coloring. Add the pepper and spaghetti and continue to sauté for 5 minutes, stirring. Stir in the rice and sauté until hot and coated with butter. Pour the boiling broth over the rice and stir well. Cover and simmer for 15 to 17 minutes until the liquid has been absorbed and the rice is tender.
♦ Fluff with a fork and stir in the parsley. Taste and season with salt and pepper.

Serves 4 to 6

MENU

Fish fillets, baked, broiled, or sautéed (page 248)
Confetti Rice Pilaf
French bread and cheese (brie, creamy blue, camembert)
Dried and fresh fruit

Mexican Rice with Peppers & Corn

Mexican Rice is a colorful, spicy side dish, or it could be a vegetarian entree with the addition of grated Longhorn or Colby cheddar cheese sprinkled on top. A heat diffuser will prevent the rice from sticking to the bottom of the pot. Put it under the pan while simmering the rice.

4 tablespoons butter
1 small onion, finely chopped
1 red or green pepper, seeded and chopped
³/4 cup corn kernels, cut from 1 or 2 ears of corn
1 teaspoon chili powder
1¹/2 cups rice
3 cups boiling water
1 teaspoon salt
¹/2 cup prepared tomato salsa, hot or mild
3 tablespoons finely chopped cilantro
Pepper to taste
6 ounces Colby or Longhorn cheddar cheese, grated, to make about 1¹/2 cups, optional

♦ In a heavy saucepan, melt the butter and sauté the onion until soft but not browned. Add the pepper and sauté for 5 minutes until soft. Stir in the corn and chili powder. Add the rice and stir to coat with butter.

♦ When the rice is hot, add the boiling water and salt, stir, and bring to a boil over medium heat. Stir and reduce the heat to low. Simmer for 15 to 17 minutes until the rice is tender and the liquid is absorbed.

♦ Remove the cover and let the rice cook for a few more minutes to dry it out a bit. Stir in the salsa and cilantro with a fork. Adjust the seasoning and add pepper to taste. Serve hot topped with a sprinkle of grated cheese.

Serves 6

MENU

Roasted or rotisserie chicken (page 245)
Mexican Rice with Peppers & Corn
Cornbread (page 260) served with butter and jalepeño jelly
Ice cream cones

Fried Rice with Chicken

Fried Rice is a one-dish dinner that combines colorful vegetables, stir-fried bits of chicken, and rice. It takes just 15 minutes if you make the rice ahead of time. A little more of this or that will stretch fried rice to please a larger group. You can add firm tofu cut into cubes, slivered snow peas, or hot sauce to make it Szechuan. Peanuts or toasted sesame seeds add crunch and protein.

1/4 cup vegetable oil
2 boned and skinned chicken breast halves, cut into thin strips
1 medium onion, coarsely chopped
3 celery stalks, cleaned and thinly sliced
1 clove garlic, minced
1 tablespoon finely minced fresh ginger root
1/2 red pepper, seeded and diced
2 eggs, slightly beaten
4 cups **cooked** rice
1/4–1/2 cup chicken broth
2 tablespoons soy sauce
1/2 teaspoon sugar
1 8-ounce can sliced water chestnuts, drained
1/2 cup frozen petite peas, defrosted in hot water and drained
3–4 scallions, thinly sliced diagonally
Salt and pepper to taste

♦ In a large skillet, heat the oil and sauté the chicken over medium-low heat until opaque and nearly cooked through, about 3 to 4 minutes. Remove from the skillet with a slotted spoon and set aside.

♦ Add the onion to the skillet and sauté for about 4 minutes, stirring to prevent it from coloring. Add the celery, garlic, and ginger and sauté for a few more minutes, stirring often. Add the pepper and sauté for a few more minutes. Add the egg, stirring quickly until softly cooked and in small pieces. Add the rice, breaking up the clumps.

♦ In a small bowl, stir together 1/4 cup of the broth, soy sauce, and sugar and add to the rice. Return the chicken to the skillet and stir together thoroughly with the water chestnuts, peas, and scallions. Heat through and adjust the seasoning with salt and pepper. Add the remaining broth if the rice is too dry. Serve immediately.

Serves 4 to 6

MENU

Fried Rice with Chicken
Strawberries with powdered sugar
Tea and nut cookies

Wild Rice & Almond Rice Pilaf

An easily roasted turkey breast needs only a good rice dish and a vegetable to make a festive weekday menu. Cultivated white mushrooms can be enhanced by adding a few shitake or portobella mushrooms that have more interesting flavors.

1/2 cup wild rice
8 tablespoons butter
2 tablespoons minced onion
1/4 pound mushrooms, chopped
1 cup long-grain white rice
2 cups boiling chicken broth
1/2 cup slivered almonds
1/4 cup minced parsley
Salt and pepper to taste

- Cook the wild rice in boiling water for about 25 minutes, or according to the package directions, until tender. Drain and reserve.

- Melt 4 tablespoons of butter in a heavy saucepan and sauté the onion and mushrooms over low heat, stirring, until the onion is soft but not colored and the mushroom juices are mostly evaporated. Add the white rice and sauté for a few minutes until hot and coated with butter. Add the boiling broth, stir, and cover. Simmer for about 15 minutes or until the liquid has been absorbed. Uncover and let the rice cook for a few more minutes to dry.

- In a sauté pan, melt the remaining butter and sauté the almonds for a few minutes until lightly colored. Add the reserved wild rice, stir, and sauté for another minute until heated through.

- Add the wild rice to the white rice with the parsley and toss with a fork to mix well. Taste and adjust the seasoning with salt and pepper.

Serves 4 to 6

MENU

Roasted turkey breast
Wild Rice & Almond Rice Pilaf
Green beans
Coffee ice cream with Chocolate Sauce (page 264)

Quick Barley-Mushroom Pilaf

*I've always loved the taste and texture of barley in soups and with mushrooms in casseroles, but pearl barley takes much too long to cook. Rice, bulgur wheat, couscous, and pasta took its place. Then I discovered **pressed** barley. The flavor is even better than I remember. Look for it in Korean or Asian groceries.*

3 tablespoons butter
¹/₂ small onion, finely chopped
¹/₄ pound white mushrooms, cut in half and thinly sliced, about 2 cups
1 cup pressed barley
¹/₂ cup rice
3 cups boiling chicken broth or salted water
Salt and pepper to taste

♦ In a heavy sauce pan, melt the butter and sauté the onion, stirring often, until softened. Add the mushrooms, increase the heat to medium, and sauté for about 3 minutes until the mushroom juices have evaporated. Add the barley and rice and sauté for a few minutes, stirring, until very hot. Add the boiling broth or water all at once, stir, and cover. Simmer for 15 to 18 minutes until the liquid is absorbed and the barley and rice are tender. Remove the cover and cook for another minute to dry out the pilaf.
♦ Fluff with a fork, season to taste with salt and pepper, and serve hot.

Serves 6

MENU

Roast beef (Roasting Chart, page 247)
Quick Barley-Mushroom Pilaf
Sautéed greens (chard, spinach, broccoli, etc.)
Chocolate-dipped dried or glacéed apricots (page 269)

Potato & Winter Vegetable Casserole

Sweet winter vegetables combine wonderfully with potatoes in this comforting casserole that goes so well with a beef, lamb, or pork roast. Turnips and parsnips seem old-fashioned, but are becoming new favorites in the cycle of culinary favorites. It's easy to prepare this dish ahead of time, then bake it at dinnertime, cooking it for a few extra minutes if it's been refrigerated.

4 tablespoons butter
1 medium-size onion,
  thinly sliced
2 large baking potatoes,
  peeled and thinly sliced
2 purple-topped turnips,
  peeled and thinly sliced
2 parsnips, peeled and
  thinly sliced
2 carrots, peeled and
  thinly sliced
³/₄ pound butternut
  squash, peeled, seeded,
  and thinly sliced
Salt and pepper to taste
2 cups chicken broth
¹/₂ cup shredded
  Parmesan cheese
Grating of nutmeg

♦ Preheat the oven to 350°F. Butter a lasagna pan or large, shallow baking dish with 1 tablespoon of the butter.

♦ In a large sauté pan, melt the remaining butter over low heat and sauté the onion until soft but not colored. Add the potatoes, turnips, parsnips, carrots, and squash, and toss gently to mix. Season with salt and pepper. When hot, add the chicken broth, bring to a simmer, and cook for about 5 minutes until the vegetables are partially cooked.

♦ Arrange the vegetables in overlapping layers in the prepared baking dish. Sprinkle the top with Parmesan cheese, a grating of nutmeg and pepper. Bake for about 30 minutes until the vegetables are tender and the top is crusted and lightly colored.

Serves 4 to 6

MENU

Roast leg of lamb (Roasting Chart, page 247)
Potato & Winter Vegetable Casserole
Mixed green salad vinaigrette
Applesauce (page 268)

Indian Potatoes & Peas

Potatoes have universal appeal, whether plain or jazzed up with some interesting spices. Indian Potatoes & Peas reminds me of the scrumptious filling in Samosas—the wonderful Indian appetizers that are stuffed and deep-fried.

2 pounds all-purpose potatoes, about 4 large
3 tablespoons vegetable oil or butter
1 large onion, chopped
1/2 teaspoon cumin seeds
1/2 teaspoon black mustard seeds
11/2 teaspoons curry powder
1/2 teaspoon ground cumin
1/8 teaspoon cayenne pepper
2 cups chicken broth
1/2 cup frozen petite peas
Salt and black pepper to taste

♦ Peel the potatoes and cut them into 1/2-inch dice. Keep them in a bowl of water to cover until ready to cook to prevent oxidation.

♦ In a large sauté pan, heat the oil or butter and add the onion. Sauté, stirring, for about 5 minutes until the onion is soft but not colored. Add the cumin seeds and mustard seeds, and sauté for a minute to bring out the flavor. Stir in the curry powder, ground cumin, and cayenne.

♦ Drain the cubed potatoes and add to the pan with the chicken broth. Cook uncovered over medium heat for about 10 minutes, or until the potatoes are soft. The liquid will evaporate as the potatoes cook. Add a little water at the end if the potatoes aren't done yet, or partially cover if the broth evaporates too quickly. Stir often towards the end to prevent the potatoes from sticking to the bottom of the pan.

♦ Stir in the peas and adjust the seasoning with salt and pepper.

Serves 6

MENU

Grilled salmon (page 248)
Indian Potatoes & Peas
Sautéed spinach
Pineapple and pomegranate seeds (in season)

Potato Pie Gratin

Potato Pie Gratin is a delightful way to satisfy a craving for potatoes. It's layered and filled with potatoes, sautéed onions, cheese, and custard. It makes a fine vegetarian main course, or a perfect accompaniment to any roast. You may use leftover baked or boiled potatoes and you can even leave the skin on for added nutrition.

Dough for a double crusted 9-inch pie (page 263) minus the sugar
2 tablespoons vegetable oil
1 large onion, sliced
12 ounces Colby or Longhorn cheddar cheese, grated, to make about 3 cups
4–5 large potatoes, cooked, cooled, and cut into thick slices
Salt and pepper to taste
3/4 cup light cream
1 egg

- Divide the dough into 2/3 and 1/3 disks. Roll out the larger piece on a lightly floured surface to form a 13-inch circle. Carefully transfer to a lightly greased 9-inch pie plate, pressing the dough into the bottom and sides. Trim the dough leaving a 1/2-inch overhang. Refrigerate until the filling is finished.
- Heat the oil in a medium-size sauté pan and sauté the onion over low heat for about 5 minutes, until softened but not colored.
- To assemble the pie, sprinkle 1/3 of the cheese in the bottom of the pie shell. Add 1/2 the potato slices and 1/2 the cooked onion. Season with salt and pepper. Top with another 1/3 of the cheese, the remaining potatoes, and the remaining onion. Season with salt and pepper. Top with the remaining cheese.
- In a small bowl, mix together the cream and egg and pour over the potatoes.
- Preheat the oven to 400°F.
- Roll out the smaller piece of dough to cover the pie. Trim the top dough to match the bottom. Press the top and bottom edges together and crimp. Brush the top lightly with milk, cut a few vent holes, and place on a heavy baking sheet.
- Bake in the lower half of the oven for about 45 minutes until nicely browned. Cool for 5 minutes and serve in wedges.

Yields 1 9-inch pie

MENU

Roast beef (Roasting Chart, 247)
Potato Pie Gratin
Coleslaw vinaigrette
Baked Apples (page 269)

Potato & Pepper Frittata

Frittatas are to Italians what omelets are to the French. A savory filling is bound with eggs, cooked in a pan, and finished in the oven. You'll need a 10-inch flameproof and ovenproof skillet, preferably nonstick. Frittatas make wonderful dinners, or can be served cool for summer picnics. Vegetable fillings could include artichoke hearts, peppers, spinach, leeks, or cooked broccoli. Savory fillings could include ham, pancetta, smoked salmon, or cooked chicken. For creaminess, add cream cheese, fresh goat cheese, or mozzarella; for zip, add Parmesan cheese. I've even topped a simple potato frittata with caviar and sour cream and served it with champagne.

3 tablespoons olive oil
2 small all-purpose potatoes, cooked, skinned, and cubed, about 2 cups
1 large roasted red pepper, drained and chopped (page 242)
2 tablespoons minced parsley
4 eggs
3 tablespoons freshly grated Parmesan cheese
Salt and pepper to taste

- Preheat the oven to 400°F.
- In a 10-inch ovenproof and flameproof skillet, heat 2 tablespoons of the olive oil. Sauté the potatoes over medium heat for about 10 minutes until golden. Add the pepper and sauté for 1 minute. Add the parsley. Sprinkle with salt and pepper and transfer to a dish.
- In a small bowl, combine the eggs, Parmesan, and salt and pepper.
- In the same skillet, heat the remaining tablespoon of oil. Pour in the eggs and cook over low heat for 1 minute, stirring occasionally, just until the bottom is set. Add the reserved potatoes and pepper and place on the upper rack of the oven for 2 or 3 minutes until set.
- Remove, cut into wedges, and serve hot from the oven.

Serves 2

MENU

Potato & Pepper Frittata
Mixed green salad
Crusty Italian bread
Frozen yogurt sundaes with fruit

Mashed Sweet Potatoes

Sweet potatoes are wonderful simply baked and topped with a bit of butter and salt, but there are times when you may want a more elegant side dish for baked ham or roasted turkey. My solution is Mashed Sweet Potatoes, enhanced with a little maple syrup to bring out the sweetness of the potatoes.

4 large sweet potatoes, peeled and cut into quarters or large chunks
3 tablespoons butter
1/4 cup maple syrup
1 teaspoon salt, or to taste
Grated zest from 1 orange
Grating of nutmeg

♦ In a large pot of boiling water, cook the sweet potatoes for about 20 minutes or until fork-tender.
♦ Drain the potatoes and transfer to a mixing bowl. Cut the butter into small pieces and add with the maple syrup to the hot potatoes. Mix, don't beat, until the potatoes are smooth and the butter is melted. Add the orange zest and nutmeg.
♦ Taste and adjust the seasoning with more maple syrup or salt to taste. Serve hot from the bowl.

Serves 6

NOTE: For a fancier version, transfer the mashed potatoes to a large pastry bag with a #9 star tip. Pipe large rosettes of potatoes into a shallow buttered baking dish. Drizzle with 2 tablespoons of melted butter. Bake in a 375°F oven for 10 to 20 minutes until hot.

MENU

Baked Ham (page 247)
Mashed Sweet Potatoes
Steamed cauliflower
Dinner rolls
Banana splits

Crisp Potato Pancakes

*O*il is the symbolic ingredient in potato latkes, or potato pancakes. It's the hot oil and thinness that make them crisp. If you don't like to stand at the cooktop and make endless potato pancakes to order, you can cook them ahead and freeze them on a cookie sheet before packing them into plastic bags for the freezer. Or make them and refrigerate. Re-heat the pancakes on a baking sheet in a single layer in a 400°F oven until very hot and crisp.

3 large baking potatoes, scrubbed
1/2 cup very finely chopped onion
2 eggs
3 tablespoons flour
1 teaspoon salt
1/2 teaspoon baking powder
Pinch of powdered ginger
Vegetable oil for frying the pancakes

♦ Grate the potatoes with the skin on (a food processor really helps!) and place them in a bowl of water to cover so they won't discolor and turn brown.

♦ In a large bowl, combine the onion, eggs, flour, salt, baking powder, and ginger.

♦ Remove the potatoes from the water in handfuls and squeeze them to remove the water. Place in a clean dish towel and squeeze out even more water.

♦ Add the potatoes to the egg and onion mixture in the bowl. Toss to mix well. Use the potato mixture immediately. Eventually the batter will become discolored, but it won't affect the taste. Stir the batter occasionally.

♦ In a large sauté pan, add about 1/4 cup of oil. When the oil is hot, use a heaping tablespoon of batter for each pancake, and spread them very thin with a spoon or fork.

♦ Cook over medium heat until well browned and crisp, about 3 minutes on each side.

♦ Drain on paper towels and serve immediately, or keep warm, but never covered, in the oven. Add more oil to the pan as you fry the pancakes in batches.

♦ Serve the pancakes hot with applesauce and sour cream.

Serves 6

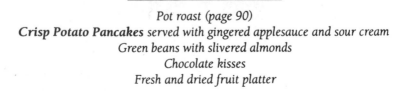

MENU

Pot roast (page 90)
Crisp Potato Pancakes *served with gingered applesauce and sour cream*
Green beans with slivered almonds
Chocolate kisses
Fresh and dried fruit platter

Savory Potato Waffles

Potato Waffles are a great dinner surprise and a perfect way to use up leftover mashed potatoes. They're reminiscent of hash-brown potatoes and potato pancakes.

1½ cups flour
1 teaspoon baking soda
½ teaspoon salt
1 cup mashed potatoes
2 cups buttermilk
2 eggs, separated
3 tablespoons vegetable oil
2 tablespoons minced chives or scallions

- Preheat the waffle iron until hot.
- In a large bowl, combine the flour, baking soda, and salt.
- In another large bowl, combine the potatoes, buttermilk, egg yolks, oil, and chives.
- In a small bowl, beat the egg whites until stiff, but not dry.
- Combine the flour mixture and the wet ingredients with a few swift but gentle strokes. Carefully fold in the beaten egg whites.
- Ladle a spoonful of batter onto the hot waffle iron and cook them according to the waffle iron directions, until the steam stops coming out of the sides and the waffles are browned and crisp.
- Serve immediately or keep warm on a cookie rack in a 250°F oven.
- Waffles can be cooled completely on a wire cookie rack and frozen in heavy plastic bags for later use. Warm them in the toaster.

Yields 8 double 4-inch waffles to serve 4 to 6

MENU

Breakfast sausages or bacon
Savory Potato Waffles
Warm sautéed apple slices sprinkled with cinnamon-sugar
Hot Chocolate (page 270)

Black Bean Chili con Carne

Chili seems the perfect dish for cool weather—a warm, spicy contrast to comfort foods like polenta, mashed potatoes, rice, or macaroni that it's served over. Con carne means with meat: ground beef, pork, turkey, or even lamb. Black beans are available dried or canned (cooked) in most supermarkets.

2 tablespoons vegetable oil

1 medium onion, chopped

2 cloves garlic, minced

1 pound ground meat (beef, pork, turkey, or lamb)

1 tablespoon yellow cornmeal

2 tablespoons chili powder

1 teaspoon salt

1 teaspoon cumin

1 teaspoon paprika

1/2 teaspoon oregano

1/4 teaspoon cayenne pepper

Black pepper to taste

1 28-ounce can chunky-style crushed tomatoes

1/2 cup water

2 cups cooked black beans (1 1-pound can), drained

1/4 cup chopped cilantro

♦ In a large pan, heat the oil and sauté the onion over low heat, stirring until soft. Add the garlic and sauté for 1 minute more. Add the meat and sauté, breaking it up, until no longer pink. Drain all the fat from the pan.

♦ Mix in the cornmeal and spices. Add the tomatoes and water, and slowly bring to a simmer. Cook, uncovered, for about 30 minutes until thickened, stirring occasionally. Stir in the beans and heat through. Adjust the seasoning with salt and pepper and more spice to taste.

♦ Stir in the cilantro and serve hot over polenta, mashed potatoes, macaroni, or rice.

Serves 4 to 6

MENU

Black Bean Chili con Carne
Polenta (page 253), Mashed Potatoes (page 254), macaroni, or Rice (page 250)
Raw vegetables: jicama, purple-top turnips, radishes, cucumbers
Frozen yogurt cones

Black & White Beans & Rice

*B*eans and rice are staples in the diet of many cultures, and for good reason. Not only do they taste great, but together they make a nutritious plant protein. Black beans from a can and white rice are the basis of this versatile dish, with a hot pepper and flavorful cumin and cilantro to add spice and color. If you add dark red kidney beans instead of black beans you'll have Red & White Beans & Rice.

3 tablespoons olive oil
1 large onion, chopped
2 cloves garlic, minced
1 jalepeño pepper, seeded and minced
1 teaspoon cumin
1 cup rice
2 cup boiling water
1 teaspoon salt, or to taste
2 cups cooked black beans, (1 1-pound can), drained
1/4 cup chopped cilantro
Pepper to taste

♦ In a large heavy sauce pan, heat the oil and add the onion. Sauté over low heat for 2 minutes until the onion is softened. Add the garlic and jalepeño pepper and continue to sauté for 2 minutes. Add the cumin and rice, stir, and sauté for about 1 minute, stirring frequently until the rice is hot. Add the boiling water and salt all at once and stir.
♦ Cover and simmer for about 17 minutes until the rice is tender and all the water has been absorbed.
♦ Rinse the black beans well in a strainer. Drain and add to the rice. Cover and cook for 1 minute to heat the beans.
♦ Stir with a fork to fluff the rice. Stir in the cilantro and season with salt and pepper to taste.

Serves 4 to 6

MENU

Barbequed ribs
Black & White Beans & Rice
Watercress and arugula salad with orange slices and red onions
Ice cream pie (page 263)

Sauces, Dressings, Marinades, Relishes, Dips & Spreads

*T*hese are the things that add zip, fun, and interest to simple foods: sauces on pasta; dressings on salads; spreads for sandwiches; dips for chips and raw vegetables; marinades to tenderize and add flavor to meats, chicken, and fish; and relishes/chutneys/salsas to give heightened flavor, color, and complexity to the tastes on a plate.

Salad dressings, prepared sauces, and relishes line the grocery and specialty shop shelves. They may save you time, but not the enjoyment of creating a home-made favorite.

Sauces

Sauces traditionally have topped and enhanced the foods we eat. But I've come to depend on marinades and chutneys or relishes to flavor and complement meats, fish, and chicken, rather than spend precious time on classic sauces. In my need for speed at dinnertime, sauces are simple, do-ahead toppings, primarily for pasta. Aside from the sauces and dressings in this chapter, the Tips & Basic Recipes chapter includes others. The winter (canned tomatoes) and summer (fresh tomatoes) tomato sauces (page 256) are sure to become household staples.

Dressings

Homemade dressings for salads are easy to make in quantity and store in the refrigerator. You can use any combination of oil and vinegar in the ratio of about 3:1. A simple vinaigrette dressing on a salad of young, tender greens is a work of art, and the perfect accompaniment to just about any dinner.

Simple, Thick, Creamy, Cheesy, and Flavorful

- ♦ To make a thickened vinaigrette, Dijon mustard or mayonnaise can be added.
- ♦ To make a thickened dressing, mayonnaise can be mixed with buttermilk to give the right consistency.
- ♦ To make cheesier dressings and vinaigrettes, add crumbled blue cheese or Parmesan.
- ♦ For flavorings, use a minced and mashed clove of garlic, a dash of Worcestershire sauce, a spoonful of horseradish, lots of chopped fresh herbs, a bit of tomato paste, anchovy paste, or wasabi (Japanese horseradish paste).

Vinegars

The word vinegar comes from two French words, *vin* (wine) and *aigre* (sour). Vinegars are culinary staples that enhance foods, sauces, and dressings. Here are some of the most popular:

White vinegar is a sharp, strong vinegar I use when the flavor is not so important or when it will be overpowered by other flavors, or it's used to acidify cooking water.

Cider vinegar is good for making chutneys since it's made from apples and has a fruity flavor.

Red wine vinegar is an essential for good vinaigrettes and deglazing pans to make sauces.

Balsamic vinegar is one of the best culinary discoveries and is now everyone's favorite ingredient. Balsamic is a dark, rich, sweet/tart vinegar made from the white grapes around Modena, Italy. The juice is cooked down, which develops the sweetness, and the vinegar is aged to develop the distinctive taste.

Rice wine vinegar is either plain and simple, or seasoned with salt and sugar. Plain, it's used in marinades and sauces. Seasoned, it is a light, non-caloric topping for salad greens, without the oil. The seasoned vinegar moistens and adds flavor to cooked sushi rice (page 250) before it's shaped into balls, or formed into logs and cut.

Oils

For Cooking

Olive oil. There's no need to use extra virgin olive oil in cooking. Find a pure, quality all-purpose Italian oil that you like, and stick with it. Olive oils can be greener in color and stronger in flavor, but for an all-purpose oil, I like Berio or Bertolli oils.

Corn oil is mild in flavor which makes it all-purpose for cooking and baking.

Vegetable oil is made from soybeans and is also mild in flavor.

Canola oil has become popular since it's a mono-unsaturated oil (like olive oil) that actually lowers cholesterol in the blood. That doesn't mean, however, that it is without calories from fat.

Safflower oil is mild and good for cooking.

Sesame oil is a pale, cold-pressed oil with a mild, nutty taste. The darker, roasted sesame oil is used as a flavoring oil rather than for cooking.

Peanut oil. This cold-pressed, mild oil is especially good for stir-fry dishes.

For Salads

These oils should be of the best quality since they're the essential ingredient of dressings. Use mild pure olive oils (from Lucca, Italy or southern France), or make combinations with vegetable oils, or flavored oils. Walnut oil is very perishable, so it should be bought fresh, in small quantities, and stored in the refrigerator. In small quantities, dark, roasted sesame oil adds a unique flavor to sauces and dressings for salads, seafood, pasta, poultry, and meat.

Marinades—Wet or Dry?

Marinades add flavor to chicken, meat, and vegetables.

Wet marinades can be as simple as a vinaigrette dressing with oil (to protect the food from drying out), vinegar (an acid that tenderizes by breaking down the tissue), and flavoring (salt, pepper, spices, fresh herbs). Some sweetness (white or brown sugar or honey) balances the acidity of marinades and gives the grilled food a browned, caramelized color and flavor. Don't overpower the delicate flavor of chicken and seafood by marinating them too long. For most recipes, a few hours should be fine. Lamb and beef can stand up to longer marinating and stronger marinades.

Dry marinades are spice blends that are rubbed into the flesh or skin of the chicken, seafood, or meat. The connection is much more direct and the flavoring is much stronger. For summer grilling, spice blends are a fantastically fast way to make chicken and fish something extra-ordinary (page 83).

Chutneys and Relishes

Chutneys are Indian relishes that add interest, depth, and zip to simple foods. They may be sweet, sour, salty, sweet and sour, or spicy. There are many varieties of chutney. They can be made with tomatoes, mangos, dates, coconut, tamarind, coriander, mint, apples, pears, etc. Most have been cooked and preserved, but chutneys can also be fresh.

Dips and Spreads

Dips and spreads may be thick, flavorful vegetable or bean pastes, or based on fattier (and fattening) cream cheese, mayonnaise, sour cream, or butter. These need lots of strong flavors to give life to simple vegetables, crackers, and sandwiches. Dips and spreads make quick hors d'oeuvres, and sometimes even become dinner, when unexpected guests arrive.

Puttanesca Sauce

Puttanesca is an assertive, flavorful, tomato-based sauce to top simple grilled fish or any pasta. If you like black olives, capers, anchovies, and garlic, you'll love this Italian specialty. The olives must be imported (either oil-cured or brined) and you should taste them to be sure you like the flavor before you go to the trouble of pitting them. A little sauce goes a long way, so freeze half for another time.

1/4 cup olive oil
1 onion, chopped
3 cloves garlic, minced
4 anchovy fillets,
   chopped
1 28-ounce can whole
   Italian tomatoes,
   drained and chopped
3 tablespoons tiny, brined
   capers, drained
Pinch of crushed red
   pepper flakes
Pepper to taste
1 cup pitted and chopped
   imported black olives

♦ In a saucepan, heat the oil over low heat and sauté the onion and garlic until softened, stirring often to prevent them from coloring. Stir in the anchovies and sauté for another minute. Add the chopped tomatoes, capers, crushed red pepper flakes, black pepper, and olives. Stir. Simmer uncovered, stirring often, until thickened, about 15 minutes.

Yields about 2 cups

MENU

*Grilled tuna or swordfish steaks (page 248) with **Puttanesca Sauce**
Pasta twists or ziti with Parmesan cheese
Mixed green salad vinaigrette
Biscotti (page 231) and espresso*

Eggplant Caponata

Eggplant Caponata is a Mediterranean relish, with similar ingredients to ratatouille: eggplant, tomato, and onion, plus celery, olives, and capers. It's a wonderful hors d'oeuvre on crackers, but also a fine accompaniment to roast chicken, grilled sausages, or, as in this menu, a condiment to make ordinary sandwiches extra-ordinary. Make it ahead of time and keep it on hand for creative meals. I've even used the leftovers on pasta in place of tomato sauce.

1 medium eggplant, cut into ½-inch cubes
2 teaspoons salt
6 tablespoons olive oil
1 onion, thinly sliced
1 clove garlic, minced
¾ cup chopped celery
2 cups chunky-style crushed tomatoes
12 pimiento-stuffed green olives, cut in half
1–2 tablespoons tiny, brined capers, drained
2 tablespoons red wine vinegar
1 tablespoon tomato paste
2 teaspoons sugar
¼ teaspoon oregano
2 tablespoons finely chopped parsley
Lots of pepper

+ Place the eggplant cubes in a colander and toss with the salt. Drain for at least 30 minutes. Dry with paper towels.
+ In a large sauté pan, heat 4 tablespoons of the oil until very hot. Add the eggplant, and cook for about 15 minutes over medium heat until soft. Use a flat-bottomed spatula often to scrape the bottom of the pan so the eggplant doesn't stick.
+ Transfer the eggplant to a bowl and add the remaining oil to the pan. Add the onion, garlic, and celery, and sauté over low heat for 10 minutes, stirring often, until softened but not colored.
+ Return the eggplant to the pan, and add the tomatoes, olives, capers, vinegar, tomato paste, sugar, and oregano. Simmer, uncovered, for about 15 minutes, until the vegetables are tender and the mixture is very thick, stirring often as it thickens. Stir in the parsley, taste, and season with pepper to taste.
+ Serve at room temperature or chilled.

Yields 1 quart

MENU

Turkey or roast beef sandwiches on crusty rolls with
Eggplant Caponata
Potato chips
Brown or Black Cows (page 205)

When you have little energy for mealtime, there's nothing wrong with bagels and cream cheese, and a super salad. A make-your-own-salad bar gives diners a choice of dressings and add-ins for the basic salad greens. Fresh fruit is refreshing in summer salads and these dressings are the perfect match.

Poppyseed Dressing

¹/₃ cup white vinegar
1 tablespoon finely
   chopped shallot
   or onion
¹/₃ cup sugar
1 teaspoon dry mustard
1 teaspoon salt
Pinch of cayenne pepper
²/₃ cup vegetable oil
2 tablespoons poppyseeds
   (or a handful of fresh
   mint leaves)

♦ In a processor or blender, combine the vinegar, shallot, sugar, mustard, salt, and cayenne. With the motor running, add the oil slowly in a thin stream until the dressing is thickened.
♦ Add the poppyseeds (or mint) and process briefly. Store in a jar in the refrigerator and shake before serving.

Yields 1¹/₂ cups

Maple Vinaigrette

¹/₄ cup Balsamic vinegar
2 tablespoons maple
   syrup
1 tablespoon Dijon
   mustard
¹/₄ teaspoon salt
¹/₄ cup olive oil

♦ Combine the vinegar, maple syrup, mustard, and salt in a deep bowl. Whisk in the oil slowly until thickened.
♦ Store in a jar in the refrigerator.

Yields ²/₃ cup

MENU

Bagels and cream cheese
Smoked salmon, trout, or bluefish
Mixed green salad with fresh cut-up fruit and berries
Poppyseed Dressing *or* **Maple Vinaigrette**
Streusel crumb coffeecake
Iced coffee

Apple-Ginger Marmalade

Apple-Ginger Marmalade makes a delicious glaze for roast chicken when it's mixed with the defatted pan juices. The marmalade is great on toast with butter or cream cheese, and it's super stirred into vanilla yogurt for dessert. Best of all, the marmalade makes wonderful holiday and hostess gifts with a loaf of homemade bread. This recipe is for ginger lovers!

3 pounds apples, peeled, cored, and chopped to make about 9 cups
1 cup peeled and finely chopped fresh ginger root
Juice and grated zest of 1 orange
Juice and grated zest of 2 lemons
2½ cups water
5½ cups sugar

♦ In a very large sauce pan, combine the apples, ginger root, orange and lemon juices, zest, and the water. Bring to a boil and simmer for 30 minutes, stirring often, until tender and soft. Stir in the sugar and boil gently, stirring often, until thickened, about 20 more minutes.

♦ Spoon immediately into sterilized canning jars. Wipe the rims clean and cover with new lids. Set aside and listen for the *ping* that lets you know a vacuum has formed and the jars have been sealed properly. Cool and label.

Yields 6 8-ounce jars

MENU

Roasted or rotisserie chicken (page 245)
Rice Pilaf (page 252)
Sautéed summer squash
*Vanilla yogurt with **Apple-Ginger Marmalade***

*Simple summer dinners can be enhanced with a spicy condiment, whether you call it a salsa or a relish. The following four recipes are easy to make ahead and require **no** cooking.*

Mango-Cilantro Salsa

1 large ripe mango,
   peeled and diced
$^1/_4$ cup minced red onion
2–3 tablespoons chopped
   cilantro
$^1/_2$ red pepper, diced
1 tablespoon Balsamic
   vinegar
1 tablespoon olive oil
$^1/_4$ teaspoon salt
Pinch of sugar

♦ Combine all the ingredients in a medium-size bowl. Stir well.
♦ Store in a jar in the refrigerator until ready to serve.

Yields about $2^1/_2$ cups

Tomato Salsa

1 teaspoon minced
   jalepeño pepper
3 scallions, chopped
1 clove garlic, minced
3 tablespoons chopped
   cilantro
2 cups chunky-style
   crushed tomatoes
1 tablespoon lime juice
2 tablespoons olive oil
1 teaspoon salt
1 teaspoon cumin
$^1/_2$ teaspoon chili powder
Pepper to taste

♦ In a medium-size bowl, combine the salsa ingredients and stir to mix throughly.
♦ Taste and adjust the seasoning, adding more spice or pepper to taste.
♦ Let the flavors mix at room temperature before serving. Store in a glass jar in the refrigerator.

Yields about $2^1/_4$ cups

Pineapple-Black Bean Salsa

1 8-ounce can crushed
  unsweetened pineapple
2 cups cooked black
  beans (1 1-pound
  can), drained
1/4 cup finely chopped
  red onion
1/4 cup finely chopped
  red pepper
1 1/2 tablespoons sugar
1 tablespoon lemon juice
1 tablespoon olive oil
1 teaspoon minced
  jalepeño pepper
2 teaspoons minced
  crystallized ginger
1 tablespoon chopped
  fresh mint
1 tablespoon chopped
  cilantro
1/2 teaspoon salt

♦ Drain the crushed pineapple
  in a strainer and press with a
  spoon to eliminate the juice. Place
  in a large bowl.
♦ Rinse the black beans well and drain. Add
  to the bowl.
♦ Add the remaining ingredients and stir. Taste and
  adjust the seasoning.
♦ Let the flavors mix at room temperature before
  serving, or store in a glass jar in the refrigerator.

Yields about 3 1/2 cups

Onion-Pepper Relish

1 cup chopped Vidalia,
  Spanish, or red onion
1/4 cup chopped
  pimientos or
  roasted peppers
1/2 cup chopped green
  pepper
1/8 teaspoon cayenne
  pepper, or to taste
2 tablespoons olive oil
1 tablespoon red wine
  vinegar
1/2 teaspoon salt
Pinch of sugar

♦ Combine all the ingredients, in
  a medium-size bowl and stir.
♦ Taste and adjust the seasoning
  with salt and pepper.
♦ Store in a jar in the refrigerator until ready
  to serve.

Yields about 2 cups

MENU

Grilled chicken (page 83)
Mango-Cilantro Salsa, Tomato Salsa,
Pineapple-Black Bean Salsa, *or* Onion-Pepper Relish
Grilled new potatoes (partially cook indoors, roll in oil and grill to finish)
Fresh fruit platter

Apple-Cranberry Chutney

A new cranberry sauce with traditional Thanksgiving fare makes the old seem new.

2 tablespoons oil
1 small onion, chopped
3 apples, peeled, cored, and chopped
1½ cups fresh cranberries
⅔ cup brown sugar
½ cup currants
2 tablespoon minced crystallized ginger
½ cup cider vinegar
1 tablespoon lemon juice
¼ cup chopped walnuts

♦ Heat the oil in a saucepan, and sauté the onion, stirring, until soft but not colored. Add the apples, cranberries, sugar, currants, ginger, vinegar, and lemon juice, and simmer, uncovered, for about 15 minutes until thickened. Stir a few times. Mix in the walnuts.

♦ Cool before spooning into glass jars or plastic containers and refrigerating. Serve chilled.

Yields about 1 pint

MENU

Shrimp cocktail (page 248)
Roasted turkey or turkey breast
Apple-Cranberry Chutney
Potato & Winter Squash Casserole (page 147)
Green beans
Pumpkin pie (page 224)

Mango-Raisin Chutney

*W*hen mangoes are at their peak—fragrant and a beautiful red/orange color—use them in fruit salads, chutneys, as a garnish for chicken salads and grilled fish, in Fruit Smoothies (page 271), or just for snacking. In Mango-Raisin Chutney, traditional chutney ingredients are used: fruit, ginger, vinegar, sugar, and spices. This will keep in the refrigerator for a week, or can be frozen in a plastic container for later use.

2 or 3 large ripe mangoes
1/2 cup cider vinegar
3/4 cup granulated sugar
1/2 cup brown sugar
2 tablespoons lemon juice
1/2 teaspoon salt
1/2 teaspoon crushed red pepper flakes, or to taste
1/4 cup minced crystallized ginger
1/2 cup raisins

♦ To prepare the mango, peel it and cut it into chunks, scraping the pulp from the seeds. You should have about 4 cups.
♦ Add the mango chunks and pulp, vinegar, sugars, lemon juice, salt, and red pepper to a large saucepan. Bring to a boil and simmer gently, uncovered, until thickened, about 25 minutes. Stir often as it thickens. Add the ginger and raisins and simmer for a few more minutes. Taste and adjust the seasoning.
♦ Cool before spooning into a glass jar or plastic container to store in the refrigerator.

Yields about 3 cups

MENU

Grilled lamb chops (page 247)
Mango-Raisin Chutney
Rice Pilaf (page 252)
Green beans vinaigrette
Lemon meringue pie

Mexican-Spiced Hummus

It's amazing what can come from a can of beans and some spices. Hummus is a versatile and delicious chick pea spread that can be used as a dip for chips or raw vegetables, a spread for turkey sandwiches or bagels, in a pita bread with chopped tomatoes and onions, or, as a sauce for potatoes and fish. Hummus is usually flavored with tahini, a sesame seed paste, but in this version, Mexican spices give it a unique and zippy taste.

2 cups cooked chick peas
  (1 16- or 19-ounce
  can), drained
¼ cup fresh lemon juice
  (from 1 large lemon)
1 clove garlic
1½ teaspoons cumin
¾ teaspoon salt
½ teaspoon coriander
⅛ teaspoon cayenne
  pepper, or to taste
Black pepper to taste
¼ cup olive oil

♦ Combine the drained chick peas, lemon juice, garlic, and spices in a processor bowl or blender. With the motor running, add the oil slowly through the feed tube and process until smooth. Taste and adjust the seasoning.

♦ To use as a sauce, thin with a tablespoon of water.

♦ Store in a covered container in the refrigerator.

Yields 2 cups

MENU

Grilled salmon (page 248)
New potatoes
Mexican-Spiced Hummus
Broccoli (page 242)
Fruit pie (page 227) and ice cream

Peanut-Sesame Dip*

*R*aw vegetables can always use another dip to add interest. This dip combines some favorite recent flavors—sesame oil, peanut butter, hot oil, and Balsamic vinegar—with mayonnaise to make a dip for vegetables or, thinned, a sauce for grilled fish, chicken, or Oriental noodles.

¾ cup mayonnaise
2 tablespoons peanut butter
2 tablespoons soy sauce
1 tablespoon roasted sesame oil
1 tablespoon Balsamic vinegar
½ teaspoon hot oil, or to taste

♦ In a small bowl, whisk together all the ingredients until smooth. Store in a glass jar in the refrigerator.

Yields about 1 cup

*To make a Peanut-Sesame Sauce, stir in a few tablespoons of hot water to thin to the consistency you like.

MENU

Peanut-Sesame Dip
Raw vegetables: snow peas, asparagus, peeled jicama sticks, carrot sticks, celery sticks
Grilled fish steaks (page 248)
Oriental noodles
Strawberry shortcakes (page 220)

Dilled Shrimp Dip

*It's always good to have a few fast hors d'oeuvres in your reper-
toire since hors d'oeuvres can sometimes become dinner. This
seafood dip makes an impressive presentation when served in a
hollowed bread bowl surrounded by a colorful assortment of vegetables. You can use crabmeat as well as shrimp.*

2 pounds cream cheese
1/4–1/2 cup sour cream
1/4 cup fresh snipped dill
Grated zest of 1 lemon
1/2 teaspoon salt, or to
  taste
2 pounds shrimp,
  cooked, peeled and
  deveined
3 scallions, chopped
Salt and pepper to taste
2 tablespoons chopped
  pimiento or roasted
  pepper
1 10-inch round bread
Assorted raw vegetables—
  pepper and carrot
  sticks, cherry tomatoes
  on toothpicks, snow
  peas, broccoli flowers,
  and cauliflower, fennel
  and celery sticks,
  jicama slices, etc.

♦ In a processor, combine the cream cheese, 1/4 cup
  sour cream, dill, and lemon zest, and process until
  smooth. Add the shrimp and scallions and process by pulsing a few times until the shrimp is
  still chunky. Adjust the seasoning with salt and
  pepper. Stir in the pimiento.
♦ If the dip is too thick, add a few more tablespoons
  of sour cream.
♦ At serving time, make a cut around the top crust
  of the bread leaving a 1 1/2-inch edge. Scoop out
  the soft bread to make a bowl. Fill with the shrimp
  dip and surround with vegetables.

Yields 6 to 7 cups

MENU

Dilled Shrimp Dip *in a bread bowl with raw vegetables*
Roasted turkey or baked ham (page 247) with condiments and rolls for sandwiches
Assorted cheese and fruit platter
Cookies and brownies (page 233)
Apple cider and Sangria (page 270)

Years ago two good friends, who are also good cooks, brought these dips to a neighborhood pitch-in. They were a hit then and remain a favorite at neighborhood gatherings still.

Linda's Spinach Spread

2 10-ounce packages frozen chopped spinach, defrosted and squeezed dry of all excess water
1 bunch parsley, stems removed and finely chopped
1 bunch scallions, green and white part, finely chopped
1/2–3/4 cup mayonnaise
Salt and lots of pepper

♦ Give the spinach an extra squeeze to eliminate any water.
♦ In a large bowl, combine all the ingredients, adding just enough mayonnaise to bind the greens. Stir together with a fork.
♦ Season well with a little salt and lots of pepper.
♦ Pack in a crock and refrigerate until serving time.
♦ Serve with crackers, vegetables, or as a wonderful sandwich spread.

Yields 4 cups

Lorie's Eggplant Dip

3 tablespoons olive oil
2 cloves garlic, chopped
1 large eggplant, cubed
1 green pepper, seeded and chopped
1 8-ounce can tomato sauce
2 tablespoons cumin, or to taste
2 teaspoons sugar
1/2 teaspoon cayenne pepper
1/4 cup red wine vinegar
1 1/2 teaspoons salt
1/4 cup chopped cilantro

♦ In a medium-size saucepan, combine all the ingredients except the cilantro. Simmer, covered, for about 20 minutes, Uncover and continue to cook for 10 minutes until soft and thick.
♦ Add to the bowl of a food processor and process until smooth. Season to taste with salt and pepper. Chill.
♦ At serving time, stir in the cilantro. Serve with vegetables or chips.

Yields about 4 cups

MENU

Whole poached salmon
Noodle kugel (page 119) or vegetable lasagna (page 128–129)
Raw vegetable platter
Assorted cheeses, crackers, breads, and rolls
Linda's Spinach Spread
Lorie's Eggplant Dip
Chocolate-dipped glacéed fruit and nuts (page 269)

Smoked Bluefish Pâté

Sandwiches are fine for a fast dinner, especially if they're not the usual tuna fish or ham sandwich. Look for smoked bluefish—peppered or plain, and make this spread for crackers or bagels, or for a sandwich filling on rye or pumpernickel. Serve with apple or pear slices.

6 ounces cream cheese
4 tablespoons butter
½ pound smoked bluefish
2 tablespoons minced onion
2 tablespoons minced parsley
1 tablespoon Dijon mustard
Pinch of cayenne pepper
Salt and black pepper to taste
2–3 tablespoons mayonnaise to make a spreadable consistency

♦ Blend the cream cheese and butter in a processor or mixer until soft. Break up the bluefish in the bowl and add the onion, parsley, and mustard. Process a few times just to combine, **not** purée. It should be thick and still chunky. Stir in the mayonnaise a few tablespoons at a time until the pâté is a spreadable consistency. Season with cayenne, and salt and pepper.

♦ Pack in a crock, cover, and refrigerate if making ahead of time. Serve on crackers or bread.

Yields about 2½ cups

MENU

Smoked Bluefish Pâté on crackers, bagels, or bread
Sliced apples and pears
Tabouleh (page 38)
Oatmeal cookies (page 230)

Sandwiches

W hen you don't have time to cook dinner, sandwiches can be a lifesaver. They can be an unexpected and delightful surprise, especially if you use a little creativity.

Bread is an essential ingredient in sandwiches, so be sure to use only the highest quality. Besides the usual kinds of bread, you might try: bagels, English muffins, rolls (crusty and soft), French baguettes, challah, croissants, rice cakes, tortillas, pita bread, lavash flat bread, and whatever else tempts you.

Hamburgers are always easy and appealing for dinner. They're even more interesting if you add different ingredients to the ground meat. For additional flavor and texture, add chopped onions, chopped spinach, a bit of salsa, grated carrots, mashed beans, or mashed tofu. You can season the meat with steak sauce, Worcestershire, or fresh herbs. Or try filling the center of the hamburger with mozzarella cheese next time you cook it.

Hamburgers—whether simple or jazzed up—can be broiled, pan fried, or grilled, for two to three minutes on each side—don't overcook them. Brown on the outside and still juicy on the inside is ideal. Top with the relishes, salsas, or condiments you like best, or add tomato slices and lettuce, guacamole and salsa, pizza sauce with mozzarella cheese, sautéed onions and peppers, or baked beans and barbeque sauce. It's hard to go wrong with hamburgers.

Pizza is another fast-food favorite that seems to taste better when it's made at home. For one thing, it will always be hotter than take-out. The sauce is easy to make (page 257) or buy. Use grated mozzarella or Monterey Jack cheese; the toppings can be whatever you choose or have on hand. The crust can be a simple yeast dough (page 260), ready-made dough from the refrigerator case or freezer of the supermarket, or from an Italian bakery. Pre-baked crusts, thick and thin, can be bought in most markets—or use pita rounds, lavash bread, or even English muffins for the crust. Pizza is usually baked on the lowest rack of a hot oven until the cheese is melted and the bottom of the crust is browned and crusty.

Even **grilled cheese sandwiches** can be a welcome dinner, especially if you dress them up with a spoon of chutney or an interesting mustard. Try giving them an international flair such as *Croque Monsieur* (page 184) with a slice of ham, cooked as you would French toast, or a Mexican grilled cheese between two tortillas and served with sour cream and salsa.

Presentation is important when it comes to dinnertime sandwiches. You might make one long, large French bread sandwich. Serve it on a large wooden board; garnish it with olives, pickles, and raw vegetables; and at the table, carve it into individual portions. The look will be impressive even if it's really just a big ham and Swiss cheese sandwich underneath.

Tomato & Cheese Pizza

*H*ere's *a basic tomato and cheese pizza you can make at home with store bought dough or homemade. Use a prepared sauce or make your own, or use chunky-style crushed tomatoes, or even fresh plum tomatoes. The crust is partially baked before adding the sauce to assure a crisp crust. This is an especially good idea if you use fresh tomatoes or like to load on the toppings.*

1/4 cup olive oil
2–3 tablespoons
  cornmeal
1 pound fresh pizza
  dough (page 260)
1 1/2 cups chunky-style
  crushed tomatoes
  or chopped plum
  tomatoes, or 1 1/2 cups
  pizza sauce (page 257)
1/2 teaspoon dried oregano
  or 2 tablespoons
  chopped fresh basil
Salt and pepper to taste
2 cups (8 ounces) grated
  mozzarella or Monterey
  Jack cheese
3 tablespoons freshly
  grated Parmesan cheese

Toppings: mushrooms,
  peppers, pepperoni,
  onions, roasted
  eggplant, olives,
  artichoke hearts

♦ Oil a heavy 16-inch round or 11 x 17-inch jellyroll pan with half of the olive oil and sprinkle evenly with the cornmeal.
♦ On a lightly floured surface, roll out the dough to fit the prepared pan. This takes some practice since the elasticity of the gluten in the yeast dough makes it shrink back. Roll the dough as much as you can starting from the center, then let gravity help you stretch the dough more. Hold it by the edge, let it hang down, and turn it around and around. Arrange it in the pan and press it into the sides. Cover the pan with a towel and let the dough rest in a warm place until puffy, about 20 minutes.
♦ Preheat the oven to 450°F.
♦ If the dough has pulled away from the edge, press it gently to the sides again with your finger tips. Brush the dough with the remaining oil and bake in the middle of the oven for 5 minutes. Don't be alarmed if the crust starts to bubble.
♦ Spread the tomatoes or prepared sauce over the dough and season with the oregano or basil, and salt and pepper. Cover with the grated cheeses and add any toppings that you like.
♦ Return to the oven and bake for 10 to 15 minutes more or until the bottom is browned and crusty, and the cheese is bubbly.
♦ Cool for a few minutes before slicing and eating.

Yields 1 16-inch round pizza

MENU

Tomato & Cheese Pizza
Mixed green salad vinaigrette
Ice cream pie (page 263) with Chocolate Sauce (page 264)

Breakfast Pizzas

Breakfast pizzas are sure to bring a smile for dinner. The crust is made of biscuit dough, topped with an egg and bacon or ham, and then baked. You can roll out the dough ahead, but prepare the pizzas at the last minute since they take just 10 minutes in the oven.

For the biscuit dough:
2 cups flour
2 teaspoons baking powder
1 teaspoon salt
4 tablespoons butter
4 tablespoons vegetable shortening
1/2 cup + 2 tablespoons milk

2 cups (8 ounces) grated Monterey Jack cheese
2 scallions, white and green, finely chopped
8 strips bacon, cooked, drained, and crumbled, or 3/4 cup diced boiled ham
2 plum tomatoes, diced and drained of excess juice
6 eggs
Salt and pepper to taste

+ Preheat the oven to 425°F. Grease 2 heavy baking sheets.
+ To make the dough, combine the flour, baking powder, and salt in a deep bowl. Cut in the butter and shortening with a pastry blender or 2 knives until it resembles coarse meal. Stir in the milk with a fork just until the dough comes together. Knead gently a few times to form a ball.
+ Divide into 6 pieces. On a floured surface, roll each piece into a 6-inch round and turn the outer edges in to form a 1/2-inch rim. Transfer to the prepared baking sheets.
+ Divide the cheese among the shells. Make a slight indent in the middle to contain the egg.
+ At serving time, crack and drop a whole egg in the center of the cheese and poke with a knife to break the yellow. Top with scallions, bacon, and tomato. Season with salt and pepper.
+ Bake for about 10 minutes until the egg is nearly set and serve immediately.

Serves 4 to 6

MENU

Breakfast Pizzas
Mixed green salad
Orange or vegetable juice
Muffins (page 197, 198) or Rugelach (page 199)

Desert Pizzas

*F*lour *tortillas are the base for refried beans, chilies, grated cheese, and tomatoes. Fast and fanciful for a quick and often requested dinner.*

3 tablespoons vegetable oil for brushing the baking sheet and tortillas

8 8-inch flour tortillas

2 cups vegetarian refried beans (1 1-pound can)

1 4-ounce can chopped green chilies, mild, medium, or hot

3 cups (12 ounces) grated Monterey Jack cheese

2 tomatoes, diced and drained of excess juice

Pitted black olive slices

- Preheat the oven to 425°F. Brush two large heavy baking sheets with oil.
- Arrange 4 tortillas on each sheet. Brush with oil.
- Divide the refried beans between the tortillas and spread evenly. Sprinkle the chopped chilies over the beans, cover with the cheese, and top with the tomatoes.
- Bake the pizzas in the middle of the oven for 10 minutes, or until the bottoms are lightly browned and the cheese is melted. Top with olives and serve immediately.

Serves 4 to 6

MENU

Desert Pizzas
Cut-up raw vegetables
Fruit Smoothies (page 271)

Barbequed Beef Sandwiches

Barbeque in 15 minutes! Thin strips of beef cook in minutes in a flavorful barbeque sauce. Any extra sauce will keep for weeks in the refrigerator. Pass the bottled hot sauce with the sandwiches for those who like their barbeque really hot.

For the sauce:
1/2 cup finely chopped onion
1 cup ketchup
1/4 cup brown sugar
1/4 cup cider vinegar
2 tablespoons Worcestershire sauce
2 tablespoons vegetable oil
1 tablespoon chili powder, or more to taste
1 teaspoon dry mustard
1/2 teaspoon pepper
Tabasco sauce to taste

1 tablespoon vegetable oil
1 pound beef sirloin tips or strips, or skirt steak, trimmed of all fat and cut into 1/8-inch slices
6 soft sandwich or hamburger rolls
Hot sauce, optional

- To prepare the sauce, combine all the sauce ingredients in a medium-size saucepan and simmer for 4 minutes. The barbequed beef uses about half the sauce—the rest can be reserved for later use. Cool before transferring to a jar and refrigerating.
- In a large sauté pan heat the oil over medium heat. Add the beef, stirring so it doesn't stick. Toss for just a minute until most of the pink is gone. Add about 1 cup of barbeque sauce and simmer for a few minutes, stirring often.
- Spoon the barbequed beef onto the rolls and serve with hot sauce.

Serves 4 to 6

MENU

Barbequed Beef Sandwiches *(on soft rolls)*
Potato chips
Coleslaw (page 243)
Brownies (page 233)

Middle Eastern Burgers

Ask your butcher to grind lean beef and lamb to make these flavorful and exotic Middle Eastern hamburgers. Cook them until pink inside.

1 slice white bread, crusts removed and cut into cubes
¹/₄ cup water
1 pound fresh lean ground beef
¹/₂ pound fresh lean ground lamb
¹/₄ cup minced fresh parsley
¹/₄ cup minced scallions
3 tablespoons chopped fresh mint leaves
2 tablespoons tomato paste
1¹/₄ teaspoons salt
¹/₄ teaspoon cinnamon
Pepper to taste
4 medium-size pita breads, cut in half

Toppings: chopped tomatoes, chopped onions, plain yogurt, mint sauce

- Prepare the grill or use a large heavy sauté pan.
- In a small bowl, soak the bread in water for 5 minutes. Drain and mash until smooth. Add to a large bowl.
- Combine the bread with all the other ingredients and mix thoroughly. Form into 8 patties.
- Cook until the outside is browned and crusty and the inside is still pink.
- Serve in pita breads with your choice of toppings.

Serves 4 to 6

MENU

Artichokes—cold with vinaigrette
Middle Eastern Burgers *in pitas with toppings*
Melon and orange salad with a sprinkle of fresh mint

Grilled Tofu-Burgers

I developed this marinade for tofu so that vegetarians and carnivores could co-exist around the mesquite-grill—some with tofu burgers and others with hamburgers. I've since used this marinade with shrimp for a great skewered and grilled dinner. Don't be put off by tofu. It's a versatile, healthy, and affordable source of protein that works in savory and sweet dishes. In addition to stir-fry dishes, the firm variety can be crumbled into chili, lasagna, or tuna fish salad; cubed and marinated for salads; or processed and mixed with vegetables and an egg for savory pies and quiches. The soft tofu can be blended into puddings, custards, and milk shakes.

1 pound extra-firm tofu, drained and cut into 6 thick "steaks"

For the marinade:
1/4 cup soy sauce
1/4 cup peanut oil
1 teaspoon hot chili garlic paste (available in Asian markets)
Pinch of coriander
2 tablespoons peanut butter
2 tablespoons honey
1 teaspoon Balsamic vinegar

6 hamburger rolls
Shredded lettuce
6 tomato slices
Mayonnaise

• Combine the marinade ingredients in a medium-size bowl. Whisk together until smooth.
• Put half the marinade in a shallow glass or plastic container. Lay the tofu on top, being sure to handle the tofu carefully so it doesn't break, and cover with the remaining marinade. Cover and marinate in the refrigerator for at least 2 hours.
• Prepare the grill.
• With a spatula, carefully place the tofu on the grill and cook for about 4 minutes on each side, basting with the sauce, until browned and a bit crusty on each side.
• Serve immediately on a roll with lettuce, tomato, and mayonnaise.

Yields 6 burgers

<hr />

MENU

Grilled Tofu-Burgers
Potato chips
Banana splits or watermelon sticks

Cowboy's Nachos

Everyone loves a chance to participate in dinner by making his or her own, or, at least assembling it. Add a spicy beef topping,chopped tomatoes, avocados, and sour cream to quick cheese nachos for a fun dinner. This gets messy, so you may need forks as well as fingers and lots of napkins.

For the topping:
1 tablespoon vegetable oil
1 small onion, finely
   chopped
1 clove garlic, minced
1/2 green pepper, seeded
   and finely chopped
1 pound lean ground beef
2 tablespoons yellow
   cornmeal
1 1/2 tablespoons chili
   powder
1 teaspoon salt
1 teaspoon cumin
1/2 teaspoon paprika
1/2 teaspoon oregano
Pepper to taste
2 tablespoons tomato
   paste
1 cup water

8 ounces tortilla chips
2 cups (8 ounces) grated
   Colby or Longhorn
   cheddar cheese

3 tomatoes, diced and
   drained of excess juice
1 ripe avocado, cut into
   chunks
1 4-ounce can pitted
   black olives, drained
Sour cream
Prepared salsa

+ Preheat the oven to 350°F.
+ To prepare the beef topping, heat the oil in a medium-size sauté pan over low heat and sauté the onion, garlic, and pepper until soft, stirring often.
+ Add the ground beef and cook until no longer pink. Drain all the fat from the meat.
+ Stir in the cornmeal and spices and sauté for 1 minute. Add the tomato paste and water and simmer for about 15 minutes until thickened.
+ Arrange the chips on a baking sheet in a single layer. Sprinkle the tops with the cheese and heat in the oven for 4 minutes or until the cheese is melted.
+ Put the spicy beef, tomatoes, avocado, olives, sour cream, and salsa in separate bowls. Transfer portions of the heated chips to dinner plates and let everyone add the toppings of his or her choice.

Serves 4

MENU

Cowboy's Nachos
Fresh fruit skewers
Chocolate milk shakes

Falafel Sandwiches

There are very few times that I make an exception to the no-fried-food rule—Falafels are one of those. These Middle Eastern special-ties, traditionally made with ground chick peas, fava beans, and spices, are as popular there as our hamburgers are here, and it's easy to taste why. Put a few falafel balls in a pita bread half, add chopped tomato, cucumber, onion, or lettuce, and top with a little tahini (ground sesame seeds, often sold next to the ground nuts and peanut butter), or with a thinned yogurt sauce.

¹/₄ cup fine-cut bulgur wheat
¹/₄ cup water
2 cups cooked chick peas (1 16- or 19-ounce can), drained
1 clove garlic
3 tablespoons dry bread crumbs
1 egg
1 tablespoon sesame seeds
1 teaspoon lemon juice
¹/₂ teaspoon salt
1 teaspoon cumin
¹/₈ teaspoon cayenne pepper
Vegetable oil for frying
6 medium- or large-size pita breads, cut in half
1 cup sesame tahini sauce or plain yogurt
Tomatoes, cucumbers, peppers, onions, and lettuce, chopped

♦ Combine the bulgur and water in a small bowl and let stand for 30 minutes.
♦ In the bowl of a food processor, add the chick peas and garlic, and process to a purée. Add the bulgur, bread crumbs, egg, sesame seeds, lemon juice, salt, and spices. Process with a few on-off pulses until well blended. Shape into 36 balls and refrigerate for at least 30 minutes.
♦ Add oil to a medium-size sauté pan to a depth of 2 inches. Heat the oil to 375°F.
♦ Fry the falafel balls in batches until golden.
♦ Drain well and keep warm on a baking sheet covered with paper towels in a 250°F oven.
♦ To make the sandwiches, place 3 falafel balls in each pita bread half. Add chopped vegetables and top with a spoonful of tahini or yogurt.

Serves 6

MENU

Falafel Sandwiches
Sliced oranges with mint and a pinch of sugar
Chocolate chip cookies (page 232)

Dilled Tuna & Tofu Sandwiches

If you're tired of ordinary tuna fish, this version is packed with added nutrition and wonderful flavor. It's great for fast dinners when time and energy are in short supply. Pita bread halves make great pockets for messy sandwich fillings.

2 6½-ounce cans solid white tuna in water
8 ounces extra-firm tofu
2 celery stalks, finely chopped
2 tablespoons minced red onion
½ cup fresh snipped dill
1 rounded tablespoon Dijon mustard
¾ cup mayonnaise, or enough to bind
Salt and pepper to taste
4 medium-size pita breads, cut in half

♦ Press the tuna to extract and drain as much water as possible. Add the tuna to a large bowl and break up with a fork.

♦ Drain the tofu, dice, and squeeze gently to extract as much water as possible. Add to the tuna with the celery, onion, and dill.

♦ In a small bowl, combine the mustard and mayonnaise. Toss with the tuna and tofu to bind.

♦ Season with salt and pepper.

♦ Spoon into the pita halves and serve.

Serves 6

MENU

Dilled Tuna & Tofu Salad Sandwiches
Cut-up carrots
Pretzels
Fruit Smoothies (page 271)

Croque Monsieur

In France, this is a culinary favorite served in every cafe and snack bar for lunch. In this country, it's just a variation on the popular ham-and-cheese sandwich—a cross between grilled ham-and-cheese and French toast. The Croque Monsieur becomes a Croque Madame with an egg (poached or fried) on top. Use more or less ham and cheese depending on how much filling you like in your sandwiches.

8 slices firm white sandwich bread, crusts removed

2 teaspoons Dijon mustard

4–8 very thin slices of lean boiled ham

8–16 thin slices of cheese (Monterey Jack, Muenster, or mozzarella)

1 egg

1/2 cup milk or half-and-half

1 1/2 tablespoons grated Parmesan cheese

2 tablespoons butter

4 poached or fried eggs, optional (for Croque Madame)

♦ Spread the mustard on one side of the bread slices.
♦ Divide the ham and cheese for 4 sandwiches. Put the sandwiches together placing the ham in the middle between the cheese.
♦ In a pie plate or shallow dish, beat the egg, milk, and Parmesan together.
♦ Allowing 1/2 tablespoon of butter for each sandwich, melt the butter in a large heavy sauté pan.
♦ Briefly dip the sandwiches in the egg-milk mixture, and sauté 2 sandwiches at a time over low heat until browned on both sides and the cheese is melted. Add more butter to the pan and continue to sauté the remaining sandwiches until golden.
♦ Serve hot with or without an egg on top.

Yields 4 sandwiches

MENU

Croque Monsieur
Cherry tomatoes
Fresh fruit salad (page 268)
Cupcakes

Grilled Reuben Sandwiches

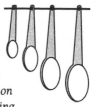

This is my much faster and flip answer to a corned beef and cabbage dinner. And everyone likes these. Classic Reuben sandwiches are made with sauerkraut, corned beef, and Swiss cheese, with Russian dressing on the side. I've substituted creamy coleslaw for the sauerkraut and dressing.

12 slices of rye or
    pumpernickel bread
Deli mustard
³/₄–1 pound lean corned
    beef, very thinly sliced
¹/₄ pound very thinly
    sliced Swiss cheese,
3–4 tablespoons butter
    for grilling the
    sandwiches
³/₄ pound creamy
    coleslaw (page 243)

+ Spread the bread generously with mustard.
+ Divide the corned beef among six slices of bread. Arrange the cheese on top and cover with the remaining slices of bread.
+ Heat half the butter in a large sauté pan. Cook a few sandwiches at a time until golden and crisp on the bottom. Turn, adding a bit more butter, and cook the other side until browned and hot.
+ Open the sandwiches, top with a spoonful of cool, creamy coleslaw, and close.
+ Cut each sandwich in half and serve hot.

Yields 6 sandwiches

MENU

Grilled Reuben Sandwiches
Dill pickles
Grapefruit and orange slices

Pan Bagna

Pan Bagna is a popular do-ahead sandwich that's great on a picnic or for an easy summer dinner. It's filled with ingredients native to the sunny Mediterranean area: tomatoes, eggplant, peppers, and olive oil. The only trick is finding a good, crusty French bread, yet one that is soft enough for a sandwich. This makes a great, messy, finger-food dinner for a summer night.

1 long crusty French bread
⅓ cup olive oil, approximately
3 large garden tomatoes, thinly sliced
8 slices grilled or roasted eggplant (page 188)
3 roasted peppers of any color (page 242)
Salt and pepper to taste
A few tablespoons chopped fresh basil or parsley
8 paper-thin slices prosciutto ham
8 thin slices cheese (provolone, Swiss, Muenster)

- Cut the bread in half horizontally and brush the cut sides with a few tablespoons of olive oil.
- Layer the bread with tomato slices, cooked eggplant, and roasted peppers, sprinkling each with salt, pepper, a little olive oil, and basil or parsley.
- Add the ham and cheese and top with the bread.
- Wrap the bread in foil and weight the sandwich for an hour with a heavy tray, bricks, or cans to allow the flavors to mellow.
- Cut in diagonal slices and serve.

Serves 6 to 8

MENU

Pan Bagna
Boiled Lobsters (page 249)
Watermelon slices and brownies (page 233)

Mediterranean Chevre & Tomato Baguette

When the garden is full of beautiful tomatoes, look no further for dinner. Buy a good loaf of French bread, chevre (fresh, soft goat cheese), fresh fruit, and a good chocolate bar. You can pretend you're on the sunny Mediterranean.

1 large French bread
¼ cup olive oil
8 ounces chevre or
   Boursin-type cheese
3 large tomatoes, peeled,
   seeded, and thinly
   sliced
½ red onion, very thinly
   sliced
Fresh basil leaves
Salt and pepper to taste

+ Preheat oven to 350°F.
+ Cut the bread in half horizontally and brush both sides with the olive oil. Crisp lightly in the oven for 5 minutes.
+ Cool the bread and spread the bottom half with the cheese. Layer the tomato and onion slices over the cheese. Top with fresh basil and season with salt and pepper. Cover with the other half of the bread.
+ Weight the sandwich with a heavy tray, bricks, or cans for 15 minutes before cutting into 8 diagonal slices to serve.

Serves 4

MENU

Mediterranean Chevre & Tomato Baguette
Mixed green salad
Fresh fruit and chocolate bars
Iced coffee or tea

Eggplant & Onion Bruschetta

Italian sandwiches have wonderful names: panino, crostini, and bruschetta. Crostini and bruschetta are based on toasted or grilled bread—the crostini are much smaller and often served as hors d'oeuvres. The toppings are usually vegetarian—you could use the Puttanesca (page 160) or Caponata sauces (page 161). This sandwich is much more than the simple sum of its parts.

½ cup olive oil

1 clove garlic, peeled and cut in half

1 medium eggplant, cut into ½-inch rounds

1 large sweet onion, peeled and cut into ½-inch slices

Salt and pepper to taste

1 Italian bread, cut into ¾-inch slices

2 ripe tomatoes, cut into thin slices

Fresh basil

♦ Preheat the broiler.

♦ Combine the oil and garlic, and let them sit for 15 minutes to flavor the oil. Brush two heavy jellyroll pans with some of the oil.

♦ Arrange the eggplant and onion slices in the pans in a single layer. Brush lightly with more oil, and sprinkle with salt and pepper.

♦ Broil the vegetables 6 inches from the heating element until lightly browned, about 5 minutes.

♦ Turn very carefully with a spatula and brush with a bit more oil. Sprinkle with salt and pepper.

♦ Broil the vegetables until lightly colored and softened. The onion may cook more quickly than the eggplant, so remove it to a platter when it's done. If necessary, turn the eggplant again, lower the pan away from the heat, and cook until softened.

♦ Remove the eggplant to the platter and cover with foil to steam and cool. This can be done ahead (and refrigerated when cooled) since the open-face sandwiches are eaten at room temperature.

♦ Turn the oven temperature down to 350°F and let it cool down for a few minutes. Brush the bread rounds lightly with the remaining oil and toast in the oven on a baking sheet for 5 to 10 minutes until a bit crisp and lightly colored, turning once.

♦ To serve, arrange a slice of eggplant and a few onion rings on each piece of bread. Top with a slice of tomato, a sprinkling of fresh basil, and salt and pepper to taste.

Serves 4 to 6

MENU

Eggplant & Onion Bruschetta
Mixed green salad with a cheesy dressing
Glazed Chocolate Pan Cake (page 208)

Corny Mexican Waffles

Savory waffles for dinner are sure to capture your family's imagination. Mexican flavors suggest serving these with chili (from a can or your freezer), or salsa and sour cream, or sprinkle them with grated Longhorn cheddar cheese. Or put the condiments out and let everyone choose his or her own toppings.

1¾ cups buttermilk
2 eggs
⅓ cup vegetable oil
1 4-ounce can chopped green chilies, mild or hot, drained
2 tablespoons snipped chives or scallion greens
1½ cups flour
½ cup yellow cornmeal
2 tablespoons sugar
1 tablespoon baking powder
½ teaspoon salt
½ teaspoon baking soda

Toppings: grated Longhorn cheddar cheese, chili, salsa, sour cream

♦ In a large bowl, combine the buttermilk, eggs, oil, chilies, and chives or scallions. Stir with a fork to mix thoroughly.
♦ In a medium-size bowl, combine the flour, cornmeal, sugar, baking powder, salt, and baking soda. Combine the wet and dry ingredients in the large bowl and stir together lightly and briefly until well mixed.
♦ Ladle a spoonful of batter onto a heated waffle iron and cook according to the waffle iron directions.
♦ Keep the waffles hot on a wire rack in a 200°F oven.
♦ If you top the waffles with cheese, do it while they're hot. Serve with chili, salsa, or sour cream.

Yields 9 double waffles to serve 4 to 6

MENU

Corny Mexican Waffles
Green salad with orange sections, red onions, and French dressing
Cafe Olé (strong coffee with hot milk and a dash of cinnamon and cocoa)

Chicken Fajitas

*P*opular restaurant fajitas are easily made at home with chicken, beef, pork, or even eggs. Dinners seem to be more fun when you can eat with your fingers.

3 chicken breast halves boned and skinned

For the marinade:
¹/₄ cup lime juice
2 tablespoons vegetable oil
1 tablespoon Balsamic vinegar
1 clove garlic, minced
¹/₂ teaspoon cumin
¹/₄ teaspoon chili powder
¹/₂ teaspoon salt
Pepper to taste

1 tablespoon vegetable oil
1 large sweet onion, cut in half and thinly sliced
1 large red pepper, seeded and cut into thin julienne strips
3 tablespoons chopped cilantro
8–10 8-inch flour tortillas

Toppings: cubed avocado, sour cream or plain yogurt, salsa

♦ Cut the chicken breasts into ¹/₂-inch strips.
♦ Add the marinade ingredients to a medium-size glass or plastic container and stir to combine. Add the chicken, toss, cover, and marinate in the refrigerator for 1 hour.
♦ Preheat the oven to 350°F.
♦ Wrap the tortillas in foil and warm them in the oven for 5 minutes before serving.
♦ Heat 1 tablespoon of oil in a large nonstick sauté pan over medium heat and add the onions and peppers. Stir-fry for just a few minutes until the vegetables are tender but crisp.
♦ Add the chicken with the marinade and stir-fry until the chicken is opaque throughout and the marinade is nearly evaporated, about 5 minutes. Stir in the cilantro.
♦ To serve, spoon portions of the chicken and vegetables on the warm tortillas and add the toppings of your choice. Wrap or roll the tortillas and eat hot with your fingers.

Serves 4

MENU

Chicken Fajitas
Beans and rice (page 155)
Tropical fruit salad (mango, kiwi, pineapple, bananas)

Breads, Coffeecakes
& Rolls

*B*ring on the bread! It can be a nutritious addition to any dinner, a great source of energizing carbohydrates, a sponge for soups and last drops of sauces or dressings, and the basis of croûtes, croutons, and garlic bread. If you have a bread machine, yeast breads can easily be part of your dinner hour. In **Rescuing the Dinner Hour**, I've avoided using yeast and tried to stick with the chemical leaveners—baking soda and baking powder.

Baking soda reacts with acid ingredients in the dough or batter (buttermilk, sour cream, yogurt, orange juice) to form carbon dioxide bubbles that make the dough rise.

Baking powder contains baking soda and an acid that reacts with water/liquid in the batter to form carbon dioxide bubbles.

Both baking soda and baking powder lose their zip and power as they sit, so buy them in small quantities and replace them a few times a year.

For quick breads, biscuits, and scones, always use a light touch, or you'll end up with a tough product. Mix the wet and dry ingredients until combined, and don't beat the batter or knead the dough excessively. The amount of liquid needed to reach the right consistency will vary slightly, and after a while you will get very good at knowing when you need to add another tablespoon or two.

Beer Bread

Bread and cheese can be a fine meal when the bread is homemade, the cheeses are unusual and interesting, and they're accompanied by a good salad and fruit. Beer bread is easy and fun to make, and it tastes great with cheddars, Swiss, and other assertive cheeses.

3 cups flour
2 tablespoons sugar
1 tablespoon + 1 teaspoon baking powder
1 teaspoon salt
$^{1}/_{2}$ teaspoon baking soda
1 12-ounce can of beer
6 tablespoons butter, melted

- Preheat the oven to 350°F. Grease and flour 1 4$^{1}/_{2}$ x 8$^{1}/_{2}$-inch loaf pan.
- Combine the flour, sugar, baking powder, salt, and baking soda. Stir in the beer until just blended—don't over mix.
- Turn into the prepared pan and drizzle the top with the melted butter.
- Bake for 50 to 55 minutes until browned and crusty and a toothpick inserted in the center comes out clean.
- Turn out of the pan and cool on a wire rack for 10 minutes before cutting into thin slices with a serrated knife. Serve with cheese.

Yields 1 loaf

MENU

Beer Bread
Assorted cheeses
Mixed green salad with raw sliced mushrooms and cherry tomatoes
Apple slices dipped in honey and granola

Currant & Caraway Scones

Scones are fast to make and bake, and they transform an ordinary sandwich into dinnertime fare. Currants are similar to raisins, but smaller, more tart, and less squishy in texture. Smoked turkey and chutney are a perfect match for these currant and caraway seeded scones. Any leftovers are delicious for breakfast, toasted with butter and honey.

3½ cups flour
½ cup sugar
1 tablespoon + 1 teaspoon baking powder
1 teaspoon salt
8 tablespoons butter
1 teaspoon caraway seeds
½ cup currants
2 eggs
¾ cup milk

♦ Preheat the oven to 425°F. Lightly grease a heavy baking sheet.

♦ In a large bowl, sift together the flour, sugar, baking powder, and salt. Cut in the butter with a pastry blender or 2 knives. Stir in the caraway seeds and currants.

♦ Beat the eggs and milk together in a small bowl, and add to the dry ingredients. Stir with a fork until the dough comes together.

♦ Turn the dough onto a lightly floured surface and knead a few times to form a ball. Add a few more tablespoons of milk if the dough seems too dry. Roll or press the dough to a ¾-inch thickness. Cut the dough with a 3-inch round biscuit cutter or glass and arrange the scones on the prepared baking sheet. Dip the cutter or glass in flour as needed to prevent sticking.

♦ Bake for about 15 minutes in the upper half of the oven until lightly colored and springy in the center. Remove to a wire rack to cool for a few minutes before serving warm with butter.

Yields 14 3-inch scones

MENU

Currant & Caraway Scones
Smoked turkey and fruit chutney (page 167)
Coleslaw (page 243)
Apple cider, hot or cold

Mexican Cornbread

Cornbread is welcome anytime of the year—for summer picnics or with barbequed foods, for sandwiches or snacks. It can be plain, or, as in this recipe, filled with wonderful goodies to make it practically a meal in itself. Leftovers are great for ham or smoked turkey sandwiches.

1¹/₂ cups flour
1¹/₂ cups yellow cornmeal
¹/₄ cup sugar
1 tablespoon baking
 powder
¹/₂ teaspoon salt
¹/₄ cup vegetable oil
³/₄ cup milk
2 eggs
1 8-ounce can creamed
 corn
1 4-ounce can mild green
 chilies, chopped
2 cups (8 ounces)
 Monterey Jack or Colby
 cheddar cheese, grated
2 scallions, chopped

♦ Preheat the oven to 400°F. Grease a 9 x 13-inch baking pan.

♦ In a large bowl, combine the flour, cornmeal, sugar, baking power, and salt.

♦ In another large bowl, combine the oil and milk and beat in the eggs. Stir in the creamed corn, chilies, cheese, and scallions. Combine the wet and dry ingredients and stir just until moistened—don't over mix.

♦ Spread the batter in the prepared pan and bake in the middle of the oven for about 30 minutes until a toothpick inserted in the center comes out clean. Cool for a few minutes before cutting into 12 squares.

Yields 12 large pieces

MENU

Barbecued ribs
Mexican Cornbread
Carrot slaw
Black or Brown Cows (page 205)

Cinnamon Sticks

These cinnamon sticks are a great treat for breakfast—and for dinner as well. So, reverse the meal order and serve a real breakfast at dinnertime when everyone's together.

For the dough:
2 cups flour
$^1/_3$ cup sugar
2 teaspoons baking powder
$^1/_2$ teaspoon salt
8 tablespoons cold butter
$^1/_2$ cup milk

For the filling:
3 tablespoons butter, melted
$^1/_4$ cup + 1 tablespoon sugar
1 teaspoon cinnamon
$^1/_2$ cup finely chopped pecans

+ In a large bowl, combine the flour, sugar, baking powder, and salt. Add the cold butter and blend with a pastry blender or 2 knives until it resembles coarse meal. Add the milk and stir with a fork until the dough begins to come together. Knead a few times until it forms a ball.
+ Enclose in plastic wrap and refrigerate to chill.
+ Preheat the oven to 375°F. Lightly grease a heavy baking sheet.
+ Divide the dough in half and roll out each piece to form an 11-inch circle on a floured surface. Brush with a tablespoon of the melted butter.
+ To prepare the filling, combine $^1/_4$ cup of the sugar, cinnamon, and pecans and sprinkle half the mixture evenly over each circle of dough.
+ Cut like a pie into 8 wedges. Starting from the outside edge, roll the dough into a long stick. Arrange seam side down, on the prepared baking sheet. Roll out the other piece of dough and assemble in the same way. Brush the tops of the sticks with the remaining butter and sprinkle with the remaining tablespoon of sugar.
+ Bake in the upper half of the oven until golden brown, about 20 minutes. Reduce the heat to 350°F during the last 10 minutes if the bottoms are browning too quickly.

Yields 16 cinnamon sticks

MENU

Vegetable juice with celery sticks
Soft scrambled eggs and bacon on soft toasted rolls
Orange slices
Cinnamon Sticks

Chocolate Chip Pan Muffins

An easy main course leaves you time to make these irresistible chocolate-studded muffins. Pan muffins eliminate the need to grease individual muffin tins—and clean them.

2 cups flour
1 cup + 2 tablespoons sugar
1 tablespoon baking powder
1/2 teaspoon salt
1 cup semisweet chocolate chips
2 eggs
1/3 cup vegetable oil
3/4 cup milk
1 teaspoon vanilla

- Preheat the oven to 400°F. Grease a 9-inch square baking pan.
- In a large bowl, stir together the flour, 1 cup sugar, baking powder, and salt. Stir in the chocolate chips.
- In a small bowl, beat together the eggs, oil, milk, and vanilla. Combine with the dry ingredients in a few swift strokes just until blended—don't over mix.
- Transfer the batter to the prepared pan and bake in the upper half of the oven for 25 minutes until golden, the center is springy, and a toothpick inserted in the center comes out clean. Remove from the oven and sprinkle with 2 tablespoons of sugar.
- Cool slightly and cut into 9 muffins. Serve warm.
- To re-heat, microwave for about 15 seconds, or until the chocolate is warm and gooey.

Yields 9 muffins

NOTE: To make **Lemon-Poppyseed Pan Muffins**, eliminate the chocolate chips and add 3 tablespoons poppyseeds and the grated zest of 1 lemon. Taste the poppyseeds before using to be sure they're fresh. Like nuts, they can become rancid with time and leave a bad aftertaste. To prevent this, store them in the freezer in an airtight container.

MENU

Artichokes (page 241) stuffed with seafood salad (page 243)
Dinner rolls
Fresh pineapple
Chocolate Chip Pan Muffins

Blueberry Pan Muffins

When it's native blueberry season, it's definitely time to make blueberry muffins. If you have a good source of blueberries, freeze the unwashed fruit in plastic bags or containers so you can enjoy blueberry muffins all year-round. Blueberry Pan Muffins are just as delicious as my favorite blueberry muffins, but in an easier and neater form.

2 eggs
1¼ cups + 2 tablespoons sugar
1 teaspoon vanilla
⅓ cup vegetable oil
2¼ cups flour
1 tablespoon baking powder
½ teaspoon salt
½ cup milk
2 cups blueberries, small are best
½ teaspoon cinnamon

+ Preheat the oven to 400°F. Grease the bottom and sides of a 9-inch square pan.
+ In a mixing bowl, beat the eggs on medium-high speed, adding the 1¼ cups sugar gradually, until light and fluffy, about 4 minutes. Beat in the vanilla. On low speed, add the oil just until blended.
+ In a large bowl, sift together the flour, baking powder, and salt. Add to the creamed ingredients alternately with the milk on low speed just until blended. Lightly fold in the blueberries. Transfer to the prepared pan.
+ In a small bowl, mix together the cinnamon and 2 tablespoons of sugar. Sprinkle the mixture evenly over the batter.
+ Bake in the middle of the preheated oven for about 35 minutes, until a toothpick inserted in the center comes out clean and the cake is springy to the touch.
+ Cool for 10 minutes before cutting. Serve warm.

Yields 9 square muffins

MENU

Sangria (page 270)
Chicken or seafood salad (page 243) in scooped-out tomatoes
Potato chips
Blueberry Pan Muffins

Cream Cheese Rugelach

*N*ot *too sweet, rugelach are small, rolled pastries usually filled with walnuts, raisins, and cinnamon. If you prepare the dough ahead of time, the rolling and baking can become a quick project. Be creative with the filling and add dates or dried apricots if you like. I've even had chocolate chip rugelach.*

For the dough:
2 cups flour
2 tablespoons sugar
2 teaspoons baking
  powder
1/2 teaspoon salt
8 tablespoons butter
8 ounces cream cheese
1/4 cup melted butter

For the filling:
1/2 cup packed light
  brown sugar
1 teaspoon cinnamon
3/4 cup finely chopped
  walnuts
1/4 cup golden raisins
1/4 cup flaked coconut
1/2 cup chopped dried
  pineapple

Sugar for the top

- To make the dough, combine the flour, sugar, baking powder, and salt in a processor bowl. Add the butter and cream cheese to the bowl and process with a few on-off turns until it resembles coarse meal. Process until it just forms a ball of dough. Enclose in plastic wrap and chill before rolling.
- At baking time, preheat the oven to 375°F.
- Divide the dough into 3 pieces. On a lightly floured surface, roll the dough, 1 piece at a time to form a 12-inch circle. Brush the dough lightly with a tablespoon of the melted butter.
- Combine the filling ingredients in a small bowl and sprinkle 1/3 of the mixture evenly over the circle of dough. With a pizza wheel or knife, cut into 12 wedges and roll up, beginning at the outer edge.
- Arrange, seam side down on an ungreased baking sheet. Repeat with the remaining dough and filling. Brush the tops lightly with the remaining butter and a pinch of sugar.
- Bake in the upper half of the oven for 20 to 25 minutes until lightly browned. Reduce the heat to 350°F during the last 10 minutes if the bottoms are browning too quickly.
- Cool on a rack. Store in a tin.

Yields 36 rugelach

MENU

Baked potatoes with toppings (page 254)
Citrus fruit salad (page 268)
Cream Cheese Rugelach

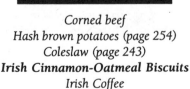

Irish Cinnamon-Oatmeal Biscuits

The oats and cornmeal add texture, and the cinnamon adds flavor to this simple drop biscuit. It's as good for breakfast and snacking as it is for dinner. When the oven temperature is this hot, the baking sheet must be heavy or it will twist and warp in the hot oven.

1¼ cups flour
½ cup + 2 tablespoons quick rolled oats
¼ cup yellow cornmeal
⅓ cup sugar
1½ teaspoons baking powder
½ teaspoon cinnamon
½ teaspoon salt
½ teaspoons baking soda
2 tablespoons butter
¾ cup buttermilk, approximately
1 egg

♦ Preheat the oven to 425°F. Lightly grease a heavy baking sheet and sprinkle with 2 tablespoons of rolled oats.
♦ In a large bowl, combine the flour, oats, cornmeal, sugar, baking powder, cinnamon, salt, and baking soda. Stir to combine. Cut in the butter with a pastry blender or 2 knives until it resembles coarse meal.
♦ In a separate bowl, whisk together the buttermilk and egg. Add to the dry ingredients, stirring with a fork just until blended and a moist dough forms.
♦ Scoop about 10 rounded serving spoons of dough onto the prepared baking sheet about 2 inches apart. Flatten the dough slightly, to about ¾-inch, with lightly floured fingers.
♦ Bake in the middle of the oven for about 12 minutes until lightly colored. Turn the oven temperature down to 400°F half way through the baking if it's browning too quickly on the bottom.

Yields 10 biscuits

MENU

Corned beef
Hash brown potatoes (page 254)
Coleslaw (page 243)
Irish Cinnamon-Oatmeal Biscuits
Irish Coffee

Christmas Scones

Even if you're not a baker, it's hard to resist the fun of homey, memory-making holiday baking. Chocolate is nearly forgotten amidst the dried and glacéed fruits, nuts, and spices that feature prominently in holiday goodies. Serve these scones for brunch or even for dessert year-round.

½ cup whole blanched almonds
1 tablespoon + ⅔ cup sugar
2½ cups flour
1 tablespoon baking powder
½ teaspoon salt
½ teaspoon ground cardamom, optional
8 tablespoons butter
½ cup currants
¼ cup finely chopped dried apricots
¼ cup finely chopped dried pineapple
1 cup light cream
1 egg
2 teaspoons vanilla

+ Preheat the oven to 425°F. Lightly grease 2 heavy baking sheets.
+ Process the almonds with the 1 tablespoon of sugar until finely ground, being careful not to let the mixture turn into paste.
+ In a large bowl, combine the almonds with the flour, baking powder, ⅔ cup sugar, salt, and cardamon. Cut in the butter with a pastry blender or 2 knives until it resembles coarse meal. Stir in the currants, apricots, and pineapple.
+ In another bowl, combine the cream, egg, and vanilla. Add to the dry ingredients and stir with a fork until the dough comes together—don't over work.
+ With a soup spoon, drop mounds of dough onto the prepared baking sheet. Wet your hands and flatten slightly.
+ Place in the upper half of the oven and immediately reduce the temperature to 400°F. Bake for 12 to 15 minutes until lightly colored.

Yields 24 2½-inch scones

MENU

Tangerines or Clementines
Scrambled eggs with chives and a dash of Tabasco
French bread toast and jam
Christmas Scones
Hot chocolate (page 270)

Holiday Fruit Bread

Baked goodies, and especially quick breads, are holiday favorites—flavored with nuts and fruits, and perfect when extra company's around for breakfast, lunch, snacks, or even dinner. Quick breads keep well, and even freeze well, so they can be made ahead of time.

2 cups flour
2 teaspoons baking powder
1/2 teaspoon salt
Grating of nutmeg (about 1/8 teaspoon)
8 tablespoons butter, at room temperature
3/4 cup granulated sugar
1/2 cup light brown sugar
2 eggs
1 teaspoon vanilla
2/3 cup milk
1 cup finely chopped mixed fruit (dried apricots, currants, dried pineapple, pitted dates, glacéed cherries)
1/2 cup chopped walnuts

- Preheat the oven to 350°F. Grease a 9 x 5-inch loaf pan (or 4 3 x 5½-inch pans).
- Sift the flour, baking powder, and salt in a large bowl, and stir in the nutmeg.
- In a mixing bowl, beat the butter until soft. Add the sugars and cream well. Add the eggs and vanilla and beat for about 5 minutes, until fluffy.
- Alternately add the milk and dry ingredients, mixing on low speed just until blended. Fold in the fruits and nuts.
- Transfer to the prepared pan and bake in the upper half of the oven for 60 to 70 minutes or until a toothpick inserted in the center comes out clean. The bread will begin to shrink away from the sides of the pan and the top will be golden. Reduce the temperature to 325°F if bread begins to brown too quickly.
- Let the bread sit for 10 minutes before running a knife around the edge and turning it out onto a wire rack. Cool completely and cut into slices to serve. Wrap in foil and then store in a plastic bag.

Yields 1 9 x 5-inch loaf or 4 3 x 5½-inch loaves

MENU

Seafood chowder (page 14) or corn chowder (page 20)
Cut-up vegetables served with hummus (page 168)
Breadsticks
Holiday Fruit Bread *served with soft cream cheese*
Tangerines or Clementines

Almond-Sour Cream Coffeecake

This almond cake is rich with almond paste and sour cream, has a fine texture, and works well for dessert with fresh fruit or ice cream. It's worth the time and expense!

8 tablespoons butter, at room temperature
²/₃ cup sugar
1 7-ounce tube almond paste, cut into chunks
2 eggs, at room temperature
1 teaspoon vanilla
1½ cups flour
1½ teaspoons baking powder
½ teaspoon salt
¼ teaspoon baking soda
½ cup sour cream, at room temperature
3 tablespoons sliced almonds

+ Preheat the oven to 350°F. Grease well and lightly flour a 9 x 5-inch loaf pan.
+ In a mixing bowl, cream the butter and sugar on high speed until very light. Beat in the almond paste until smooth and light, about 5 minutes.
+ Add the eggs and vanilla, beating for 5 more minutes, until fluffy.
+ Sift the dry ingredients into a large bowl and add alternately with the sour cream to the creamed ingredients, mixing on very low speed, until thoroughly combined.
+ Transfer the batter to the prepared pan, sprinkle with the almonds, and bake in the middle of the preheated oven, about 55 minutes, until a toothpick inserted in the center comes out clean and the cake begins to pull away from the sides of the pan. The center of the cake should be springy.
+ Cool on a rack for 15 minutes, turn out of the pan, cool completely, and wrap in foil.
+ At serving time, slice the cake and serve with sliced, sweetened strawberries and whipped cream.

Yields 1 9 x 5-inch loaf

MENU

Scrambled eggs with cream cheese and chives on toasted English muffins
Bacon
Orange juice and coffee
Almond-Sour Cream Coffeecake *with strawberries and whipped cream*

Cakes, Pies, Cobblers, Crisps, Cookies & Bars

D esserts are a joyful ending to the dinner hour, and not necessarily a time-consuming element. In my house, it's hard to offer my children only a piece of fruit since they consider fruit a snack between meals or something to top their breakfast cereal. I have a stash of chocolate bars which will sometimes suffice for dessert if I call it a "Chocolate Tasting," or the chocolate can be chopped up and served over ice cream or frozen yogurt. When I don't have time to bake, there are many convenient solutions.

Fresh fruit can be embellished in many ways. Cut-up and skewered on bamboo sticks, it can be served on a pretty platter with bowls of coconut, chopped nuts, jimmies, or granola for rolling, or a bowl of vanilla yogurt for dipping. The old favorites of strawberries and confectioners' sugar, or strawberries with sour cream and brown sugar for dipping, are still popular.

When fresh fruit is looking less than at its peak, there is always frozen fruit (sweetened strawberries and raspberries) to top angel cake, poundcake, and ice cream or frozen yogurt. Citrus fruit is nearly always available since it keeps so well.

Fruit Smoothies are similar to milkshakes but with fruit (fresh or frozen) and yogurt as the thickener rather than ice cream (page 271).

Brown Cows (root beer and vanilla ice cream) and **Black Cows** (cola and vanilla ice cream) are reminders of my childhood, and great fun for dessert.

Ice cream, frozen yogurt, sherbet, sorbet, ices, juice bars, and **ice cream treats** (sandwiches, bars, and sundae cups) are always in the grocery freezer, or you can make homemade ice cream sandwiches with your choice of ice cream and soft cookies. Wrapped individually in plastic, they make fine desserts or snacks.

In the dairy case, there are ready-made desserts like puddings, tapiocas, and rice pudding. Or you can shake up an instant pudding from a packaged mix with milk. Yogurt, in so many new flavors and combinations, has taken over the role that puddings once played in our diets.

There are innumerable cookies, cakes, pies, and baked desserts at the bakery, in the supermarkets and in take-out shops to make your dinner hour easier.

Baked Desserts

There are days in the winter when I'd rather bake than cook—smell the aroma of baking and feel the warmth of the oven. At times like that I think of a really easy dinner (spaghetti and salad, or a rotisserie chicken and cut up vegetables for dipping) and use my limited time making a pie or cake that bakes during dinner. I may have plenty of leftovers in the refrigerator that need no more than a good salad and a homemade dessert to make dinner seem new and special.

Pies are especially easy if I've made the pie dough ahead of time and chilled it in the refrigerator, or if I have a frozen crust on hand.

Layer cakes with frosting seem too time consuming for quick dinner hours, but single layer cakes, loaded with texture and flavor, with baked toppings or glazes, make just the right amount of dessert and are do-able during a hectic week. Save the meringue layers, mousseline buttercreams, and piped decorations for the weekend guests.

Some Baking Tips

Pies

Use cold butter and ice water in making the pie dough. Handle the dough as little as possible so it doesn't become elastic and tough. Pies like to be baked on the lower shelf of the oven so the bottom crust gets browned and crisped. The crust should be a nice golden color, not pale. Reheat fruit pies on the bottom rack of a 375°F oven for 15 minutes.

Cakes

Try to have all your cake ingredients at room temperature. The butter and milk can go in the microwave for a few seconds, and the eggs can be quickly warmed in hot water. This warmer temperature makes it easier for the butter and sugar to cream, and for the sugar to dissolve so it's not gritty between your fingers. The shortening, sugar, and eggs form a light emulsion that incorporates air to help the cake rise.

Butter gives cakes a fine flavor; shortening, which is already light and emulsified, makes cakes light in texture; and oil makes them very moist and a little denser.

Flour

For cakes and cookies, use an all-purpose, unbleached white flour, not bread flour or self-rising flour. Cake flour produces a lighter textured cake, and can be imitated by substituting 2 tablespoons of cornstarch for 2 tablespoons of flour in each cup of flour used in the recipe. Bread flour has more gluten/protein that helps the yeast raise the bread dough, but it produces heavy cakes. All flour should be fluffed before scooping into a measuring cup and leveled off.

Mixing the Batter

When making cakes, the time to beat the batter is when you are creaming the butter, sugar, and eggs. After that, turn the mixer on a low speed and add the dry and wet ingredients alternately, just until thoroughly blended. Stop the mixer to scrape the bottom of the bowl to be sure the batter is mixed thoroughly. Overbeaten batter cakes will develop holes.

Preparing the Pan

Use solid vegetable shortening for greasing cake pans and baking sheets since it has a higher burning point than butter. If the recipe calls for greasing **and** flouring, sprinkle the bottom of the pan with flour, shake it around, and knock out the excess. This makes it easier to remove the cakes and gives them a browned edge.

Helping the Cake Rise Evenly

Pour the batter into the prepared pan and spread it 1/2-inch up the sides and all around the pan, or tilt the pan if the batter is loose, so the batter goes 1/2-inch up the sides. This gives the cake a start in its rising.

Bake cakes in the middle to upper half of the oven so the tops brown more readily. Opening the oven door frequently to check on the cake will cause a large loss of heat and uneven temperatures while the cake struggles to rise. Have a toothpick ready and make your testing quick.

Ready or Not—How to Know When the Cake is Done

+ A toothpick inserted in the center will come out clean—with no wet, gummy batter adhering to it.
+ The cake may be golden or the top will spring back when gently pressed.
+ The cake will begin to pull away from the sides of the pan.
+ If you listen closely, the cake will sound *quiet*, without the sound of the moisture evaporating—really!

Storing Cakes

Frosting protects cakes from drying out, so cover the cut, unfrosted surface of cakes with plastic wrap to store. Frosted cakes may be stored in the refrigerator, but they should be brought to room temperature before serving so the frosting doesn't have a waxy consistency.

Brownies, bars, and unfrosted cakes should be covered with plastic wrap and stored in a heavy plastic bag.

Cookies

Cookies always seem best when they're freshly baked, so bake them as you need them. Keep some dough in the refrigerator or freezer in a labeled plastic container. Since cookies take only a short time to bake, it's very important not to open the oven door frequently to check on them. That makes the oven temperature drop and causes the heating element to come on to compensate for the heat loss, and that **burns the bottom of the cookies**. Bake cookies in the upper half of the oven away from the heating element. The best way to prevent burned bottoms, is to preheat the oven 25°F higher than the baking temperature, **if** you can remember to turn it down as soon as you put the baking sheet in the oven. That will compensate for the 25°F drop in temperature when you open the oven door. Some of the new, double-layer baking sheets are supposed to eliminate the burning problem. You can duplicate this by using two baking sheets, one on top of the other. Quality baking sheets should be heavy stainless steel.

Glazed Chocolate Pan Cake

This has become the only chocolate cake I make for quick week-day dinners, although it's good enough for company any time. The ganache glaze is a quick alternative to cake frostings. Use good chocolate for the best results.

For the cake:
1/3 cup unsweetened
    Dutch cocoa*
1/3 cup hot water
1 cup flour
1 teaspoon baking
    powder
1/4 teaspoon baking soda
1/4 teaspoon salt
2 eggs, at room
    temperature
1 cup granulated sugar
1/2 teaspoon vanilla
1/4 cup vegetable oil
2/3 cup buttermilk

For the glaze:
1/4 cup heavy or whipping
    cream
3 ounces dark, bitter-
    sweet chocolate,
    chopped
1/4 teaspoon vanilla
1/4 cup confectioners'
    sugar

- Preheat the oven to 375°F. Lightly grease a 9-inch square cake pan.
- In a small bowl, mix the cocoa and hot water until smooth. Set aside.
- In another bowl, sift the flour, baking powder, baking soda, and salt together.
- In a mixing bowl, beat the eggs with the granulated sugar until light and fluffy, about 4 minutes.
- Mix in the cocoa mixture, vanilla, and oil on low speed, scraping the bottom of the bowl with a spatula until thoroughly blended. On low speed, add the dry ingredients and buttermilk alternately, mixing just until blended. Scrape the bottom of the bowl again. Transfer the batter to the prepared pan.
- Bake in the upper half of the oven for about 40 minutes until a toothpick inserted in the center comes out clean. Cool on a wire rack for 10 minutes while you prepare the glaze.
- Heat the cream in a small heavy saucepan until nearly boiling. Remove from the heat, add the chocolate, cover, and let it sit for 5 minutes. Add the vanilla and stir until smooth. Sift the confectioners' sugar over the chocolate and stir until smooth.
- Pour the glaze over the warm cake and spread it evenly to the edges. Cut the cake into 9 3-inch squares and serve slightly warm or at room temperature.

Yields 1 9-inch square cake

* If you use Hershey's cocoa, eliminate the baking powder and use 1 teaspoon baking soda.

MENU

Grilled lamb chops (page 247)
Grilled marinated vegetable kebabs
Wheat Pilaf (page 252)
Glazed Chocolate Pan Cake

Gingerbread Cake with Blueberries & Cream

Gingerbread cakes are old-time favorites that are compatible with our contemporary need for simplicity and ease. This cake is not too sweet, has a wonderful texture, and is loaded with flavor. For a fancier dessert, it pairs wonderfully with whipped cream and fruit (blueberries, poached or even canned pears, kiwi slices, mangoes, bananas). This is a cake I love for breakfast with lots of dark coffee. The crystallized ginger gives it great zip and a real ginger flavor.

1/3 cup vegetable shortening
1/2 cup sugar
1 egg, at room temperature
1/4 cup dark molasses
1 cup flour
1 teaspoon cinnamon
1 teaspoon powdered ginger
1 teaspoon unsweetened cocoa
1/2 teaspoon baking soda
1/4 teaspoon salt
1/3 cup hot coffee
3 tablespoons minced crystallized ginger

1 pint blueberries
1 cup heavy cream, sweetened and whipped at serving time

+ Preheat the oven to 350°F. Grease an 8-inch round cake pan.
+ In a mixing bowl on medium speed, beat the shortening and sugar together until creamed. Beat in the egg until light and smooth, about 4 minutes. On low speed, slowly beat in the molasses.
+ In another bowl, sift together the flour, cinnamon, ginger, cocoa, baking soda, and salt. Add alternately with the hot coffee, mixing on low speed just until blended. Add the crystallized ginger.
+ Transfer the batter to the prepared pan and bake in the upper half of the oven for 35 minutes or until the top is springy and a toothpick inserted in the center comes out clean.
+ Cut into wedges and serve slightly warm or at room temperature with blueberries and whipped cream on top.

Yields 1 8-inch round cake

MENU

Pot roast (page 90)
Sautéed spinach
Noodles
Mixed green salad vinaigrette
Gingerbread Cake with Blueberries & Cream

Ladyfinger Cheesecakes with Fresh Fruit

When you'd like a cake for dessert, but it's too hot to turn on the oven, use convenient ladyfingers for this easy summer dessert. Ladyfingers are usually the basis of rich finales like tiramisu, the Italian dessert with rich mascarpone double-cream cheese, whipped cream, and liqueurs; or trifles layered with cake, egg-enriched custard, and fruits. In this dessert the filling is made with cream cheese and just about any light-colored fruit juice concentrate (orange, lemonade, or even piña colada or dacquiri mixes), and topped with fresh fruits. These quick Ladyfinger Cheesecakes are best if you make them a few hours ahead of serving time.

1 package of ladyfingers (12)

6 ounces cream cheese

3 to 4 tablespoons lemonade or orange juice concentrate, or orange liqueur

3 tablespoons confectioners' sugar, or to taste

Fresh raspberries, blueberries, sliced peaches, kiwis, or strawberries

♦ Separate the ladyfingers and open them up like sandwiches.

♦ In a mixing bowl, prepare the filling by beating the cream cheese and juice concentrate (or liqueur) together to a thick but spreadable consistency. Add the sugar to taste.

♦ Spread about 2 teaspoons of the cheese mixture on each half of each ladyfinger. Sandwich the fruit between the ladyfinger halves.

♦ Arrange the cakes on a platter and cover with plastic wrap. Refrigerate for at least a few hours to combine the flavors.

♦ Dust with confectioners' sugar before serving.

Yields 12 cheesecakes

MENU

Hamburgers (page 173)
Pasta salad (pages 47, 48, 49)
Garden tomato slices
Ladyfinger Cheesecakes with Fresh Fruit

Orange Angel Cake

This dessert cake is heavenly, especially when served with sliced strawberries sprinkled with sugar. It's similar to angel cake—made with beaten egg whites—but does have a stick of butter and baking powder for leavening as well. The texture is both moist and airy. The subtle flavor of the cake can be changed by steeping fresh ginger, coffee beans, lemon peel, or anise seeds in the milk instead of orange peel. Do try it!

1¹/₂ tablespoons + 1³/₄ cups flour
1¹/₂ tablespoons + 1¹/₄ cups + ¹/₄ cup sugar
1 cup milk
Zest from 1 orange
8 tablespoons butter, at room temperature
1 teaspoon vanilla
¹/₄ cup cornstarch
2 teaspoons baking powder
¹/₂ teaspoon salt
4 egg whites, at room temperature

- Preheat oven to 350°F.
- In a small bowl, mix together 1¹/₂ tablespoons of flour and 1¹/₂ tablespoons of sugar. Grease a heavy 9-inch bundt pan and lightly dust with the flour/sugar mixture. Shake out the excess.
- Combine the milk and orange zest in a small saucepan and bring to a boil over low heat. Remove from the heat, cover, and let sit until cool. Remove the zest.
- In a mixing bowl, beat the butter, adding 1¹/₄ cups of sugar slowly, until well creamed, about 4 minutes. Add the vanilla and ¹/₄ cup of the milk and beat well.
- In a large bowl, sift 1³/₄ cups flour, cornstarch, baking powder, and salt together. Add to the creamed mixture alternately with the remaining milk.
- In a clean bowl with clean beaters, beat the egg whites, adding the remaining ¹/₄ cup of sugar slowly, until stiff peaks form. Fold half the whites into the batter to lighten it, then fold in the remainder until the batter is homogenized and there are no streaks of egg white.
- Transfer the batter to the prepared pan and bake in the middle of the oven for 55 to 60 minutes until golden and a toothpick inserted in the center comes out clean.
- Cool for 10 minutes. Turning out onto a rack to cool completely. Slice and serve plain or with sugared fresh-sliced strawberries.

Yields 1 9-inch bundt cake

MENU

Oven-baked salmon fillets (page 248)
Boiled new potatoes
Roasted peppers (page 242), vinaigrette
Orange Angel Cake

Carrot-Walnut-Cinnamon Cake

Simple menus allow time for favorite desserts, even if that means baking. It's great if you can time it so that dessert is baking while you're enjoying dinner. This carrot cake is spiced with cardamom as well as cinnamon, and I use butter instead of oil. Most carrot cakes are covered with cream cheese frosting, but this one's good enough to stand alone. Frostings take more time and are loaded with fat and calories, so my recent strategy is to make really flavorful, textured cakes that need just a dusting of powdered sugar if anything at all. This is another cake I find irresistible at breakfast time.

8 tablespoons butter, at room temperature
1 cup granulated sugar
2 eggs, at room temperature
1 teaspoon vanilla
1 cup flour
1 teaspoon baking soda
1 1/2 teaspoons cinnamon
1/2 teaspoon cardamom
1/2 teaspoon salt
1 1/2 cups grated carrots
1/2 cup walnuts, coarsely chopped
Confectioners' sugar for the top

• Preheat the oven to 350°F. Grease and lightly flour a 9-inch square baking pan.
• In a mixing bowl, beat the butter with the granulated sugar until well creamed. Add the eggs, one at a time, beating until very light and pale, about 4 minutes. Beat in the vanilla.
• In a large bowl, sift together the flour, baking soda, cinnamon, cardamom, and salt. On low speed, add to the creamed mixture and mix just until blended. Stir in the carrots and nuts.
• Transfer the batter to the prepared pan, spreading the batter to the corners and sides. Bake in the upper half of the oven for 40 to 45 minutes until the center is springy and a toothpick inserted in the center comes out clean.
• Cool on a rack before cutting into 9 pieces. Dust with confectioners' sugar if desired or spread with cream cheese frosting if you must.*

Yields 1 9-inch square cake

* To prepare cream cheese frosting combine 2 ounces of cream cheese, 1 tablespoon of butter, 1 cup of confectioners' sugar, and 2 teaspoons of milk.

MENU

Fish sticks
Risotto (page 252)
Cherry tomatoes and celery sticks with a dressing dip
Carrot-Walnut-Cinnamon Cake

Peanut Butter Cake

In honor of school days and happy childhood memories, try this easy ending for a dinner that is sure to please any school-age child, and adults, too. If you can't eat peanut butter without jelly, skip the chocolate chips and serve each cake slice with a spoonful of jelly on the side.

4 tablespoons butter, at room temperature
3 tablespoons peanut butter, at room temperature
3/4 cup granulated sugar
1 egg
1/2 teaspoon vanilla
1 cup flour
1 teaspoon baking powder
1/4 teaspoon baking soda
1/4 teaspoon salt
1/2 cup buttermilk
1/2 cup semisweet chocolate chips
Confectioners' sugar
Jam or jelly of your choice, optional

♦ Preheat the oven to 350°F. Grease and flour a 9-inch round cake pan.
♦ In a mixing bowl, beat the butter, peanut butter, and granulated sugar until well creamed. Add the egg and vanilla and beat until light, about 4 minutes.
♦ In a large bowl, sift the flour, baking powder, baking soda, and salt. Add alternately with the buttermilk to the creamed mixture, mixing on low speed just until blended. Stir in the chocolate chips.
♦ Transfer the batter to the prepared pan and bake in the middle of the oven for about 40 minutes until the center is springy, the cake pulls away from the sides of the pan, and a toothpick inserted in the center comes out clean. Cool completely in the pan on a wire rack.
♦ At serving time, sift confectioners' sugar over the top and cut into wedges.

Yields 1 9-inch round cake

MENU

Baked chicken (page 245)
Oven-Roasted Potatoes (page 255)
Peas and carrots
Peanut Butter Cake

Candy Bar Streusel Crumb Cake

A streusel topping with crushed candy bars takes the place of frosting on this rich, buttermilk cake. It's an easy dessert to go with a simple, no-cook menu.

1 cup flour
1 teaspoon baking powder
1/4 teaspoon baking soda
1/4 teaspoon salt
4 tablespoons butter, at room temperature
1/2 cup granulated sugar
1/2 teaspoon vanilla
1 egg
2/3 cup buttermilk

For the streusel:
1 tablespoon butter
3 tablespoons flour
1/4 cup brown sugar
1/2 cup crushed chocolate toffee or peanut butter candy bars, about 2 candy bars

◆ Preheat the oven to 350°F. Grease a 9-inch round baking pan.
◆ In a large bowl sift together the flour, baking powder, baking soda, and salt.
◆ In a mixing bowl, beat the butter and granulated sugar together until well creamed. Add the vanilla and egg and beat for 4 minutes until light. On low speed, alternately add the buttermilk and the dry ingredients just until blended. Transfer the batter to the prepared pan.
◆ Using the same bowl, prepare the streusel by combining the streusel ingredients and blending them together with 2 knives or a pastry blender. Sprinkle evenly over the cake batter.
◆ Bake in the center of the oven for about 35 minutes until the center is springy, the cake begins to pull away from the sides of the pan, and a toothpick inserted in the center comes out clean.
◆ Cool on a wire rack before cutting into wedges and serving from the pan.

Yields 1 9-inch round cake

MENU

Bagels, cream cheese, and smoked fish (with onions, capers, tomatoes)
Green salad with fresh fruit (page 162)
Candy Bar Streusel Crumb Cake
Iced coffee

Autumn Caramel Pecan Cake

Autumn is a time to relish the changing colors, the sunshine of Indian summer, and the markets' colorful scene of pumpkins, cider, apples, and gourds. In the fall, menus change to heartier dishes and baked desserts like Autumn Caramel Pecan Cake. The squash or pumpkin purée gives it added flavor and moistness. The availability of canned pumpkin makes this cake a year-round dessert.

2 cups flour
1¹/₂ teaspoons baking powder
¹/₂ teaspoon baking soda
¹/₂ teaspoon salt
1 teaspoon cinnamon
2 eggs
1¹/₂ cups granulated sugar
1¹/₂ teaspoons vanilla
¹/₂ cup vegetable oil
1 cup squash or pumpkin purée, fresh or canned

For the glaze:
4 tablespoons butter
¹/₂ cup light brown sugar
2 tablespoons milk
1 cup coarsely chopped pecans

Whipped cream, optional

- Preheat the oven to 350°F. Lightly grease a 9 x 13-inch baking pan.
- Combine the flour, baking powder, baking soda, salt, and cinnamon in a large bowl.
- In a mixing bowl, beat the eggs, sugar, and vanilla for about 4 minutes, until very light. On low speed, add the oil and mix until incorporated. Alternately add the flour mixture and the squash purée, until thoroughly mixed. Transfer the batter to the prepared pan and spread it evenly.
- Bake in the upper half of the oven for 45 to 55 minutes or until a toothpick inserted in the center comes out clean and the cake is springy to the touch.
- For the glaze, combine the butter, brown sugar, and milk in a small saucepan, and boil for 1 minute until golden and slightly thickened. Pour over the hot cake and spread evenly. Sprinkle with the pecans and cool on a rack. Serve slightly warm with an optional spoonful of whipped cream.

Yields 1 9 x 13-inch cake

MENU

Pork roast (Roasting Chart, page 247)
Polenta (page 253)
Brussels sprouts
Autumn Caramel Pecan Cake

Chocolate Roulade Yule Log

Chocolate Roulade Yule Log is a traditional Christmas dessert, usually filled with buttercream frosting. This version fills a light chocolate roll cake with chocolate ganache and whipped cream. It's a special dessert worth making any time of the year. You can pre-pare the cake a day ahead, but fill and assemble it the day you plan to serve it.

1 tablespoons butter
Flour for dusting parchment paper

For the cake:
3 whole eggs, separated
2 egg whites
Pinch of salt
1/2 + 1/4 cup granulated sugar
1/2 teaspoon vanilla
1/3 cup flour
1/4 + 1/4 cup unsweetened cocoa
1/2 teaspoon baking powder
2 tablespoons milk

- Preheat the oven to 375°F. Grease an 11 x 16-inch jellyroll pan with half the butter. Line with parchment paper and grease the paper well with the remaining butter. Dust with flour and shake out the excess.
- Put the 5 egg whites in a large mixing bowl with a pinch of salt.
- In another mixing bowl, beat the 3 egg yolks, adding 1/2 cup of sugar gradually until light, about 3 minutes. Add the vanilla and mix well.
- Sift the flour, 1/4 cup cocoa, baking powder, and salt together into a large bowl. Add alternately with the milk to the creamed mixture.
- With clean beaters, beat the egg whites until frothy, gradually adding the remaining 1/4 cup sugar until the whites are stiff but not dry. Mix a large spoonful into the chocolate batter, and fold in the remaining whites until there are no lumps of egg white. Spread evenly in the prepared jellyroll pan.
- Bake in the middle of the oven for 15 to 17 minutes until the center is springy and a toothpick inserted in the center comes out clean. Cool for 5 minutes.
- Sift 1/4 cup cocoa onto a clean dish towel and turn the cake onto the towel. Carefully remove the parchment paper. With a serrated knife, trim 1/2 inch from the 2 short sides to facilitate rolling. Roll the cake lengthwise in the towel.

For the ganache filling:
1/2 cup heavy or whipping
cream
5 ounces bittersweet
chocolate, chopped

For the whipped cream
filling:
1/2 cup heavy or whipping
cream
3 tablespoons confec-
tioners' sugar
1/2 teaspoon vanilla

♦ To prepare the filling, heat the cream to a simmer
in a small saucepan. Remove from the heat, add
the chocolate, cover, and set aside for 5 minutes.
Stir until smooth and cool to room temperature.
♦ To assemble, unroll the cake and spread an even
layer of chocolate ganache over the entire surface, pushing the cake together if there are cracks.
♦ In a small bowl, whip the remaining heavy cream
with the confectioners' sugar and vanilla until
stiff. (If you overwhip the cream, stir in an additional tablespoon of the heavy cream to lighten
the consistency.)
♦ Spread the whipped cream over the chocolate
layer and carefully re-roll the cake, turning it onto
a long, narrow, serving platter with the seam side
down.
♦ Keep chilled and cut into diagonal slices at serving time.

Yields 1 14-inch yule log cake to serve 8 to 10

MENU

Vegetable or cranberry juice
Roast beef (Roasting Chart, page 247) with horseradish sauce
Oven-roasted potatoes (page 255)
Steamed greens (chard, beet greens, kale)
Chocolate Roulade Yule Log

Fourth of July Cake

Strawberries, blueberries, and whipped cream, make this a red-white-and-blue finale for the Fourth of July. Even without the topping the buttermilk-orange cake is moist and rich.

For the cake:

1 egg

3/4 cup sugar

1/2 teaspoon vanilla

1/3 cup vegetable oil

1/3 cup orange juice

1/3 cup buttermilk

1 1/2 cups flour

1 teaspoon baking powder

1/2 teaspoon baking soda

1/2 teaspoon salt

4 ounces red currant jelly, melted

1 pint large strawberries, sliced into fans

1 cup blueberries

1 cup whipping cream, sweetened and whipped at serving time

- Preheat the oven to 350°F. Lightly grease and flour a 9 x 2-inch round cake pan. A 9-inch parchment round will help you remove the baked cake. Grease and flour the parchment paper.
- In a mixing bowl, beat the egg and sugar together until creamed and light, about 4 minutes. Add the vanilla and mix well. With the mixer on low speed, add the oil.
- In a small bowl, combine the orange juice and buttermilk.
- In another bowl, sift the dry ingredients together.
- Alternately add the liquid and dry ingredients to the creamed mixture, mixing on low speed, just until thoroughly blended.
- Transfer the batter to the prepared pan and bake in the middle of the oven for 40 to 45 minutes until a toothpick inserted in the center comes out clean.
- Cool on a rack for 10 minutes, then turn out of the pan to cool completely on a wire rack. Remove the parchment paper.
- Cover well with plastic wrap until a few hours before serving. Brush the top and sides with some of the melted jelly. Arrange fans of strawberries over the top and sprinkle with blueberries. Carefully and lightly brush the fruit with the remaining melted jelly to give it a shiny glaze. The jelly should be melted and warm, not hot, or it will cause the fruit to "weep" and get very juicy.
- Cut, serve, and top each piece with a large spoonful of whipped cream.

Yields 1 9-inch cake

MENU

Lobsters (page 249)
Corn-on-the-cob
Coleslaw (page 243)
Fourth of July Cake

Red-Hot Apple Cake

I'm reminded to make this favorite family dessert when Valentine's Day candy displays appear in the stores. Red-Hot Cinnamon Hearts spice and color the apple filling which is enclosed in a cookie crust and baked in a pie plate. No matter the form, my husband's family has always called this, Red-Hot Apple Cake. Pie or cake, it's delicious. Tradition dictates that Red-Hot Apple Cake be made with canned apples that come already poached.

½ cup vegetable shortening
⅓ cup granulated sugar
½ teaspoon vanilla
1 egg
1½ cups flour
½ teaspoon baking powder
½ teaspoon salt

For the filling:
1 20-ounce can sliced apples, unsweetened
½ cup granulated sugar
½ cup brown sugar
2 tablespoons quick-cooking tapioca granules
2 rounded tablespoons red-hot cinnamon heart candies
½ teaspoon cinnamon

- Preheat the oven to 350°F. Lightly grease a 9-inch pie plate.
- For the crust, beat the shortening with the granulated sugar in a mixing bowl until well creamed. Add the vanilla and egg and beat until light, about 4 minutes.
- In another bowl, combine the flour, baking powder, and salt and add to the creamed mixture, mixing until a dough forms.
- Press ⅔ of the dough into the bottom and sides of the prepared pie plate.
- To prepare the filling, combine the apples, granulated sugar, brown sugar, tapioca, candy hearts and cinnamon in a large bowl. Stir well and allow to sit for 15 minutes.
- Spoon the filling into the crust. Pat the remaining dough into flat pieces and cover as much of the apple surface as possible.
- Place the pie plate on a heavy cookie sheet and bake in the middle of the oven for 50 to 60 minutes until nicely browned.

Yields 1 9-inch pie

MENU

Beef au Poivre (page 89)
Baked potatoes (page 254)
Sautéed mushrooms
Broccoli (page 242)
Red-Hot Apple Cake

Strawberry Cream Shortcakes

Strawberry shortcakes are harbingers of spring and summer, and a must in your dessert repertoire. Shortcakes can be the basis of many fruit desserts topped with whipped cream.

2 cups flour
$^1/_2$ cup sugar
1 tablespoon baking powder
$^1/_2$ teaspoon salt
4 tablespoons cold butter
1 cup light cream
1 egg

For the topping:
1 quart strawberries
$^1/_4$ cup sugar
2 tablespoons orange liqueur or fresh lemon juice
$1^1/_2$ cups heavy or whipping cream, sweetened and whipped at serving time

- Preheat the oven to 425°F. Lightly grease a heavy baking sheet.
- In a large bowl, combine the flour, sugar, baking powder, and salt. With a pastry blender or 2 knives cut in the butter until it resembles coarse meal.
- In a small bowl, combine the cream and egg and stir into the dry ingredients, mixing gently with a fork just until blended.
- With a large spoon, scoop out rounded mounds of dough and arrange on the prepared baking sheet a few inches apart. Press gently with floured fingers until 1-inch thick.
- Bake in the upper half of the oven for 12 to 14 minutes, reducing the heat to 400°F halfway through. Remove to a wire rack to cool.
- Rinse and slice the strawberries into a medium-size bowl. Add the sugar and liqueur or lemon juice, and set aside to macerate for 30 minutes.
- Mash half the berries and stir together.
- To assemble, cut the shortcakes in half and arrange on a plate. Mound with the sweetened strawberries and juice, and top with the whipped cream.

Yields 8 shortcakes

MENU

Grilled lamb chops with mint jelly (page 247)
Mashed Potatoes (page 254)
Asparagus
Strawberry Cream Shortcakes

Cranberry Cream Cheese Poundcake

*D*ried cranberries have become the darlings of today's bakers and cooks. The sweetened and dried berries are fabulous as snacks, on cereal, in breads and sauces, or paired with other fruits in compotes, stews, or stuffings. They're becoming widely available in supermarkets and produce stores. Try them with walnuts in this cream cheese, orange flavored poundcake. Without the fruit and nuts this is a great basic poundcake.

8 tablespoons butter, at room temperature
3 ounces cream cheese, at room temperature
1 cup sugar
1 teaspoon vanilla
2 eggs
1^1/$_2$ cups flour
1^1/$_2$ teaspoons baking powder
^{1}/$_2$ teaspoon salt
^{1}/$_3$ cup milk
^{1}/$_4$ cup dried cranberries
Grated zest of 1 orange
^{1}/$_4$ cup coarsely chopped walnuts

- Preheat the oven to 375°F. Grease a 4^1/$_2$ x 8^1/$_2$-inch loaf pan. Line the bottom and ends with a 4^1/$_2$ x 18-inch strip of parchment paper to facilitate removing the baked cake. Grease the paper and lightly dust with flour.
- In a mixing bowl, beat the butter and cream cheese together, adding the sugar gradually. Beat on medium speed until well creamed. Add the vanilla and eggs, and continue to beat for 4 more minutes, until very light.
- In a large bowl, sift the flour, baking powder, and salt together.
- In a mixing bowl on low speed, alternately add the flour mixture and milk to the creamed ingredients, just until blended. Stir in the cranberries, zest, and nuts.
- Transfer the batter to the prepared loaf pan. Place in the upper half of the oven and immediately reduce the temperature to 350°F. Bake in the middle of the oven for about 1 hour until the cake is golden and a toothpick inserted in the center comes out clean. Reduce the temperature to 325°F if the cake is browning too quickly.
- Cool for 15 minutes before turning out onto a wire rack to cool completely. Remove the paper and store the cake wrapped in foil. Cut in slices to serve.

Yields 1 pound cake

MENU

Baked ham (page 247)
Baked sweet potatoes or yams
Pickled beets and sweet pickles
Cranberry Cream Cheese Poundcake

Cannoli Cake with Apricots & Chocolate

This cake reminds me of the scrumptious Italian pastries with their flavorful ricotta or custard fillings. But this dessert requires no frying or baking since it's a cake made with store-bought ladyfingers and layered with chocolate and fruit-studded ricotta cheese.

18 whole ladyfingers, separated into halves
2 pounds ricotta cheese
1/2 cup granulated sugar
1 teaspoon vanilla
3 tablespoons orange-flavored liqueur or dark rum
1/3 cup semisweet chocolate chips, chopped
1/3 cup candied fruits (apricots, pineapple, cherries, etc.)

For the topping:
1 cup heavy or whipping cream
1 tablespoon orange-flavored liqueur
2 tablespoons confectioners' sugar
Chocolate chips or candied fruit for garnish

♦ Line a deep, 2-quart round container with plastic wrap. Arrange ladyfinger halves in a concentric circle in the bottom of the container, filling up the entire space. Arrange ladyfinger halves around the outside edge (the filling will prevent them from falling into the center).
♦ In a large bowl, combine the ricotta, sugar, vanilla, orange-flavored liqueur, chocolate, and candied fruits.
♦ Spoon half the mixture over the ladyfingers. Top with more ladyfingers halves. Cover with the remaining cheese mixture and the remaining ladyfingers.
♦ Enclose in plastic wrap and chill for 4 hours.
♦ At serving time, uncover and turn the cake out onto a serving plate. Lift off the container and remove the plastic wrap carefully.
♦ In a small bowl, beat the cream and orange-flavored liqueur with the confectioners' sugar until stiff peaks form. Pipe the whipped cream over the cake using a pastry bag. Decorate with chocolate bits or candied fruits.

Serves 8 to 10

MENU

Grilled steaks or chops (page 247)
Grilled new potatoes (partially cooked inside, brushed with oil, and grilled)
Spinach salad
French bread
Cannoli Cake with Apricots & Chocolate

Apple Caramel Surprise Pie

*P*ies are always fun to make, and more than anything, they
epitomize home baking. I always use Golden Delicious apples in my
apple pies since they're available year-round and they always bake well. I
have many apple pie recipes, but this one is a favorite. It's always a surprise
to those who rave about it to find out that the secret ingredient is marshmallows!
I'm reluctant to reveal the secret for fear that you won't try it—but trust me, the
marshmallows blend with the apple juices, cinnamon, brown sugar, and butter to make
a creamy caramel that coats the apples inside the homey brown crust.

*Dough for a double-crusted
9-inch pie (page 262):*
2 cups flour
2 tablespoons granulated
  sugar
1/2 teaspoon salt
2/3 cup shortening or 10
  tablespoons butter, or
  a combination
6–7 tablespoons ice water

For the filling:
2 pounds (about 5)
  Golden Delicious
  apples, peeled, cored,
  and sliced to make
  about 5 cups of
  sliced apples
2 tablespoons cornstarch
3/4 cup light brown sugar
1 teaspoon cinnamon
12 large marshmallows,
  cut in half
2 tablespoons butter

1 tablespoon milk
2 tablespoons granulated
  sugar

+ Roll 2/3 of the dough into a 13-inch circle on a
  lightly floured surface. Lightly grease the pie plate
  and fit the dough into the bottom and sides without stretching it. Trim the edges leaving a 1/2-inch
  overhang. Refrigerate and save the trimmings for
  the top crust.
+ Preheat the oven to 425°F.
+ To prepare the filling, combine the apples with
  the cornstarch, brown sugar, and cinnamon. Toss
  and stir gently to combine thoroughly.
+ Arrange the marshmallows in a single layer in
  the bottom of the pie plate. Add the apples on
  top and dot with bits of butter.
+ Brush the edges of the dough lightly with milk.
  Roll out the top crust on a lightly floured surface
  and arrange over the pie, pressing the edges
  together lightly. Trim the top dough to match the
  bottom and save any trimmings. Crimp the edges
  to make a decorative border. Brush the top lightly
  with milk, add any extra dough shapes, brush
  again with milk, and sprinkle with granulated
  sugar. Cut a few vent holes in the top.
+ Place the pie plate on a heavy cookie sheet and
  bake on the bottom shelf of the oven for 10 minutes. Reduce the temperature to 375°F and continue to bake until the apples are tender and the
  crust is nicely browned, about 45 minutes.

Yields 1 9-inch pie

MENU

Baked halibut or swordfish (page 248)
Rice Pilaf (page 252)
Tomato slices vinaigrette with fresh basil
Apple Caramel Surprise Pie

Jack-o'-Lantern Pie

*Jack-o'-Lantern Pie is a spiced pumpkin-custard pie that's
decorated with whipped cream to **look** like a jack-o'-lantern.
Use fresh or canned pumpkin, but when buying fresh, look
for the sweet, small, cooking pumpkins, not the large ones that
we carve for Halloween.*

Dough for a 10-inch pie
crust (page 262):
1½ cups flour
1 tablespoon granulated
sugar
½ teaspoon salt
8 tablespoons butter
or ½ cup vegetable
shortening, or a
combination
4 tablespoons ice water

For the filling:
1½ cups fresh or canned
puréed pumpkin
3 eggs
¾ cup dark brown sugar
2 tablespoons maple
syrup
1 teaspoon cinnamon
½ teaspoon ground
ginger
¼ teaspoon grated
nutmeg
¾ cup heavy or whipping
cream

½ cup heavy or whipping
cream, sweetened and
whipped to decorate or
garnish the pie

+ Combine the flour, granulated sugar, and salt in
a medium bowl. Cut in the shortening with a
pastry blender or 2 knives until it resembles
coarse meal. With a fork, stir in the water until a
dough forms. Turn the dough out onto a lightly
floured surface and gently knead until the dough
forms a ball. Enclose in plastic wrap and chill.
+ On a lightly floured surface, roll out the dough
to a 14-inch circle. Fit the dough into a lightly
greased pie plate, pressing it into the bottom and
sides. Trim the edges and press into a decorative
border. Chill the crust while you prepare the
filling.
+ Preheat the oven to 425°F.
+ In a medium-size bowl, whisk together the pumpkin purée, eggs, brown sugar, maple syrup, and
spices. Stir in the cream until smooth and thoroughly blended. Pour the filling into the pie shell
and smooth the top.
+ Bake the pie on the bottom rack of the oven for
15 minutes. Reduce the temperature to 325°F
and continue to bake until the filling is set and
the center no longer looks wet, about 45 to 50
minutes.
+ Cool on a wire rack, cover, and refrigerate.
+ At serving time, decorate the top of the pie with
whipped cream in a jack-o'-lantern design.

Yields 1 10-inch pie

MENU

Barbequed pork chops
Baked beans
Coleslaw (page 243)
Jack-o'-Lantern Pie

Southern Peanut Pie

Homemade pie crusts are always best, but for the sake of time and convenience, there are frozen pie shells or ready-for-the-pie-plate crusts in the dairy case. This nut pie includes peanut butter as well as peanuts and is served with the customary whipped cream.

Dough for a 9-inch pie crust (page 262):
1¼ cups flour
1 tablespoon granulated sugar
½ teaspoon salt
3 tablespoons butter
3 tablespoons vegetable shortening
3–4 tablespoons ice water

For the filling:
3 eggs
½ cup granulated sugar
⅓ cup peanut butter
1 teaspoon vanilla
¾ cup dark corn syrup
1 cup unsalted cocktail peanuts

½ cup heavy or whipping cream, sweetened and whipped at serving time

- Combine the flour, granulated sugar, and salt in a medium-size bowl. Cut in the butter and shortening with a pastry blender or 2 knives until it resembles coarse meal. With a fork, stir in the water until a dough forms. Turn it out onto a lightly floured surface and gently knead until the dough forms a ball. Enclose in plastic wrap and chill.
- On a lightly floured surface, roll out the dough to form a 13-inch circle. Fit the dough into a lightly greased pie plate, pressing it into the bottom and sides. Trim the edges and press into a decorative border.
- Preheat the oven to 425°F. Place the pie shell on a heavy baking sheet.
- In a small bowl, whisk together the eggs, granulated sugar, and peanut butter until well mixed. Add the vanilla and corn syrup. Stir in the peanuts. Spoon into the unbaked pie shell.
- Bake in the lower half of the oven for 15 minutes. Reduce the temperature to 350°F and continue to bake for about 35 minutes or until set.
- Cool on a wire rack and refrigerate.
- Serve the pie with a large spoonful of whipped cream.

Yields 1 9-inch pie

MENU

Teriyaki Beef with eggplant and pepper skewers (page 93)
Grilled corn-on-the-cob (brush with oil and grill briefly)
Sliced tomatoes and red onions
Southern Peanut Pie

Maple Pecan Pie

Maple syrup adds a new dimension to pecan pie and makes a sweet old favorite even better. Be sure the nuts are fresh and tasty before you use them. Store pecans in the freezer to keep them fresh.

Dough for a 9-inch pie crust (page 262):

1¼ cups flour
1 tablespoon granulated sugar
½ teaspoon salt
3 tablespoons butter
3 tablespoons solid vegetable shortening
3–4 tablespoons ice water

For the filling:
3 eggs
⅓ cup maple syrup
⅔ cup dark corn syrup
½ cup brown sugar
4 tablespoons butter, melted
½ teaspoon vanilla
¼ teaspoon salt
1½ cups pecan halves, coarsely chopped

½ cup heavy or whipping cream, sweetened and whipped at serving time

- Combine the flour, granulated sugar, and salt in a medium-size bowl. Cut in the butter and shortening with a pastry blender or 2 knives until it resembles coarse meal. With a fork, stir in the water until a dough forms. Turn it out onto a lightly floured surface and gently knead until the dough forms a ball. Enclose in plastic wrap and chill.
- On a lightly floured surface, roll out the dough to form a 13-inch circle. Fit the dough into a lightly greased pie plate, pressing it into the bottom and sides. Trim the edges and press into a decorative border. Chill while you prepare the filling.
- Preheat the oven to 425°F.
- To prepare the filling, beat the eggs, maple syrup, brown sugar, corn syrup, butter, vanilla, and salt together in a mixing bowl. Stir in the pecans.
- Pour into the prepared pie shell. Bake on a heavy baking sheet in the bottom half of the oven for 10 minutes. Reduce the oven temperature to 375°F and continue to bake for about 40 minutes until the crust is browned and the filling is set.
- Cool on a rack before refrigerating.
- Serve with a spoonful of the whipped cream.

Yields 1 9-inch pie

MENU

Meatloaf
Mashed Potatoes (page 254)
Green beans
Maple Pecan Pie

Sugar-Crusted Rhubarb Pie

Celebrate spring with a seasonal menu and a rhubarb pie finale. Rhubarb is in the markets for a limited time, so enjoy it while you can. It's easy to cut into pieces and stew briefly in orange juice and sugar for a simple dessert.

Dough for a 9-inch double-crusted pie (page 262):
2 cups flour
2 tablespoons sugar
1/2 teaspoon salt
1/2 teaspoon cinnamon
5 tablespoons butter
1/3 cup vegetable shortening
6–7 tablespoons ice water

For the filling:
Rhubarb stalks cut into 3/4-inch pieces to make 4 cups
1/4 cup flour
1–1 1/4 cups sugar
Grated zest of 1 orange or 2 tablespoons chopped kumquat skin
1 tablespoon butter

For the glaze:
1 tablespoon milk
2 tablespoons sugar

+ Combine the flour, granulated sugar, salt, and cinnamon in a medium-size bowl. Cut in the butter and shortening with a pastry blender or 2 knives until it resembles coarse meal. With a fork, stir in the water until it forms a dough. Turn the dough onto a lightly floured surface and gently knead until the dough forms a ball. Divide the dough into 2/3 and 1/3 and flatten. Enclose in plastic wrap and chill.
+ On a lightly floured surface, roll out the dough to form a 13-inch circle. Fit the dough into a lightly greased pie plate, pressing it into the bottom and sides. Trim the edges leaving a 1/2-inch hanging over the side. Chill the crust while you prepare the filling.
+ Preheat the oven to 450°F.
+ Put the rhubarb in a large bowl. In another small bowl, combine the flour, sugar, and zest. Toss with the rhubarb and transfer to the pie plate. Dot the rhubarb with 1 tablespoon of butter.
+ Moisten the edge of the bottom crust. Roll out the remaining dough so it overhangs the pie plate. Trim the top dough to match the bottom. Pinch the edges together and crimp. Brush the top crust with milk and sprinkle with sugar. Cut a few vent holes with a knife.
+ Bake the pie on a heavy baking sheet in the lower half of the oven for 10 minutes. Reduce the temperature to 350°F and continue to bake for about 40 minutes until browned and bubbly.
+ Cool on a rack and serve warm or cold.

Yields 1 9-inch pie

MENU

Lamb chops, grilled or broiled, served with mint or onion jelly (page 247)
Potato gnocchi
Steamed asparagus
Sugar-Crusted Rhubarb Pie

Summer Fruit Cobbler

Cobblers are old-fashioned summertime desserts, similar to fruit pies, but with only a top crust of biscuits or shortcake, and not quite as thickened. Use your favorite summer fruit, or a combination of peaches, plums, nectarines, cherries, or even a few berries. This is best still warm from the oven when the crust is a bit crisp. You can make the dough ahead of time, enclose in plastic wrap, and refrigerate until you're ready to make the cobbler.

2 tablespoons butter
2 pounds peaches, nectarines, and plums to make 4 cups pitted, skinned, and cut fruit
³/₄ cup sugar
1¹/₂ tablespoons cornstarch or 3 tablespoons flour
1 tablespoon lemon juice
¹/₂ teaspoon cinnamon

For the crust:
¹/₃ cup vegetable shortening, or 5 tablespoons butter, at room temperature
3 tablespoons sugar
1 egg
¹/₂ teaspoon vanilla
1 cup flour
¹/₂ teaspoon baking powder
Pinch of salt
3 tablespoons milk

+ Preheat the oven to 375°F. Lightly butter a 9-inch pie plate with 1 teaspoon of the butter.
+ In a large bowl, combine the prepared fruit, sugar, cornstarch, lemon juice, and cinnamon, stirring to mix well. Turn the fruit into the prepared pie plate and dot with the remaining butter.
+ To prepare the crust, beat the shortening and sugar together in a mixing bowl. Add the egg and vanilla, and beat until light.
+ Combine the flour, baking powder, and salt in a small bowl, and add alternately with the milk to the shortening/sugar mixture until a dough forms.
+ Drop spoonfuls of the dough symmetrically over the fruit, covering as much surface as you can but leaving a 2-inch vent hole in the center.
+ Bake on a cookie sheet in the upper half of the oven until the crust is browned, the filling is bubbly and the fruit is tender, about 45 minutes.
+ Serve slightly warm with vanilla ice cream.

Serves 6

MENU

Vinaigrette marinated grilled shrimp, scallop, and pepper skewers
Pasta with chopped fresh tomatoes and basil
Summer Fruit Cobbler

Apple-Cranberry Crisp

Apples and cranberries are a perfect match when they're sweetened and baked with a cornmeal streusel topping.

1½ pounds Golden
  Delicious apples,
  peeled, cored, and
  sliced to make 4 cups
2 cups fresh cranberries
1 cup sugar
1 tablespoon flour

For the topping:
1¼ cups flour
¼ cup fine yellow
  cornmeal
½ cup granulated sugar
½ cup brown sugar
1 teaspoon cinnamon
8 tablespoons butter
¾ cup milk

Vanilla frozen yogurt or
  ice cream

♦ Preheat the oven to 375°F. Lightly grease a 10-inch round baking dish or pie plate.
♦ In a large bowl, combine the apples, cranberries, sugar, and flour. Turn into the prepared baking dish.
♦ To prepare the topping, combine the flour, cornmeal, sugars, and cinnamon in a small bowl. Cut in the butter with a pastry blender or 2 knives until it resembles coarse meal.
♦ Spread the topping evenly over the fruit and press gently.
♦ Bake in the middle of the oven for about 45 minutes until the topping is golden and the fruit is bubbly and tender.
♦ Serve warm with frozen yogurt or ice cream.

Serves 6 to 8

MENU

Acorn squash halves, microwaved and filled with spicy chili
Cucumber sticks with yogurt for dipping
Bread sticks
Apple-Cranberry Crisp

Cinnamon Oatmeal Cookies

Homemade cookies make even a simple dinner something special. Sesame seeds are the special ingredient that gives these soft cookies flavor and crunch. Try these with vanilla ice cream to make homemade ice cream sandwiches.

12 tablespoons butter, at room temperature
3/4 cup granulated sugar
1/2 cup brown sugar
2 eggs
1 teaspoon vanilla
1 1/2 cups flour
1 teaspoon cinnamon
1/4 teaspoon grated nutmeg
3/4 teaspoon baking soda
1/2 teaspoon salt
1 cup quick rolled oats
1/2 cup sesame seeds
1/2 cup currants

- Preheat oven to 375°F. Lightly grease a baking sheet.
- In a mixing bowl, beat the butter with the sugars until well creamed. Add the eggs and vanilla and beat together.
- In a large bowl, combine the flour, cinnamon, nutmeg, baking soda, and salt. Add to the creamed mixture until well blended. Stir in the oats, sesame seeds, and currants.
- Drop rounded tablespoons of dough onto the baking sheet.
- Bake in the upper half of the oven for 10 to 12 minutes, until the edges are browned and crisp.
- Cool the cookies on a wire rack.

Yields 3 dozen cookies

MENU

Roasted chicken (page 245)
Baked sweet potatoes
Sautéed greens (spinach, chard, kale, etc.)
Grapefruit halves
Cinnamon Oatmeal Cookies

Espresso Biscotti Cookies

*B*iscotti are the Italian almond-anise cookies that are double baked, sliced and crisped, only to be dunked in espresso or cappuccino for dessert. In Espresso Biscotti Cookies I've added lemon zest and instant espresso powder with the toasted almond and crushed anise seeds. Rather than bake them in the traditional way I've formed small round cookies with a melon baller and baked them at two temperatures to make them as crisp as traditional biscotti. These are a wonderful finish to an Italian menu.

¹/₃ cup whole almonds	◆ Preheat the oven to 325°F.
1 egg	◆ On a baking sheet, toast the almonds lightly for 10 to 12 minutes. Remove from the oven and cool completely before chopping.
¹/₂ cup sugar	
¹/₂ cup vegetable oil	
¹/₂ teaspoon anise seeds, crushed	◆ Turn the oven temperature up to 350°F. Lightly grease 2 heavy baking sheets.
1 teaspoon grated lemon zest	◆ In a large mixing bowl beat together the egg and sugar until light, about 3 minutes. On low speed beat in the oil, anise seed, lemon zest, and espresso powder.
1 teaspoon instant espresso powder	
1¹/₂ cups flour	◆ In another bowl mix the flour, baking powder, and salt together. Add to the mixing bowl and combine on low speed until thoroughly mixed. Stir in the almonds. The dough will be sticky.
1 teaspoon baking powder	
¹/₄ teaspoon salt	

◆ Using a 1-inch diameter melon baller, scoop out balls of dough and arrange them, 1¹/₂ inches apart, on the prepared baking sheets. Bake in the upper half of the oven for 15 minutes. Reduce the temperature to 300°F and bake for another 15 minutes to crisp the cookies. If you're baking these in 2 batches, remember to heat the oven to 350°F again before baking the second batch of cookies.

◆ Cool the cookies completely on a wire rack before storing in an air tight tin.

Yields about 40 1¹/₂ inch cookies

MENU

Antipasto salad (cheese, sausages, artichoke hearts, brined peppers, etc.)
Spaghetti and meatballs (page 88)
Focaccia
Mixed green salad
Espresso Biscotti Cookies
Espresso or cappuccino

Chocolate Chunk Cookies

No home can be without a recipe for chocolate chip cookies and this is the best one so far. Butter gives the cookies great flavor and the shortening gives them the crispy edges. And there are no nuts to obscure the main point—chocolate! Use semisweet chocolate chips or chop bittersweet or milk chocolate bars into chunks. A combination of chocolate gives the cookies the best and most unique flavor.

8 tablespoons butter, at room temperature
1/2 cup vegetable shortening
3/4 cup brown sugar
3/4 cup granulated sugar
2 eggs
1 teaspoon vanilla
2 3/4 cups flour
1 teaspoon baking soda
1/2 teaspoon salt
3 cups chopped chocolate, semisweet, bittersweet, or chocolate chips

♦ Preheat the oven to 400°F.
♦ In a mixing bowl, beat the butter and shortening together. Beat in the sugars, then add the eggs and vanilla and beat until light and fluffy.
♦ In a separate bowl, combine the flour, baking soda, and salt, and mix well. Beat into the creamed mixture. Stir in the chocolate. Store the dough in the refrigerator, or divide into 3 pint containers and save for later use.
♦ Arrange heaping tablespoons of dough on an ungreased baking sheet. Place in the upper half of the oven and immediately reduce the temperature to 375°F.
♦ Bake the cookies for 10 to 14 minutes (depending on your oven and the size of the cookies) until the edges are set and lightly browned, and the centers are still slightly soft. Try not to open the oven door often.
♦ Remove from the oven and cool for 1 minute before transferring to a wire rack to cool.
♦ Eat the cookies while the chocolate is still warm and gooey. Store any extras in a covered tin, when they're completely cool.

Yields 4 to 5 dozen cookies

NOTE: You can turn these into Chocolate Chunk Bars by pressing the dough into a greased 11 x 16-inch jellyroll pan. Bake in the middle of a 350°F oven for about 20 minutes until lightly browned and a toothpick inserted in the center comes out clean. Cool for 10 minutes and cut into bars.

MENU

*Toasted garlic bread with mozzarella or Jack cheese melted on top,
and a slice of avocado or tomato
Spinach and lettuce salad vinaigrette*
Chocolate Chunk Cookies

Chocolate Chip Brownies

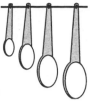

If you love chocolate, few desserts will satisfy your chocolate craving faster than Chocolate Chip Brownies. They're very rich and fudgy and easy to make with a 12-ounce package of chocolate chips. A scoop of peppermint ice cream on top makes them even more decadent.

8 tablespoons butter
12 ounces semisweet chocolate chips
2 tablespoons water or coffee
2 eggs
3/4 cup sugar
1 teaspoon vanilla
1 cup flour
1/4 teaspoon salt
1/4 teaspoon baking soda
1/4 teaspoon baking powder

♦ Preheat the oven to 350°F. Grease a 9-inch square baking pan.
♦ In a small saucepan, melt the butter and add half of the chocolate chips and all of the water. Leave on the lowest heat for just a minute, then remove from the heat and cover.
♦ In a mixing bowl, beat the eggs until light, adding the sugar gradually until pale and thickened. Add the vanilla and mix together.
♦ Stir the chocolate until smooth and add to the mixing bowl. Stir together gently with a rubber spatula, scraping the bottom of the bowl.
♦ In another bowl, mix the flour, salt, baking soda, and baking powder together. Sift into the chocolate mixture and gently fold into the batter with the remaining chocolate chips.
♦ Spread evenly in the prepared pan and bake in the middle of the oven for about 35 minutes until the center looks done, a toothpick inserted in the center comes out nearly clean, and the brownies begin to pull away from the sides of the pan. Don't over bake.
♦ Cool for 15 minutes before cutting into 9 3 inch squares.

Yields 9 3-inch brownies

MENU

Hamburgers with tomato and onion slices
French fries and onion rings
A pickle tasting
Chocolate Chip Brownies *with peppermint ice cream*

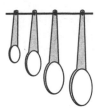

Turtle Cookie Bars

This fabulous, rich cookie bar will remind you of "turtle" candies—caramel and pecans enrobed in chocolate. What a cheery end to a simple dinner.

For the crust:
1/2 pound butter
1/4 cup confectioners' sugar
1 cup flour
1/4 teaspoon salt
1/4 teaspoon baking powder

For the caramel:
2 tablespoons butter
2 tablespoons light corn syrup
1/4 cup granulated sugar
1/4 cup light brown sugar
2 tablespoons buttermilk
1/8 teaspoon baking soda
1/4 teaspoon vanilla

1 cup pecan halves
1 1/2 cups semisweet chocolate chips

♦ Preheat the oven to 350°F. Lightly grease a 9-inch square baking pan.
♦ In a food processor, combine the crust ingredients and process until a ball of dough forms.
♦ With floured fingers, press the dough into the bottom of the prepared pan and 1/2-inch up the sides.
♦ Bake in the upper half of the oven for about 20 minutes, until lightly colored.
♦ While the crust is baking, prepare the caramel by combining the butter, corn syrup, sugars, buttermilk, and baking soda in a heavy saucepan. Heat over medium heat and stir until the butter melts and the mixture begins to boil. Boil, stirring constantly, for about 3 minutes, until golden in color. Don't let it burn!
♦ Remove the caramel from the heat, add the vanilla, and stir.
♦ Arrange the pecans in a single layer over the partially baked crust and pour the caramel evenly over the nuts without disturbing them.
♦ Return the pan to the oven and bake an additional 10 minutes until the caramel is bubbly and the crust is browned.
♦ Cool for a few minutes before sprinkle the chocolate chips evenly over the filling. After 5 minutes the chocolate should be melted enough to spread over the pecans.
♦ Cool for a few hours to let the chocolate set completely. Cut into 16 squares.

Yields 16 cookie bars

MENU

Chicken Salad (page 243)
Sliced tomatoes and avocados
Potato chips
Turtle Cookie Bars

Chocolate Fondue with Fruits & Cake

This elegant, do-it-yourself dessert is always a hit for holidays or when you're entertaining a crowd, Arrange a platter of cake squares and fresh, dried, and glacéed fruit, then heat a pot of cream and chocolate to make a ganache sauce. Use bamboo skewers for dipping the fruit and cake into the luscious chocolate. It's easy and decadent! Use any leftovers for hot fudge sauce.

1³/4 cups heavy cream
12 ounces bittersweet chocolate, chopped or semisweet chocolate chips
¹/4 cup light corn syrup
1 tablespoon Grand Marnier or orange-flavored liqueur, optional
Strawberries, banana slices, whole grapes, dried apricots, crystallized ginger, candied pineapple, or other fruit that's not too juicy
Angel cake or fruit cake, cut into squares

♦ In a heavy saucepan over low heat, warm the cream until nearly boiling. Add the chopped chocolate or chips, cover, and remove from the heat. Let it sit for 5 minutes.
♦ Uncover and stir gently until the chocolate is melted and the fondue is smooth. Stir in the corn syrup and Grand Marnier and serve with a platter of fruit and cake.
♦ Dip the fruit and cake when the chocolate fondue is warm, never hot. Keep it warm by putting it in a sauté pan of hot water when it cools and thickens too much.

Yields about 3¹/2 cups, enough for 8 to 10 people

MENU

Shrimp cocktail (page 248) and smoked fish platter
Beef tenderloin with sautéed white and some exotic mushrooms
Mashed potato stuffed potato skins (page 254)
Matchstick carrots and peppers, sautéed
Mesclun, endive, and watercress salad vinaigrette
Chocolate Fondue with Fruits & Cake
Champagne

Meringue Starbursts

It's always amazing to see and taste what egg whites and sugar can become. Meringues can be turned into baskets to hold ice cream and berries, or into sweet starbursts, plain or bottomed with chocolate, to serve like cookies. Meringues don't like humidity and heat, so choose a dry, cool day to make them, and store them in an airtight container. A pastry bag with a star tip will give the starbursts a professional look. Bake the meringues on foil and peel them off after they're slowly baked, dried, and crisp.

4 extra-large egg whites
¹/₈ teaspoon cream of tartar
1 cup sugar
12 ounces semisweet chocolate, melted, optional

- Preheat the oven to 350°F. Line a heavy baking sheet with foil.
- In a mixing bowl, using a whisk attachment, beat the egg whites with the cream of tartar on high speed until soft peaks form. Very gradually add the sugar, beating on high speed until very thick and glossy and the meringue stands in stiff peaks.
- Transfer the meringue to a pastry bag with a large (#8) star tip. Pipe rows of stars on the foil 1 inch apart. Use 2 baking sheets if necessary.
- Place the baking sheet in the middle of the oven and immediately reduce the temperature to 200°F. Leave the meringues in the oven for 6 hours. Turn off the oven and let them cool completely. They should be crisp throughout. Peel the starbursts carefully off the foil and store in a tin.
- A few hours before serving, melt the chocolate in the microwave or in a heavy pan set over hot water. Dip the bottoms of the starbursts into the chocolate and lay them on wax paper. Set aside for a few hours until the chocolate is set and firm and you can peel the starbursts off the paper.

Yields approximately 45 starbursts

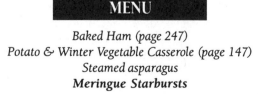

MENU

Baked Ham (page 247)
Potato & Winter Vegetable Casserole (page 147)
Steamed asparagus
Meringue Starbursts

Tips & Basic Recipes

ooking is always more enjoyable if your kitchen is organized, your pantry is stocked with basic ingredients, and your cooking tools work well.

Cooking Equipment, Utensils & Necessities

Cooking equipment and utensils are personal matters. What's right for one person may not be right for another. Utensils, pots, and pans become your friends after years of reaching for just the right tool or vessel. You'll remember some of the wonderful meals you prepared with them and in them. I can only suggest quality, heavy pots and pans that retain heat and cook evenly, whether it is enamel over cast iron, nonstick, or stainless steel with center cores of copper and aluminum. They all have advantages and disadvantages.

Quality cookware costs a great deal of money, but should be considered an investment for a lifetime of cooking, and a family heirloom beyond. Buy the best quality available and build up your supply of equipment pot by pot and knife by knife. Fine kitchen tools and the proper equipment help you produce good results which make cooking and baking that much more fun.

Candy Thermometer

Cutting Boards—I recommend a portable wooden board with a fruit side and a savory (onion/garlic) side, *and* a dishwasher-safe board for cutting poultry and meats. Wash these well and eliminate food smells by rubbing with coarse salt and a lemon and then with soapy water. Rinse well and dry before storing.

Food Mill for eliminating the seeds and skin of cooked tomatoes and apples in homemade tomato sauce and applesauce. Foley is the reliable classic.

Heat Diffuser. A metal plate with holes that sits under a pot or pan and tempers the heat. It acts like a double boiler to prevent foods from sticking to the bottom of pots or pans. Use it when heating milk, melting chocolate, or cooking rice.

Instant-Read Meat Thermometer. Unlike other traditional meat thermometers, these don't cook with the meat but are inserted in the thick part of the meat and test the temperature in seconds. They're the answer to successful meat cookery.

Kitchen Scale to measure ounces and grams. It helps with recipes that call for one-half pound of this or 8 ounces of that. A handy ounce/gram equivalency guide on a label stuck to the scale will make the conversion easier if you can't remember how many grams to the ounce or the pound.

Here are some useful equivalents:

1 ounce = about 30 grams
450 grams = 1 pound
1 pound = 16 ounces
1 pint = 1 pound
2 tablespoons = 1 fluid ounce
1 tablespoon = 3 teaspoons
1/4 cup = 2 ounces = 4 tablespoons
1/2 cup = 4 ounces = 8 tablespoons
1 cup = 8 ounces = 16 tablespoons
2 cups = 1 pint
4 cups = 1 quart
4 quarts = 1 gallon
1 stick of butter = 1/2 cup = 8 tablespoons
1 egg = approximately 1/4 cup
1 lemon = about 1/4 cup juice
1 lime = about 2 tablespoons juice
16 ounces cheese = approximately 4 cups grated cheese

Knives for chopping, boning, paring, or slicing are essential to food preparation and should be made of high-carbon stainless steel. Use a quality sharpener to keep them sharp. Good knives make cooking a pleasure—dull ones are frustrating and dangerous. A serrated knife is useful for slicing tomatoes and a heavy serrated knife is a necessity for slicing crusty bread.

Large Stainless Steel Spoons—whole and slotted—for stirring and scooping. To taste a soup or sauce, spoon some of the liquid into a small second spoon. Taste from the small spoon and keep the larger one for stirring the pot.

I use **Parchment Paper** to cover and protect delicate chicken breasts and fish cooked at high temperatures. It's also used in baking to line cake pans and cookie sheets to make removing cakes and cookies easier. Parchment paper comes in rolls and sheets and is available in most cookware stores.

Pastry Scraper for moving dough around the work surface.

Stainless Steel Strainers are costly but long-lasting and stay clean since they're dishwasher-safe. Buy a small and large size.

Stainless Steel Surgical Scissors for cutting everything from roasted chickens to string and for trimming the pie dough around the edges.

Vegetable Peeler for vegetables and citrus peels.

Wooden Spoons and Flat-Bottom Spatulas for stirring savory foods and a separate set for stirring sweet foods. Wood doesn't get hot to the touch but it does absorb the flavors of the foods it stirs and these are very difficult to eliminate. It can be helpful to label your utensils for use with either sweet or savory foods so that your applesauce doesn't taste like shrimp and garlic.

Zester for making grated zest of citrus fruits for cakes, marinades, salads, and flavoring.

Serving Platters and Bowls

Presentation makes such a difference in turning an ordinary meal into something memorable. Simple spaghetti looks spectacular on a decorative platter topped with chopped green parsley or basil, a few chopped red tomatoes, and black olives. Vegetables in plain white serving bowls will sell much faster than vegetables in a saucepan or the microwave pouch. Or use vegetables as a colorful garnish around the main course on a large serving platter. Porcelain bowls are fired at a higher temperature and are much less likely to chip than more rustic earthenware bowls. Platters that are oven- and microwave-safe give you greater heating and serving possibilities.

Storage Containers

These need not be fancy new containers. You can clean a yogurt, cottage cheese, or plastic deli container. The only necessity is a tight-fitting lid. Be sure to label the contents of these recycled containers so you're clear about the contents of your refrigerator or freezer.

Basic Recipes

EGGS

- Buy fresh eggs without cracks and refrigerate them for up to 2 weeks. Check the date on the carton. Eggs that crack should be used as soon as possible for baking or in a dish that will be fully cooked.
- Fresh eggs can be frozen for later use. Freeze egg whites or yolks in labeled plastic containers.
- If you plan to use the egg whites for meringues or cakes, be careful not to let the yolks mix with the whites when you separate the eggs or they won't whip up and increase in volume.
- To freeze 4 egg yolks or 2 whole eggs, mix in $^1/_8$ teaspoon salt or $1^1/_2$ teaspoons sugar so the eggs won't thicken or gel.
- If you're concerned about fat in your diet, you may substitute 2 whites for 1 whole egg in baking.
- One egg equals approximately $^1/_4$ cup.

Omelets

2 fresh eggs
1 tablespoon water
$^1/_4$ teaspoon salt
Pepper to taste
1 tablespoon butter
$^1/_3$ cup filling: grated cheese, cream cheese and chives, julienned ham, creamed spinach, sautéed mushrooms, leftovers, etc.

- In a small bowl, mix the eggs, water, salt, and pepper with a fork.
- Heat an omelet pan or 10-inch nonstick sauté pan over medium heat and add the butter. When very hot, add the eggs and whisk quickly with a fork for a few seconds until lumpy. Immediately turn the heat to low and let the eggs cook slowly, lifting the edges and tipping the pan to allow the liquid egg to spill over and cook.
- Before the egg is completely set, add any filling you like in a strip in the middle. Heat until warm, then turn the omelet out of the pan onto a plate, folding over the sides so the filling is enclosed. The heat of the eggs will continue to cook the eggs and warm the filling.

Hard-Cooked Eggs

These eggs are the basis of egg salad and deviled eggs. They're cooked but not boiled. This method leaves the yolk bright yellow in color, soft, and buttery tasting. They're so good plain, you won't bother to devil them.

6 fresh eggs
$^1/_2$ teaspoon salt
Water

- Put the eggs in a medium saucepan, add the salt, and cover by 1-inch with water. Bring to a boil over medium heat and cover.
- Remove from the heat and let the eggs sit for 13 minutes.
- Drain immediately and run cold water over them until cool. Leave the eggs in the cold water as you crack them against the side of the pan. Peel the shells and refrigerate.

Poached Eggs

- Grease a saucepan and add 2 inches of water. Bring to a boil.
- Break a very fresh egg into a small bowl without cracking the yolk and slip it carefully into the water. Simmer for 3 to 5 minutes or until the white is set and the yolk is still soft.
- Remove with a slotted spoon and drain on paper towels.

VEGETABLES

Artichokes

These are wonderful vegetables available from late-March through the summer. Cook them and serve hot with butter or cool with a vinaigrette dressing. To cook them:

4–6 firm, medium artichokes
Water to cover (although they will float)
$1/4$ cup white or cider vinegar
$1/4$ cup olive oil
1 celery stalk
$1/4$ bunch parsley
1 tablespoon salt

- Cut the stem and $3/4$ inch off the top of the artichoke. Rinse well and trim the tips of the leaves with a scissors.
- Combine the water, vinegar, oil, aromatics, and salt in a large pot. Bring to a boil and add the prepared artichokes. Boil, partially covered, about 30 minutes (25 minutes for small and 35 minutes for large) or until a leaf pulls out without much resistance. Bite the bottom of the leaf and pull off the flesh. It should be tender and soft, but not mushy. Remove from the water.
- Spread the leaves apart, remove the center cone, and spoon out the prickly center "choke" with a grapefruit spoon. The bottom is the prized treat at the end.

Oven-Dried Tomatoes

Oven-dried tomatoes, like sun-dried tomatoes, are made with plum or Roma tomatoes that are meatier than slicing tomatoes. The long drying process in a low oven intensifies the tomato flavor as the tomatoes reduce in size and become chewier, but not brittle. The drying time will vary depending on the size of the tomatoes.

20 ripe plum tomatoes
2 tablespoons olive oil
Coarse salt

- Preheat the oven to 250°F.
- Cut the tomatoes nearly in half, opening them like a book. Lay them very close together, cut side up, on wire racks in a jellyroll pan. Rub the cut surface lightly with olive oil and sprinkle with coarse salt.
- Place in the middle of the oven. Dry them for 8 to 10 hours, maybe more, checking periodically, until they lose their juiciness, are leathery, and no longer squishy.
- Cool completely.
- To use them for sandwiches, salads, or on crackers with fresh cheese, it's best to pack them in layers in a glass jar with olive oil to cover

Oven-Dried Tomatoes
(continued)

completely. They will keep for at least a week this way. You may flavor the oil with a clove of garlic, whole peppercorns, or a bay leaf. If the olive oil congeals in the refrigerator, warm slightly in warm water, or for a few seconds in the microwave.

Roasted Peppers & Eggplant

Roasting brings out the sweetness in vegetables and imparts a unique, rich flavor to the flesh. Roasted peppers make a colorful side dish, and a fine addition to composed salads and sandwiches.

Use large sweet green, red, orange, yellow, or purple
    sweet peppers

+ Preheat the broiler and set the rack 4 to 6 inches from the heat. Line a heavy cookie sheet or jellyroll pan with foil to avoid messy clean-up.
+ Rinse, core, and seed the peppers. Jab the peppers and eggplant a few times with a sharp knife. Arrange in a single layer on the foil.
+ Broil until the skin is blackened and blistered. Turn until all sides are blistered. You may also blacken and blister peppers on a grill or over an open gas flame to get the same roasted flavor.
+ As the peppers are roasted or grilled, and the eggplant has become soft, collapsed, and blackened, transfer to a large bowl and cover with a plate. This will steam the peppers and make removing the skins effortless.
+ When completely cool, peel the skins. Roasted peppers can be refrigerated or even frozen for later use. They are wonderful packed in olive oil and garlic and used in salads or sandwiches.

Broccoli

A stir-fry and steaming method cooks broccoli perfectly. You may use chicken broth instead of water for added flavor, but skip the salt.

1 bunch broccoli
3 tablespoons vegetable or peanut oil
1 teaspoon salt
1/2 cup water

+ Rinse the broccoli and shake dry. Cut off the stem end and break up the flowers into bite-size pieces. Peel the stem with a peeler or knife, and cut into rounds or sticks.
+ In a large sauté pan with a cover, heat the oil over medium-high heat and add the salt. When hot, add the cut-up broccoli. It will make lots of sputtering noises. Immediately stir and toss for about 15 seconds until the green color is brighter. Stirring will prevent the broccoli from burning. Have the water ready and pour into the pan with a great whoosh of steam. Cover quickly and reduce the heat to medium.
+ Check in 5 minutes and test with a fork to see it if is done. Some like broccoli crisp-tender, others more tender. Taste and continue cooking 1 minute more if needed. Don't overcook the broccoli or it will turn a terrible color and lose its flavor. If you're preparing broccoli for a cold dish or garnish, you can retain the green color by plunging the broccoli into ice water to chill and then drain.

Mayonnaise-based salads are summer favorites, but they're perishable and need to be refrigerated. For a slimmer dressing, you may want to mix mayonnaise with some plain yogurt to bind the salad, but that does change the flavor. A spoonful of Dijon mustard gives a mayonnaise dressing additional flavor and zip. These are the basic proportions. Add just enough dressing to bind the ingredients well.

Coleslaw

6 cups shredded cabbage (1½ pounds), best done with
    a knife
1 large carrot, grated
½ green pepper, seeded and julienned
1 large celery stalk, thinly sliced
3 scallions, thinly sliced
1 cup mayonnaise
2 tablespoons cider vinegar
2 tablespoons sugar, or to taste
1 teaspoon salt

• Toss the vegetables together. In a small bowl, combine the mayonnaise, vinegar, sugar, and salt, and stir until smooth. Mix the vegetables and dressing together. Refrigerate.
• Mix well before serving. Coleslaw is best eaten the day it is made.

Chicken Salad

4 cups boned cooked chicken (from one whole chicken—page 9
    or 4 poached chicken breasts—page 245–46)
3 celery stalks, thinly sliced
2 scallions, thinly sliced
1 cup mayonnaise
2 tablespoons vinegar of your choice (cider, Balsamic, malt, wine,
    etc.)
Salt and pepper to taste
Optional additions: red or green peppers, blanched vegetables,
    seedless grapes, dried fruit, a spoonful of chutney
Optional toppings: cooked and crumbled bacon, nuts,
    cherry tomatoes, avocado, crumbled blue cheese

• Cut the chicken into bite-size pieces.
• In a large bowl, combine the chicken, celery, and scallions.
• In a small bowl, stir together the mayonnaise and vinegar. Add any optional ingredients to the chicken with enough dressing to bind. Season to taste with salt and pepper.
• Refrigerate and serve slightly chilled.
• At serving time, add toppings of your choice.

Seafood Salad

1 pound cooked seafood—crabmeat, shelled shrimp, lobster
2 or 3 celery stalks, thinly sliced
2 scallions, thinly sliced
¾ cup mayonnaise, or enough to bind
1 tablespoon fresh lime juice
½ teaspoon dry mustard
Optional toppings: avocado, caviar, hard-cooked egg slices

- Cut the seafood into bite-size pieces. Combine with the celery and scallions.
- In a small bowl, stir together the mayonnaise, dry mustard, and lime juice.
- Combine the seafood and dressing. Top with avocado, caviar, or egg slices.

Potato Salad

5 or 6 medium all-purpose potatoes (not russets)
3 tablespoons wine vinegar
1 teaspoon salt
1 teaspoon sugar
2 celery stalks, thinly sliced
3 scallions, thinly sliced
1 cup mayonnaise
1 tablespoon Dijon or coarse-grained mustard
Salt and pepper to taste
On the side: hard-cooked egg slices, blanched green beans,
    cherry tomatoes, drained white tuna

- Cook the potatoes for about 20 minutes in boiling salted water until tender. Drain, peel, and cut them into large chunks. Place in a bowl. Sprinkle the warm potatoes with vinegar, salt, and sugar. Cover with a plate and let the potatoes cool. Add the celery and scallions.
- In a small bowl, combine the mayonnaise and mustard and add to the potatoes, stirring gently until well mixed. Taste and adjust the seasoning with salt and pepper.
- For a summer meal, serve on a large platter with egg slices, green beans, tomatoes, and tuna.

Egg Salad

6 hard-cooked eggs (page 240), peeled and coarsely chopped
2 celery stalks, finely chopped
3/4 cup mayonnaise
1/2 teaspoon dry mustard
1 tablespoon pickle relish, optional

- Combine the eggs, celery, mayonnaise, and mustard, and stir gently to mix. Season to taste with salt and pepper. Add pickle relish if you like.

Tuna Salad

1 6½-ounce can solid white tuna in water, well drained
3/4 cup finely chopped celery
1/2 cup mayonnaise, or enough to bind
Optional additions: 2 tablespoons finely chopped onion,
    1 hard-cooked egg, chopped
Pepper to taste

- Press the tuna to extract as much water as possible. Add to a small bowl and break up with a fork. Combine with the celery and mayonnaise and mix thoroughly.
- Mix in any additions you like and season with pepper.

Roasted Whole Chicken

1 3–4 pound whole chicken
Salt and pepper to taste
Flavorings of your choice to put in the cavity: onion, fresh herbs,
fresh ginger, garlic, etc.

- Preheat the oven to 425°F.
- Remove the giblets from the chicken cavity and wash the chicken inside and out. Pat dry with paper towels. Pull off any excess fat and skin. Sprinkle the cavity with salt and pepper and add any flavorings you like. Tie the legs together and twist the wings back so they provide a flat base for the chicken.
- Arrange the chicken, back side up, on a buttered rack in a large roasting pan. Season with salt and pepper.
- Roast the chicken for about 30 minutes. Turn the chicken breast side up and roast about 25 more minutes, basting a few times, until nicely browned. The juices should run clear when you poke the thigh with a fork.
- Transfer the chicken to a platter and let it rest, breast side down, for 10 minutes before carving or cutting into quarters for serving.

Baked Chicken

Bake a cut-up whole chicken, or any of the parts you like. Baked potatoes take the same amount of time, so put them in the oven with the chicken and dinner, with a salad or vegetables, will be ready with very little effort.

1 tablespoon vegetable oil
1 3–4 pound frying chicken, cut into 8 pieces
1/3 cup unflavored dry bread crumbs
3/4 teaspoon salt
Pepper to taste
1/2 teaspoon paprika
2 tablespoons butter

- Preheat the oven to 375°F. Add the oil to a shallow 9 x 13-inch baking dish or roasting pan and spread to oil the bottom.
- Trim the chicken pieces of all excess fat and skin. On a piece of wax paper, combine the bread crumbs, salt, pepper, and paprika. Roll the chicken in the crumbs and arrange skin side up in the prepared baking dish. Dot the tops with small pieces of butter.
- Bake in the middle of the oven for 1 hour until browned, basting a few times with the accumulated juices. Remove from the baking dish and serve on a platter.

Poached Chicken Breasts for Salad

*Chicken salads may use the meat from a whole cooked chicken (**Grandma's Chicken Soup,** page 9) or the boned and skinned meat from a roasted or rotisserie chicken, but the most elegant salads use poached chicken breasts. Poaching doesn't mean boiling. By barely simmering the breasts in a flavorful stock, they remain moist and tender and perfect for salads.*

8 cups water
^{1}/$_4$ cup vegetable oil
1 onion, cut into quarters
^{1}/$_4$ bunch parsley, tied together
1 celery stalk
1 tablespoon salt
Peppercorns
6 chicken breast halves

• Trim the chicken breasts of all excess fat and skin.
• In a large sauté pan, combine the water, oil, onion, parsley, celery, salt, and peppercorns. Bring to a boil, cover, and simmer for 15 minutes to add flavor to the liquid. Add the chicken and return to a simmer. Over very low heat, barely simmer for 2 or 3 minutes.
• Remove from the heat, cover, and allow the chicken to cool in the broth. It will continue to cook in the hot liquid. When cooled, remove the skin and bones from the breasts.

Oven-Poached Chicken Breasts

Oven-poaching in a hot oven is another technique (also used with fish) which produces a very flavorful and perfectly cook chicken breast.

4–6 chicken breast halves
1 tablespoon butter
Salt and pepper, to taste
^{1}/$_4$ cup minced shallots
^{1}/$_2$ cup dry white wine
Parchment paper to cover

• Trim the chicken breasts of all excess fat and skin.
• Preheat the oven to 450°F. Use half the butter to lightly grease a shallow glass baking dish.
• Arrange the chicken breasts in a single layer, skin side up, in the prepared dish. Sprinkle with salt, pepper, and the shallots. Pour the wine into the bottom of the dish. With the remaining butter, lightly grease one side of the parchment paper and lay it over the chicken breasts, buttered side down.
• Bake in the oven for about 20 minutes, until the chicken is no longer squishy, but firm and opaque throughout. If you poach boned and skinned chicken breasts, they will take just 10 to 12 minutes.
• Cool before you remove the paper, skin, and bones.

Grilled Chicken Breasts

*When chicken breasts are cooked over high heat, they need the protection of the skin. Without the skin, the chicken must be brushed with an oil-based marinade or mayonnaise to keep it moist (see **Grilled Tuscan Chicken Breasts**, page 78). Chicken with the bone in will take longer to cook than boned and skinned chicken breasts, which need just a few minutes on each side until they're opaque throughout and perfectly cooked. Over-cooking makes chicken breasts tough and chewy.*

Roasting Chart for Beef, Lamb & Pork

Beef	Rib Roast	300F°	25 minutes per pound to 130°	Rare
			Cook to 140°	Medium
Beef	Boneless Roast	350F°	13 minutes per pound to 130°	Rare
Beef	Tenderloin	450F°	30 minutes total or to 130°	Rare
			Cook until 140°	Medium
Lamb	Leg	350F°	20 minutes per pound to 150°	Medium
Lamb	Rack	400F°	13 minutes per pound to 140°	Medium-Rare
Pork	Roast	350F°	22 minutes per pound to 160°	Medium
Pork	Tenderloin	425F°	22 minutes per pound to 160°	Medium

Meat should be at room temperature before roasting. If very lean, rub the meat lightly with oil and season with salt and pepper. Set the roast, fat side up, on a rack in a roasting pan. When the instant-read meat thermometer reaches the desired temperature, set aside to rest for 15 minutes before carving. Remember that the meat will continue to cook for 10 to 15 minutes as it sits. It's better to undercook than overcook the meat. If necessary, you can return roasts to the oven.

Broiled or Grilled Chops & Steaks

Rib or loin chops and steaks (beef, lamb, pork, veal)
Salt and pepper to taste

* Preheat the broiler or prepare the grill.
* Trim the excess fat from chops. If very lean, rub with a small amount of olive oil. Season with salt and pepper.
* Broil or grill the meat about 4 inches from the heat.
* If the meat is ³/4-inch thick, cook for 4 minutes on each side; if 1-inch thick, broil or grill 5 minutes on each side; for 1¹/2-inch thick, 6 minutes on each side for medium-rare. Expert grillers can test how well cooked meat is by poking it with a fork or finger. Squishy means the meat is raw, hard means it is well done, and if the meat is springy or resistant to the touch it is somewhere in between. You will get good at this with experience.

Baked Ham

Use a bone-in, fully cooked ham—12 to 14 pounds
(This is a good time to ask your friend the butcher which ham is the best.)

* Preheat the oven to 350°F.
* Score the top of the ham, stick with a few whole cloves, and bake for 30 minutes.
* Make a thick glaze with brown sugar, mustard, marmalade, and bourbon. Cover the top of the ham, and bake for 1¹/2 hours, basting often.

High Temperature Oven-Cooked Fish	*Fish is delicate and quick-cooking, so it needs some protection when it's baked at high temperatures. It should to be covered with its own skin, or with oil, vegetables, or parchment paper. The rule of cooking is 10 minutes per inch of fish, or until the fish is opaque throughout or begins to flake. There are two method of cooking fish fillets or fish steaks, one with liquid and one without. In both, preheat the oven to 450°F.*

Oven Poaching: Lightly oil a shallow glass baking dish. Lay the fish in the dish skin side down. Season with salt, pepper, minced shallots, and any spices or herbs you like. Pour 1/2 cup liquid (wine, stock, heavy cream) into the bottom of the dish. Cover the fish with a piece of buttered parchment paper. Bake for 10 minutes per inch of fish until it is opaque throughout. Remove the fish and cook down the liquid in a sauté pan over high heat to make a sauce.

Oven Baking: If you're using a fish fillet with skin, line a heavy baking pan with foil and arrange the fish skin down on the foil. The skin will adhere to the foil when you cut the fish for serving. If the fish fillet has been skinned, lightly grease the baking pan and arrange the fish on it. Lightly rub the fish with oil or a skim of flavored mayonnaise (mostly oil). Season with salt and pepper. Bake for 10 minutes per inch of fish until it is opaque throughout.

Grilled or Broiled Fish Steaks	*Grilling or broiling works well with fish steaks that don't fall apart easily and with varieties that have a higher fat content: salmon, swordfish, and tuna. Rub the fish with a little oil or a skim of mayonnaise, and grill or broil 4 inches from the heat source for about 10 minutes per inch of fish total. Thick fish steaks (1 to 1 1/2 inches) should be turned after 6 or 7 minutes. Thin steaks don't need to be turned at all.*

Pan-Sautéed Fish Fillets	*Thin, delicate fish fillets should be treated with care and cooked for just minutes in a sauté pan. Heat the pan, add butter or oil, and sauté for 2 minutes. Turn with a wide spatula and continue to sauté until the fish is opaque and begins to flake. You may roll the fish in flour or crumbs or leave it plain and season with salt and pepper. Serve with lemon wedges.*

Shrimp—Cooked & Deveined	*Cooking shrimp is really poaching them—simmering in a flavorful liquid. Shells add flavor to cooked shrimp, so if you're cooking them to add to a finished dish, remove the shells and devein **after** you've cooked them. If you're cooking the shrimp with other ingredients, remove the shells and devein first. After pulling off the shell, hold the shrimp and make a shallow slit along the back curve from one end to the other. This exposes the vein, or dark intestinal tract. Lift it out with a toothpick and rinse the shrimp.*

Shrimp *(continued)*

6 cups water
1 cup dry white wine
1/2 onion, cut up
1 celery stalk, cut up
1 clove garlic, peeled and cut in half
Parsley stems
1 bay leaf
2 teaspoons salt
1/2 teaspoon peppercorns
1 1/2 pounds shrimp

- Combine the water, wine, onion, celery, garlic, parsley, bay leaf, salt, and pepper in a medium-size saucepan. Bring to a boil, cover, and simmer for 20 minutes to flavor the water.
- Whether the shrimp is fresh or frozen, drop it into the stock. Return the liquid to a simmer, stirring, and cook for about 1 minute until the color changes to pink and the shrimp curve into a crescent, but before they curl into a tight spiral. The shrimp should be opaque and white in the middle, and firm but not hard when you squeeze them. Don't overcook. Drain immediately, chill in ice water, and drain again.

Boiled Lobster

Buy lobsters the day you plan to cook and eat them. Store them in the refrigerator while you boil a large pot of salted water that will hold the lobsters without crowding. There should be enough water to amply cover them. Before you cook the lobsters, make sure they are alive. Find a brave soul who will plunge them, head first, into the boiling water. You may also kill the lobsters before boiling by plunging the tip of a knife between the head and body to sever the spinal cord, but I find this impossible to execute. Cover the pot, and when the water returns to a boil, cook the lobsters:

8 minutes for 1 pounders
12 minutes for 2 pounders
16 minutes for 3 pounders

Drain and serve with hot melted butter and lemon wedges. Provide a nutcracker or hammer to crack them, little forks or picks, and lots of napkins. A large bowl for juice and shells helps to keep things cleaner.

Cleaning Squid (Calamari)

Cleaning squid is easy but smelly. You may prefer to buy it cleaned, although it will cost a bit more. Cut the prized tentacles in front of the eyes and the ink sac. Grab the head and pull the insides out, including the "plastic" quill that forms a sort of backbone and structure for the squid. Squeeze the body from the bottom (like a tube of toothpaste) to eliminate any other insides. Rub the dark skin off between your fingers. Cut the body into 1/2-inch rings.

Couscous

Couscous is also known as Moroccan pasta—a grain-shaped precooked pasta made of ground durham wheat (semolina).

2 cups water
2 tablespoons butter
$1/2$ teaspoon salt
$1^1/3$ cups couscous

- In a medium-size saucepan, bring the water, butter, and salt to a boil. Add the couscous, stir, and cover.
- Remove from the heat and let stand for 5 minutes. Fluff with a fork and serve immediately.

Serves 4

- For a more authentic Moroccan couscous, you may flavor the water with a pinch of saffron, a pinch of tumeric, and a cinnamon stick. Stir in 1 cup cooked chick peas with the couscous and continue as above.

Boiled Rice

Long-grain white rice is so easy to cook, there's no need for instant rice. The ratio of water to rice is 2:1—twice as much water as rice.

2 cups water
1 teaspoon salt
1 tablespoon butter or oil, optional
1 cup long-grain white rice

- In a medium-size saucepan, combine the water, salt, butter, and rice. Over medium-high heat bring to a boil. Stir, scraping the bottom of the pan, reduce the heat to low, cover, and simmer for 15 minutes until nearly all the water is absorbed.
- Remove the cover and simmer a few more minutes to dry the rice more. Fluff with a fork and serve immediately.

Serves 4

Sticky Rice for Sushi

Sushi is made from a short-grain, polished white rice that is slightly sweet and very sticky when cooked. It's available in any Asian grocery and in some supermarkets. Ask for advise about ingredients and techniques for sushi-making. Some sticky rice recipes recommend soaking, draining, more soaking, and cooking, but I've found that the traditional cooking method is fine. It's how you handle and season the rice after cooking that creates its unique character. If you're making sushi (sticky rice wrapped in seaweed papers with pickled and fresh vegetables, crabmeat, etc.) or simply rolling the seasoned rice in balls to serve with pickled ginger and wasabi (horseradish paste), you begin the same way. For sushi, I double this recipe.

2 cups water
1½ cups short-grain sticky rice
⅓ cup seasoned rice vinegar (salt and sugar added), approximately

• In a medium-size saucepan, combine the water and rice. Bring to a boil, stir, and reduce the heat to low. If you put this over a heat diffuser (page 238) it will prevent the rice from sticking to the bottom and forming a crust. Simmer, covered, for about 18 minutes or until the water is absorbed. Remove from the heat and let the rice stand for 10 minutes.
• With a fork, fluff the rice and turn it into a shallow wooden bowl. Fan the rice with a fan or a piece of cardboard while you sprinkle on the seasoned vinegar. Keep turning and fanning to cool the rice as it absorbs the vinegar. Another pair of hands is helpful. When cool, cover the bowl with a damp towel until you're ready to make the sushi or balls of rice. Don't refrigerate. In working with the rice, be sure to keep a bowl of water nearby and wet your hands so the rice doesn't stick to them.

Yields about 4 cups

Brown Rice

Brown rice is more nutritious than white because the bran hasn't been removed, and it has a nuttier flavor than white rice. The long cooking makes it less convenient for quick dinners. For quicker cooking you can soak the rice overnight or from early morning to cut the cooking time in half.

Traditional cooking:
3 cups water
1 tablespoon butter or oil
1 teaspoon salt
1 cup long-grain brown rice

• In a medium-size saucepan, combine the water, butter, and salt. Bring to a boil and stir in the rice.
• Cover and simmer for about 45 minutes until the water is absorbed and the rice is tender.

Quick cooking:
2 cups water
1 cup long-grain brown rice
1 tablespoon butter
1 teaspoon salt

• In a medium-size saucepan, combine the water and brown rice and soak overnight or all day.
• To cook, add the butter and salt to the pan and bring to a boil. Stir well, cover, and simmer for about 20 minutes until the water is absorbed and the rice is tender.

Rice Pilaf

Pilaf is really a technique for cooking rice or other grains. In this basic recipe, rice is sautéed in butter or oil along with some onion and vermicelli or thin spaghetti, then cooked in boiling liquid. The rice doesn't stick together so the pilaf has a light, unique texture. You can add cooked vegetables, chicken, or meats, and fresh herbs or spices at the end of cooking to create a one-dish meal.

4 tablespoons butter
1/3 cup vermicelli or thin spaghetti, broken into 1/2-inch pieces
1 1/2 cups rice
3 tablespoons minced onion
3 cups boiling broth or water
3/4 teaspoon salt (omit if using canned broth)

- Melt the butter in a heavy saucepan over low heat. Add the vermicelli and sauté until lightly colored, about 2 minutes.
- Stir in the rice and onion and sauté for about 3 minutes, stirring often, until the rice is very hot, the vermicelli is browned, and the onion is soft.
- Stir in the boiling broth and cover tightly. Simmer for about 15 minutes until the water is absorbed. Remove the cover and continue to cook for a few minutes to dry out the pilaf.
- Fluff with a fork and serve hot.

Serves 4 to 6

Wheat Pilaf

4 tablespoons butter
1/2 cup vermicelli or thin spaghetti, broken into 1/2-inch pieces
1 cup bulgur (cracked wheat), medium- or fine-cut
3 tablespoons finely chopped onion
2 cups boiling broth or water
1/2 teaspoon salt (omit if using canned broth)

- Melt the butter in a heavy saucepan. Add the vermicelli and sauté for 2 minutes, stirring, until it changes color.
- Add the bulgur and onion and sauté for 3 more minutes, stirring often, until the onion is soft and the vermicelli is golden.
- Pour the boiling broth over the bulgur and stir well. Reduce the heat to low and simmer for 15 to 20 minutes until the liquid has been absorbed and the bulgur is tender.
- Fluff with a fork and serve hot.

Serves 4

Risotto

Risotto is a famous Italian dish that uses Arborio rice, an Italian short-grain variety. The rice can be cooked like long-grain rice, with 2 parts water to 1 part rice for 18 minutes, but the risotto technique is different. It is more like a pilaf. Risotto requires nearly constant stirring, and the slow addition of simmering liquid as it is absorbed. The result is a rich, creamy dish that's worth the effort if you have the patience.

Risotto
(continued)

3 cups chicken broth
2 tablespoons butter or olive oil
1/4 cup minced onions
1 cup Arborio rice
1/4 cup dry white wine
1/4 cup freshly grated Parmesan cheese
Salt and pepper to taste

• Heat the broth in a medium-size saucepan and keep it at a simmer.
• In a large heavy saucepan, over low heat, melt the butter or heat the oil. Add the onion and sauté, stirring, until soft but not colored. Add the rice and sauté for about 3 minutes until the rice is hot. Add the wine and stir until it is almost completely absorbed.
• Add 1/2 cup hot broth to the rice, stir, and simmer until the liquid is absorbed. Continue adding broth, 1/2 cup at a time, stirring until the liquid is absorbed before adding more.
• Taste and keep adding broth until the rice is creamy and tender to the bite. This will take about 25 minutes.
• Stir in the Parmesan cheese and season to taste with salt and pepper.

Polenta

Polenta is really cornmeal mush, sweet or savory. You can cook the yellow cornmeal in water or broth and flavor it with Parmesan cheese, or you can cook it in milk and water and serve it for breakfast sweetened with sugar. Most restaurants chill the savory polenta in a jellyroll pan, cut it into shapes, and fry it so it has a crustiness or bake it with a sprinkle of cheese. This famous Italian dish is perhaps most satisfying and delicious freshly made and served soft. As it sits it will solidify.

The proportions are approximately 4 cups of liquid to 1 cup of yellow cornmeal. The only trick is sprinkling the cornmeal into the boiling liquid **slowly** *so it doesn't lump. Alternatively, you can mix the cornmeal with the cold water, and add it to the boiling liquid without fear of lumping.*

3 cups broth or milk
1 cup cold water
2 tablespoons butter
1/2 teaspoon salt
1/2 teaspoon sugar
1 cup yellow cornmeal

• In a medium-size saucepan, combine the broth or milk, water, butter, salt, and sugar. Heat to a simmer.
• Whisking constantly, add the cornmeal very slowly in a thin steady stream.
• Simmer the mixture for about 15 minutes, stirring constantly with a flat wooden spatula or spoon, scraping the sides and bottom of the pan so the polenta doesn't burn. It should become thick and creamy.
• Serve immediately, topped with butter and sprinkled with Parmesan cheese. If you serve it for breakfast, top it with sugar and milk.

Baked Potatoes & Toppings

For baked potatoes use russets or Idahos that have a drier, mealier texture. Or Yukon Gold potatoes that have a rich, creamy texture. Potato skins are full of vitamins and fiber, so eat them as well. Before you bake potatoes, scrub them, dry them, and rub them with butter. It's a good idea to poke them with a knife in a few places, especially if you're cooking them in the microwave rather than the oven.

- For oven baking, put the potatoes in a 350F° oven for 1 hour or until soft.
- Microwaves cook potatoes in 10 to 15 minutes, but the texture is different and the skin doesn't get crisp. As a compromise, you could microwave the potatoes for 5 minutes and then bake them for about 25 minutes until soft.
- For a treat, remove the insides of the cooked potato and mash them with butter and milk. Stuff the mashed potatoes into the potato skins and return to the oven briefly to heat and crisp slightly. Fast food places in this country and in Europe turn baked potatoes into complete meals topped with a choice of goodies: chili, tomato sauce and cheese, baked beans, creamed or curried vegetables, sour cream and bacon, etc.

Mashed Potatoes

Everyone loves mashed potatoes. They can be made with russets or all-purpose potatoes, and prepared as rich or lean as you like with butter, cream, half-and-half, or milk. Mashed potatoes are best made fresh, and literally mashed, not overly beaten, and never processed. A few lumps make them authentically homemade!

2 pounds (about 4) large baking or all-purpose potatoes
1/2–3/4 cup milk or light cream
4 tablespoons butter
Salt and pepper to taste

- Prepare a large pot of boiling, salted water.
- Peel the potatoes, cut in quarters and add to the boiling water. Cook, partially covered, 15 to 20 minutes, until tender when stuck with a fork.
- Warm the milk or cream briefly in a small saucepan or microwave.
- Drain the potatoes and toss them with the butter to melt. Mash the potatoes with a hand masher, in a food mill, or, easiest, in a mixing bowl with a flat attachment.
- When mashed and free of most lumps, add the milk or cream slowly, mixing until the potatoes reach the consistency you like. Season with salt and pepper. Don't overwork mashed potatoes or they will become gummy.

Hash-Brown Potatoes

Hash-browns can be made with freshly cooked potatoes, but usually are the answer to leftover boiled potatoes. These tend to disappear from the pan before they ever get to the table.

4 white all-purpose potatoes, peeled and cut into 3/4-inch cubes
1/4 cup vegetable oil
Salt and pepper

Hash-Brown Potatoes
(continued)

- Cook the potatoes in a large pot of boiling salted water until nearly tender, about 5 to 10 minutes. Drain and set aside.
- In a large sauté pan, heat the oil over medium heat. Add the drained potatoes to the hot oil, shaking the pan to prevent them from sticking. Cook over medium heat, turning often with a spatula and scraping the sides.
- Season well with salt and pepper.

Serves 4 to 6

Oven-Roasted Potatoes

3 tablespoons vegetable oil
$1/2$ teaspoon paprika
6 all-purpose potatoes, peeled and cut into quarters
Salt and pepper to taste

- Preheat the oven to 375°F.
- Add the oil and paprika to a shallow baking dish and heat for 5 minutes in the oven. Add the potatoes and toss well to coat on all sides.
- Bake for about 45 minutes, turning often, until crisp on the outside and tender on the inside when poked with a fork. Season well with salt and pepper.

Cooking Dried Beans

Common wisdom used to be that dried beans needed to be soaked overnight in 4 times as much water, then drained and simmered in 4 times as much fresh water until done. Alternatively, the beans were boiled for a minute, allowed to sit for a few hours, and simmered in fresh water until done. But beans can be cooked without soaking in nearly the same amount of time and with better taste and texture.

1 pound dried beans
1 teaspoon salt
8 cups water

- Pick over the beans to remove any stones. Rinse and drain. Add to a deep saucepan with salt and water to cover by 3 inches. Bring to a boil, skim the surface, reduce the heat, and cook at a simmer, partially covered, until done.
- Some beans will take 30 minutes (lentils), others about $1 1/2$ hours (black, kidney, pinto, and small white beans), while still others may take up to 2 hours (chick peas). Add more water if needed. Fresher beans will take less time, and old ones will take longer. To test, remove a few from the water and blow on them to see if the skins curl back. Taste to be sure they're tender but not mushy.
- Cooked beans can be frozen with some of the cooking water in labeled plastic containers, so it's a good idea to make a large batch and have some ready for another time.

Summer Tomato Sauce

A smooth tomato sauce made with an abundance of fresh plum tomatoes.

1 onion, peeled and cut into quarters
3 cloves garlic, peeled and chopped
1 celery stalk, cut in pieces
4 pounds plum tomatoes, cut in half
1/4 cup red wine vinegar
1/2 cup olive oil
1 28-ounce can tomato purée
1 tablespoon brown sugar
1 tablespoon salt
1/4 bunch parsley, tied together with string
Pepper to taste

- Combine all the ingredients in a large sauce pot. Bring to a boil slowly and simmer, partially covered, for about 45 minutes.
- Remove the parsley stems and put the sauce through a food mill to eliminate the tomato skins and seeds to extract all you can.
- If you want a thicker sauce, return to the sauce pot and cook down further. Taste and adjust the seasoning.
- Store in 2-cup portions in the refrigerator or freezer.

Yields about 8 cups

Chunky Winter Tomato Sauce

*This is a basic staple year-round. This favorite sauce is perfect for any pasta, lasagna, and pizza. Don't be put off by the corn syrup—it's a perfect foil to the acid tomatoes. If you like a smooth tomato sauce, use cans of **crushed** plum tomatoes and call this simply Winter Tomato Sauce.*

3 tablespoons + 1/2 cup olive oil
1 large onion, finely chopped
2 cloves garlic, minced
2 28-ounce cans peeled whole Italian tomatoes with juice
1 28-ounce can tomato purée
1/2 cup light corn syrup
1 tablespoon salt
1 teaspoon oregano
1 teaspoon pepper
1/2 cup freshly grated Parmesan cheese

- Heat 3 tablespoons of the oil in a large saucepan. Sauté the onion and garlic for about 5 minutes over low heat until softened but not colored.
- Stir in the tomatoes, purée, corn syrup, and seasonings. Bring to a simmer and cook, partially covered, for about 20 minutes, or until thickened. Break the tomatoes up into chunks as they cook.
- Add the Parmesan cheese and continue to simmer uncovered for 5 minutes.
- Stir in the olive oil and adjust the seasoning.

**Chunky Winter
Tomato Sauce**
(continued)

- Cool before dividing into plastic 2-cup containers and refrigerating. If freezing, be sure to leave enough "head room" to allow for expansion so the container or jar doesn't break.

Yields about 10 cups

NOTE: To make mushroom or meat sauce, sauté ½ pound mushrooms or meat (ground beef, pork, or sausage) with the onions. Pour off any meat fat before adding the tomatoes.

Quick Pizza Sauce

Enough for 2 large pizzas, and nearly as fast as opening a can of commercial sauce.

1 28-ounce can chunky-style crushed tomatoes
3 tablespoons olive oil
1 large clove garlic, minced
½ teaspoon oregano
Salt and black pepper to taste
¼ teaspoon crushed red pepper flakes

- Combine all the ingredients in a medium-size saucepan and simmer uncovered for about 5 minutes.
- Store in the refrigerator after it has cooled.

Yields about 3 cups

Bechamel Sauce

A basic white sauce for topping vegetables and as a basis for macaroni and cheese sauce.

3 tablespoons butter
3 tablespoons flour
1½ cups milk, heated to boiling
Salt to taste
Grating of nutmeg

- In a small saucepan, melt the butter over low heat and add the flour. Whisk constantly and cook for a few minutes to eliminate the flour taste. Add the hot milk slowly, whisking often. Cook until the sauce thickens and comes to a boil. Whisk frequently as it thickens.
- Season to taste with salt and a grating of nutmeg. The sauce should cool before you store it, covered, in the refrigerator where it will keep for a few days.

Yields 1¾ cups

Vinaigrette

Vinaigrette is a simple vinegar and oil-based dressing. The mustard emulsifies the dressing and prevents the oil and vinegar from separating. Different vinegars and oils add their own subtle flavor to the dressing. You may want to flavor the vinaigrette with fresh herbs, spices, garlic, onion, etc., but the basic recipe is the same. If you make salads frequently, it's best to make a double batch of dressing and store it in a jar in the refrigerator, since it keeps for weeks.

1/4 cup red wine vinegar
1 rounded tablespoon Dijon mustard
3/4 teaspoon salt
Pepper to taste
2/3 cup oil (a mild olive oil or a combination of olive oil and
    vegetable oil)

• In a small deep bowl, whisk together the vinegar, mustard, salt, and pepper. Add the oil very slowly, whisking constantly and quickly, until an emulsified, thickened dressing forms.
• Store in the refrigerator.

Yields 1 cup

Mayonnaise in the Food Processor

For convenience and speed, I mostly use commercial mayonnaise, but homemade mayonnaise is a real treat. It's easily prepared in a processor or even a blender. The most important step is getting the ingredients to room temperature because if they are cold the mayonnaise won't emulsify and thicken. Put the egg in hot water to warm if you've forgotten to take it out of the refrigerator. The lemon juice and mustard should also be at room temperature.

1 whole egg, at room temperature
2 tablespoons fresh lemon juice or vinegar, at room temperature
1/2 teaspoon salt
Pinch of sugar
1 tablespoon Dijon mustard, at room temperature
1 1/2 cups vegetable oil
Fresh herbs, optional

• In a processor bowl or blender, combine the egg, lemon juice, salt, sugar, and mustard with the motor running. Add the oil very slowly through the feed tube. A thick emulsion will form. Add fresh herbs if you like, and process briefly.
• For a thinner consistency, add a few tablespoons of hot water through the feed tube and process briefly.
• Store in a covered jar in the refrigerator for up to 5 days.

Yields about 2 cups

Russian Dressing	1 cup mayonnaise
	$^1/_3$ cup chili sauce
	Chopped pimiento to taste
	1 tablespoon finely chopped onion, optional
	Dash of hot sauce

* Combine the ingredients.
* Store in a covered jar in the refrigerator.

Blue Cheese Dressing	1 cup mayonnaise
	$^3/_4$ cup buttermilk
	1 cup crumbled blue cheese
	$^1/_2$ clove garlic, mashed and pressed to a paste
	Pinch of cayenne pepper and sugar

* Combine all the ingredients in a bowl and mash together with a fork until blended but still a bit lumpy. Taste and adjust the seasoning.
* Store in a covered jar in the refrigerator.

French Dressing

Red and slightly sweet, French dressing makes a good chicken marinade as well as a topping for a lettuce and cottage cheese salad.

$^1/_3$ cup ketchup
$^1/_3$ cup cider vinegar
2 tablespoons sugar
$^1/_2$ teaspoon salt
$^1/_2$ teaspoon Worcestershire sauce
Pepper to taste
$^1/_2$ clove garlic, minced
$^2/_3$ cup vegetable oil

* In a deep bowl, whisk together the ketchup, vinegar, sugar, salt, Worcestershire, and pepper. Add the oil slowly, whisking constantly, until thickened.
* Store in a covered jar in the refrigerator.

Ranch Dressing	1 cup mayonnaise
	$^1/_3$ cup buttermilk
	$^1/_3$ cup freshly grated Parmesan cheese
	1 clove garlic, mashed and pressed to a paste
	$1^1/_2$ tablespoons red wine vinegar
	$^1/_4$ teaspoon Worcestershire sauce
	Pepper to taste

* Combine the ingredients in a bowl and stir to mix well. Taste and adjust the seasoning.
* Store in a covered jar in the refrigerator.

BREADS

Pizza Dough

1 cup warm water
Pinch of sugar
1 package active dry yeast
2½ cups flour, approximately
1 teaspoon salt
2 tablespoons olive oil

• In a small bowl, combine ½ cup water, sugar, and yeast. Proof for 5 minutes until the yeast is bubbly and active.
• In a large bowl, combine 1½ cups of flour and the salt. Add the proofed yeast, olive oil, and remaining ½ cup warm water. Stir with a large wooden spoon until smooth. Stir in ½ cup more flour.
• Turn the dough out onto a floured surface and knead, adding the remaining flour as needed, until smooth and elastic and no longer sticky. This should take about 5 minutes.
• Put the ball of dough into an oiled bowl, turning the dough to coat on all sides. Cover with a clean dish towel and let rise in a warm place for about 1 hour until doubled in size.
• Punch down the dough and roll out to form a disk. Cover and rest for 10 minutes before shaping into a pizza pan.

Yields about 1 pound of dough, enough for an 18-inch round or an 11 x 17-inch pizza

Cornbread

Another simple, pleasing addition to the menu to make dinners more special.

1 cup flour
1 cup yellow cornmeal
¼ cup sugar
1 tablespoon baking powder
½ teaspoon salt
1 cup milk, at room temperature
1 egg, at room temperature
2 tablespoons melted butter or vegetable oil

• Preheat the oven to 400°F. Grease a 9-inch square baking pan.
• In a medium-size bowl, combine the flour, cornmeal, sugar, baking powder, and salt.
• In a small bowl, combine the milk, egg, and melted butter or oil.
• Mix the wet and dry ingredients together lightly with a fork, stirring gently just until blended.
• Spread in the prepared pan and bake in the upper half of the oven until the cornbread is springy to the touch and begins to pull away from the sides of the pan. This should take about 18 minutes.
• Cut into 9 squares and serve hot with butter.

Biscuits

An easily prepared and quickly baked treat that enhances a simple dinner.

2 cups flour
1 tablespoon baking powder
1 teaspoon sugar
$^1/_2$ teaspoon salt
4 tablespoons vegetable shortening or butter
$^3/_4$ cup milk, approximately

+ Preheat the oven to 450°F. Lightly grease a heavy baking sheet or 9-inch cake pan.
+ In a large bowl, combine the flour, baking powder, sugar, and salt. Cut in the shortening or butter with a pastry blender or 2 knives until it resembles coarse meal. Add the milk, tossing lightly with a fork until the mixture almost forms a ball. Use a light hand here or the biscuits will be tough.
+ On a lightly floured surface, knead the dough gently a few times, and press out to $^1/_2$-inch thickness.
+ With a $2^1/_2$-inch round cutter or glass dipped in flour, cut out 9 or 10 biscuits. Arrange on the sheet or in the pan. If the biscuits are close together, they will be softer—far apart and they will be crustier.
+ Bake in the upper half of the oven for about 15 minutes. Turn down the oven to 425°F halfway through so the bottoms don't burn. Serve hot with butter.

Yields 9 or 10 biscuits

NOTE: For drop biscuits, add a few more tablespoons of milk to the dough to make a slightly looser batter. Drop 9 or 10 biscuits from a large spoon onto the baking sheet or into the cake pan.

Garlic Bread

1 loaf Italian bread, cut diagonally $^3/_4$ of the way through into 1-inch slices
4 tablespoons butter, at room temperature
1 large clove garlic, minced
$^1/_2$ teaspoon seasoned salt
$^1/_4$ cup Parmesan cheese, optional

+ Preheat the oven to 350°F.
+ In a small bowl, combine the butter, garlic, seasoned salt, and Parmesan cheese, and mix with a fork until spreadable.
+ Arrange the bread on a large sheet of aluminum foil. Spread a thin skim of garlic butter in the cuts of the bread. Enclose the bread in foil and bake on a baking sheet for 10 minutes to warm the bread and melt the butter. Open the foil to expose the top of the bread and bake for another 5 minutes until slightly crisp.

Croûtes & Croutons

Croûtes are toasted slices of bread, used as the base for sandwiches and hors d'oeuvres. Croutons are toasted cubes of bread that are used as toppings for salads and soups. A drizzle of olive oil and salt make croûtes or croutons unusually good. Both depend on good French or Italian bread for an authentic taste.

12 slices of bread (³/₄-inch thick) or 8 cups bread cubes (³/₄-inch),
    crusts removed if you like
3–4 tablespoons olive oil
¹/₄–¹/₂ teaspoon coarse salt

• Preheat the oven to 350°F.
• In a jellyroll pan, arrange the bread slices in a single layer or add
  the cubes. Brush the slices with the oil and sprinkle with salt, or
  toss the bread cubes with the oil and sprinkle with salt. Spread out
  to a single layer.
• Bake the croûtes or croutons for 35 to 40 minutes until dry and
  crisp, tossing and turning occasionally to color evenly.
• Cool completely before storing in a tin.

Pita Crisps

*Pita crisps are similar to croûtes. They add a crunchy texture to the
dinner menu, and make good scoopers and pushers for other foods on the
plate. Flavor the crisps by adding herbs and spices to the butter or oil.*

4 6-inch pita breads
3 tablespoons oil or butter, at room temperature
¹/₄–¹/₂ teaspoon coarse salt
Dried herbs or spices of your choice: cayenne pepper, chili pow-
    der, cumin, curry powder, spice blends, etc.

• Preheat the oven to 350°F.
• Cut around the edge of the breads with a scissors or knife and
  open them up so that you have 2 disks from each pita bread. Arrange
  the pita bread halves on a heavy baking sheet.
• Combine the oil or butter with the salt and any flavoring you like.
  Brush or spread the oil or butter on the bread.
• Bake for about 5 minutes or until crisp. Serve hot.

Yields 8 crisps

DESSERTS

Pie Crust— Sweet & Savory

*The secret of a good pie crust is in the handling—too much and the crust
will be tough. Butter crusts are flavorful and crisp; shortening crusts are
tender and flaky. To combine the best of both, I use half butter and half
shortening. For a more tender crust, replace the water with sour cream,
use 1 teaspoon of vinegar with the water, or use 1 egg yolk in place of 2
tablespoons of water. To make a sweet crust, add 1 or 2 tablespoons of
sugar to the flour. Keep the dough chilled so the pastry is easier to work
with. The dough freezes well, so make a few at a time.*

For a single-crust 9-inch pie:
1¹/₄ cups flour
1 tablespoon sugar, optional
¹/₄ teaspoon salt
6 tablespoons butter or ¹/₃ cup shortening, or a combination
3–4 tablespoons of ice water

Pie Crust
(continued)

For a double-crust 9-inch pie:
2 cups flour
2 tablespoon sugar, optional
$^1/_2$ teaspoon salt
10 tablespoons butter or $^2/_3$ cup shortening, or a combination
6–7 tablespoons ice water

• In a large bowl or food processor, combine the flour, sugar, and salt. Add the butter or shortening, and work with a pastry blender or 2 knives, or the on-off switch of the processor, until the mixture resembles coarse meal.
• Add the water slowly, tossing with a fork until the dough begins to come together, or add the water all at once through the feed tube of the processor with the motor running, and process until the dough begins to come together.
• Turn the dough out on a lightly floured surface and knead gently 2 or 3 times until it forms a ball. Flatten into a disk, enclose in plastic wrap, and chill until you're ready to roll it out.
• Lightly grease a 9-inch pie plate. Roll out the dough on a lightly floured surface to form a 13-inch circle. Start from the center and work out, turning it often so it doesn't stick. Roll onto the rolling pin or fold in quarters to lift it into the prepared pie plate. Carefully fit the dough into the plate, pressing it into the bottom and sides without stretching. Trim the edges with scissors, leaving a $^3/_4$-inch overhang which can be tucked under for a thicker edge on a single-crust pie. Crimp the edges decoratively, and chill until ready to fill and bake.
• To pre-bake the crust, known as baking "blind," line the chilled shell with foil and fill with uncooked beans or rice. Bake on the bottom shelf of a pre-heated 400°F oven for 10 minutes. Remove the foil and beans, poke the bottom of the crust a few times with a fork, and bake for 5 more minutes until lightly colored. Reserve the cooled beans in a labeled jar to use as permanent pie weights.

Crumb Crust

Baked crumb crusts are the basis of quick desserts that are filled with pudding or ice cream. Cheesecakes are often baked in crumb crusts as well. The crumbs are usually made from graham crackers, but can also be made from vanilla or chocolate wafers, zwieback, ginger snaps, or amaretti.

For a 9-inch pie (or a 10-inch springform):
1$^1/_2$ cups graham cracker crumbs
$^1/_4$ cup confectioners' sugar
4 tablespoons melted butter

• Preheat the oven to 300°F.
• Combine the crumbs, sugar, and butter in a small bowl, mixing well. Turn into a pie plate and pat into the bottom and up the sides of the plate.
• Bake in the middle of the oven for 15 minutes. Cool before adding the filling.

Chocolate Sauce

An all-purpose sauce for ice cream and cakes. For a thick hot fudge, use the higher amount of cocoa. For a thinner sauce, use the lesser amount.

4 tablespoons butter
3/4 cup light brown sugar
1/2 cup granulated sugar
1 cup heavy cream
2 tablespoons light corn syrup
3/4–1 cup unsweetened cocoa, sifted

- In a medium-size saucepan, melt the butter over low heat and add the sugars, cream, and corn syrup. Heat to boiling, stirring often, until the sugar is dissolved.
- Remove from the heat and whisk in the cocoa until smooth.
- Cool before dividing into 2 8-ounce jars. Store in the refrigerator.

Vanilla Custard Sauce

This sauce is really a thinned pastry cream rather than a custard. It uses flour as a thickener as well as egg yolks. The flour makes it more fool-proof than more temperamental custards that will curdle if heated too much. Pastry creams are very versatile since they can be used in fruit tarts or thinned for a sauce.

3 egg yolks
1/4 cup sugar
2 tablespoons flour
1 cup milk
1/2 teaspoon vanilla
Optional flavorings for a sauce: heavy cream, fruit liqueurs,
    chopped bittersweet chocolate, very strong espresso coffee

- In a heavy saucepan, whisk together the yolks and sugar. Add the flour with a few tablespoons of the milk and whisk until smooth.
- Heat the remaining milk and whisk into the sugar mixture. Bring to a boil over medium-low heat, whisking constantly as it thickens.
- Cook gently for 1 minute to cook the flour and eliminate the flour taste.
- Remove the pastry cream from the heat and transfer to a bowl. Stir in the vanilla. Flavor or thin to desired consistency with cream, liqueurs, melted chocolate, or espresso.
- Cover and refrigerate until ready to use.

Baked Custard

An easy old-fashioned dessert that seems forgotten these days. Try it with a spoonful of maple syrup on top and it's reminiscent of Crème Caramel.

3 cups milk
4 eggs
1/2 cup sugar
1/4 teaspoon salt
1 teaspoon vanilla
Maple syrup, optional

- Preheat the oven to 350°F.

Baked Custard
(continued)

- Heat the milk in a saucepan over low heat, or in the microwave, until nearly at a simmer.
- In a large bowl, whisk together the eggs, sugar, and salt. Slowly whisk in the hot milk. Stir in the vanilla.
- Pour the mixture into eight 1/2-cup custard cups. Place in a shallow baking dish of hot water to come halfway up the sides of the custard cups. This is a "water bath," or *bain marie*, that helps the custard cook slowly and evenly.
- Bake in the middle of the oven for 35 to 40 minutes, or until nearly set and a knife inserted off center comes out clean. The custard will continue to cook and set as it cools.
- Remove the custard from the water bath and cool completely before covering and refrigerating. Serve chilled and with a teaspoon of maple syrup on top if you like.

Vanilla Cake

8 tablespoons butter, at room temperature
1 cup sugar
2 eggs, at room temperature
1 teaspoon vanilla
2 1/4 cups flour
1 tablespoon baking powder
1 teaspoon salt
1 cup milk, at room temperature

- Preheat the oven to 350°F. Grease 2 8-inch round cake pans. To facilitate removing the baked cake, line the greased pans with 8-inch parchment paper rounds, then grease and lightly flour.
- In a mixing bowl, beat the butter, adding the sugar gradually. Add the eggs, one at a time, and then the vanilla. Beat on medium-high speed for about 5 minutes until the mixture is pale and light and the sugar is no longer gritty between your fingers.
- In another bowl, sift together the flour, baking powder, and salt. On low speed, add the dry ingredients alternately with the milk to the creamed ingredients, until just blended.
- Divide the batter between the prepared pans and bake in the upper half of the oven for 30 to 35 minutes until golden and the top is slightly springy to the touch.
- Cool for 10 minutes before removing from the pans and transferring to wire racks to cool completely. Peel off the paper before frosting.

Yields 2 8-inch round layers

Chocolate Cake

1/4 cup vegetable oil
3/4 cup sour cream
2 eggs, at room temperature
1 cup coffee
2 cups flour
2 cups sugar
1 teaspoon baking soda
1/2 teaspoon baking powder
1/2 teaspoon salt
4 ounces unsweetened chocolate, melted and cooled

Chocolate Cake
(continued)

• Preheat the oven to 350°F. Grease 2 9-inch round cake pans. Line with a 9-inch parchment paper rounds, grease, and lightly flour.
• In a mixing bowl, combine the oil, sour cream, eggs, and coffee. Mix until well blended.
• In another bowl, sift together the flour, sugar, baking soda, baking powder, and salt. Add to the mixing bowl with the wet ingredients and mix to combine. Add the melted chocolate and beat on high speed for 4 minutes, scraping the bottom of the bowl occasionally. Pour into the prepared pans and spread evenly.
• Bake in the upper half of the oven for 35 to 40 minutes, or until the cake begins to pull away from the sides of the pan and a toothpick inserted in the center comes out clean.
• Cool for 10 minutes before removing from the pans and transferring to wire racks to cool completely. Peel off the paper before frosting.

Yields 2 9-inch layers

Cake Frosting

Even cake mixes taste better and more homemade with this easy cake frosting. If you have extra frosting, put it in a labeled plastic container and freeze it to use later for cupcakes. This recipe makes enough for a small 8-inch layer cake, but if you love loads of icing on your cake or have made a larger cake, double the recipe. Butter gives the frosting the best flavor, but you could substitute some vegetable shortening for a fluffier consistency.

8 tablespoons butter, at room temperature
2 cups confectioners' sugar
1/2 teaspoon vanilla
1 egg white
4 ounces melted bittersweet chocolate, optional

• In a mixing bowl, combine the butter, sugar, vanilla, and egg white. Mix on low speed until combined. Scrape the bottom of the bowl, and beat on high speed for about 5 minutes, until light and fluffy. You may want to thin with a few teaspoons of warm water to make a mayonnaise-like consistency.
• For chocolate frosting, beat in the melted chocolate.

Sugar Cookies

Roll out the dough and cut into any shapes you like. Sprinkle with colored sugars before baking or paint with a colored confectioners' sugar/milk glaze after baking and cooling.

12 tablespoons butter, at room temperature
1 cup sugar
1 teaspoon vanilla
1 egg
3 cups flour
1 teaspoon baking powder
1/2 teaspoon salt
1/4 cup milk

• In a mixing bowl, beat the butter and add the sugar gradually, mixing until creamed. Add the vanilla and egg, and beat until smooth.

Sugar Cookies
(continued)

- Mix the flour, baking powder, and salt together. Add alternately with the milk to the creamed butter and sugar, mixing until a dough forms.
- Enclose in plastic wrap and chill briefly to make handling and rolling easier. The dough shouldn't be cold, just chilled.
- Preheat the oven to 375°F.
- Cut the dough into quarters and roll out on a lightly floured surface to the thinness you like. Cut the dough into shapes and transfer to heavy baking sheets. No need to grease the sheets since the butter in the dough will prevent the cookies from sticking.
- Bake in the upper half of the oven until lightly colored, about 8 to 10 minutes, depending on the thickness of the dough. Transfer to a wire rack to cool completely before storing in an airtight tin.

Yields 3 dozen 4-inch cookies

Cheesecake

Rich and full of calories, cheesecake has become an occasional treat, cut into small pieces and topped with lots of fresh fruit. Cheesecake can be prepared ahead of time and frozen if it is wrapped well. Thaw in the refrigerator overnight, or cut into individual pieces as needed.

Graham cracker crumb crust (page 263)

For the filling:
1½ pounds cream cheese, at room temperature
1 cup sugar
1 teaspoon vanilla
3 eggs, separated

- Preheat the oven to 300°F. Press the crumbs into the bottom and 1 inch up the sides of a 10-inch springform pan.
- To prepare the filling, combine the cream cheese, sugar, and vanilla in a mixing bowl, and beat on medium speed until well blended. Add the egg yolks, one at a time, mixing well after each addition.
- In a separate bowl with clean beaters, beat the egg whites until stiff. Fold into the cream cheese mixture.
- Pour into the prepared springform pan and place on a heavy baking sheet. Bake in the middle of the oven for about 1 hour until the filling seems nearly set when you wiggle the pan.
- Turn off the oven, open the oven door, and let the cheesecake cool slowly before removing to a wire rack to cool completely. Refrigerate and serve chilled with optional toppings.
- Glaze at serving time with melted red currant jelly and fresh berries, or make a mountain of chocolate curls (scrape a vegetable peeler over chocolate bars).

Fruit Salad	• Some fruits do better in fruit salad than others: melons, pineapple, oranges, grapefruit, grapes, mango, papaya, kiwi, blueberries. • Some fruits are best added just before serving because they get mushy or turn brown: raspberries, sliced strawberries, bananas. • Apples and pears turn brown when cut and exposed to the air, so these should be added at the end or sprinkled with lemon juice to prevent oxidation.

Poached Fruit

Poaching is a technique that cooks foods gently and slowly. For fruits, that means barely simmering in a sugared, acidified liquid. Pears and peaches are usually the fruit of choice because they provide a single serving dessert that can be embellished with a custard, fruit sauce, or chocolate sauce.

4 cups water
1 cup dry white wine
¹/₂ cup sugar
1 cinnamon stick or 3 slices of fresh ginger root
4 Bartlett pears or 8 peach halves, peeled just before poaching

• In a large saucepan, combine the water, lemon juice, sugar, and cinnamon. Bring to a boil, add the pears or peaches, and simmer over low heat for about 15 minutes.
• Remove the fruit from the liquid and set aside to cool. Cook the liquid down to a syrupy sauce, or use it as the base for a drink make with sparkling water.

Applesauce

Homemade applesauce freezes well in plastic containers and tastes especially good when the glut of fall apples is just a memory and the new crop is months away. Macintosh apples make the smoothest, creamiest applesauce, but a combination of varieties gives a complexity of flavor. Since apples vary so much, it's best to sweeten to taste and add cinnamon as a flavor enhancer only if needed. There's no need to peel and core the apples if you use a food mill that will eliminate the skins and seeds.

3 pounds Macintosh apples, cut into eighths
1 cup water
³/₄ cup sugar, or to taste
Squeeze of fresh lemon juice
¹/₂ teaspoon cinnamon, or to taste

• Combine the apples and water in a large saucepan. Bring to a simmer, cover, and cook for about 20 minutes, stirring occasionally, until the apples are soft and have broken down.
• Put the apples and juice through a food mill and return to the pan. Add sugar to taste, lemon juice, and cinnamon if desired. The heat of the applesauce will melt the sugar. You can cook it down to a thicker sauce if you like. Stir often.
• Cool before transferring to covered containers and refrigerating.

Baked Apples

Baked apples are even faster when they're microwaved, and nearly as delicious.

6 large Rome Beauties or other baking apples
1/2 cup light brown sugar
1 tablespoon butter
1/2 cup water

+ Preheat the oven to 350°F.
+ Core the apples from the bottom but don't cut through the top. A melon baller does a good job of scooping out the center. Peel 1 inch of skin all around the opening. Jab each apple a few times around the sides, and place close together in a shallow baking dish.
+ Fill the centers with the sugar and dot with bits of the butter. Add the water to the dish, cover loosely with foil and bake in the oven for about 1 hour or until soft.
+ To microwave, cover the apples with wax paper and cook on high power for about 15 minutes, turning a few times, until the apples are soft. Baste with the juices in the dish.
+ Reduce the juices and serve over the apples. Serve warm or chilled with a spoonful of heavy cream over the top.

Chocolate-Dipped Fruit

+ Chocolate-dipped fruit (and nuts) is an elegant dessert, and one of the easiest you can make. Be sure to use good quality chocolate. You can buy bittersweet chocolate in 10 pound blocks from candy suppliers. Break it up with a hammer, and store it in a dry place in covered plastic containers.
+ When melting chocolate, use a heavy saucepan and place on top of a heat diffuser or in a sauté pan of hot water, keeping the temperature low and the process slow. Chop the chocolate to melt it quicker, and never let even a drop of water get into the chocolate or it will "seize" and stiffen and be useless for dipping.
+ The fruits should be self-contained so they don't get juicy or turn brown, and they must be dry before dipping. Big, whole strawberries are the most spectacular, especially if you dip them in white chocolate first, let the chocolate set, and then dip the white tips in dark chocolate. Glacéed or dried apricots, crystallized ginger, and dried pineapple also work well for dipping.
+ Heat the chocolate, stirring as it melts, and use it immediately when it's smooth. Dip the fruit (or nuts) in the chocolate and arrange in a single layer on a baking sheet lined with wax paper. When the chocolate is set and firm, peel the fruit off of the paper and arrange on a platter. A few minutes in the refrigerator helps to set the chocolate. If you use strawberries, it's best to eat them the day you make them.

Iced Tea

Almost as easy as the mixes, and flavored or sweetened the way you like.

2 regular or 3 herbal tea bags
1 cup boiling water
$^1/_4$ cup sugar, or to taste
6 cups cold water
Fresh mint or lemon juice to flavor

• Combine the tea bags and boiling water, cover, and steep for 5 to 10 minutes. Remove the tea bags, stir in the sugar, and add to a pitcher with the cold water. Flavor with mint or lemon, and adjust the sweetness to taste.

Yields almost $^1/_2$ gallon

Hot Chocolate

1 tablespoon unsweetened cocoa
1 tablespoon brown sugar
1 tablespoon white sugar
$1^1/_2$ cups hot milk
Mini-marshmallows, optional

• In a large mug, combine the cocoa and sugars. Add a few table-spoons of the milk and stir until smooth. Add the remaining milk and stir well. Serve with mini-marshmallows if you like.

Sangria

Sangria is a sweetened citrus fruit and wine punch that originated in Spain but is perfect for summer dining and picnics anywhere.

$^1/_4$ cup sugar
$^1/_4$ cup hot water
2 lemons, thinly sliced
2 oranges, thinly sliced
$^1/_2$ cup orange juice
$^1/_4$ cup orange liqueur or brandy
1 bottle dry red or white wine
Sparkling water to taste

• In a large pitcher, combine the sugar and hot water and stir to dissolve the sugar. Add the lemon and orange slices and mash a bit to extract some of the fruit juices.
• Add the orange juice, liqueur or brandy, and the wine. Stir well and set aside. At serving time, add sparkling water to fizz and lighten the punch and serve over ice in wine goblets.

Serves 4 to 6

Fruit Smoothies

Just as flavored yogurts have become contemporary substitutes for puddings, Fruit Smoothies have become a healthier alternative to milkshakes. They're a blend of yogurt and fruit, with fruit juice and sometimes ice to thin. This is a Rebe Glass special.

1 8-ounce container fruit yogurt of your choice
1/2 banana, cut up
1/2 cup frozen sliced strawberries with sugar
1/2 cup cut-up fruit of your choice (mangoes, peaches, fresh strawberries, berries)
1/2 cup cold orange juice

• In a blender, combine the yogurt, banana, frozen strawberries, and your fruit of choice. Blend until smooth, adding additional orange juice to thin to the consistency you like.
• Serve immediately in tall glasses.

Yields 2 drinks

Lemonade Shake-Ups

These are reminiscent of the popular and refreshing summer state fair drinks.

2 large lemons
6 tablespoons sugar
2 cups water
6 ice cubes

• Cut the lemons in half and squeeze the juice into a quart jar. You should have about 1/2 cup of lemon juice.
• Cut up the squeezed lemons and add them to a the jar. Add the sugar, water, and ice cubes. Shake up until cold and the sugar is dissolved.
• Pour over ice in glasses.

Yields 1 quart

Index